A History of Women
in Men's Clothes

In loving memory of my mother Pamela Shopland and all those who lost their lives to Coronavirus in 2020.

A History of Women in Men's Clothes

From Cross-Dressing to Empowerment

Norena Shopland

First published in Great Britain in 2021 by
Pen & Sword History
An imprint of
Pen & Sword Books Ltd
Yorkshire – Philadelphia

Copyright © Norena Shopland 2021

ISBN 978 1 52678 767 5

The right of Norena Shopland to be identified as Author of this work has been asserted by her in accordance with the Copyright, Designs and Patents Act 1988.

A CIP catalogue record for this book is available from the British Library.

All rights reserved. No part of this book may be reproduced or transmitted in any form or by any means, electronic or mechanical including photocopying, recording or by any information storage and retrieval system, without permission from the Publisher in writing.

Typeset by Mac Style
Printed and bound in Great Britain by
CPI Group (UK) Ltd, Croydon, CR0 4YY

Pen & Sword Books Limited incorporates the imprints of Atlas, Archaeology, Aviation, Discovery, Family History, Fiction, History, Maritime, Military, Military Classics, Politics, Select, Transport, True Crime, Air World, Frontline Publishing, Leo Cooper, Remember When, Seaforth Publishing, The Praetorian Press, Wharncliffe Local History, Wharncliffe Transport, Wharncliffe True Crime and White Owl.

For a complete list of Pen & Sword titles please contact

PEN & SWORD BOOKS LIMITED
47 Church Street, Barnsley, South Yorkshire, S70 2AS, England
E-mail: enquiries@pen-and-sword.co.uk
Website: www.pen-and-sword.co.uk

Or

PEN AND SWORD BOOKS
1950 Lawrence Rd, Havertown, PA 19083, USA
E-mail: Uspen-and-sword@casematepublishers.com
Website: www.penandswordbooks.com

Contents

Introduction		vi
Chapter 1	To See Lovely Things	1
Chapter 2	Individuals Not Distinguished	12
Chapter 3	It Was Just a Lark	23
Chapter 4	Family Life	34
Chapter 5	For Love, or Hate	45
Chapter 6	A Nymph of the Pave	54
Chapter 7	Usurping His Occupation	67
Chapter 8	Hard Labour	78
Chapter 9	For Nefarious Purposes	89
Chapter 10	Soldiers	100
Chapter 11	Sailors	110
Chapter 12	A Pair of Pretty Legs	121
Chapter 13	Exposed to Ridicule and Insult	135
Chapter 14	A Skirt for Each Leg	146
Chapter 15	Loving Women	158
Chapter 16	Questioning Gender	170
Conclusion		181
Notes		184
Bibliography		200
Index		202

Introduction

It is an acknowledged fact that women's history lags a long way behind that of men. At the time of writing, the biographical content of women on Wikipedia, the world's largest encyclopaedia, consists of approximately 18 per cent. Where women do appear, particularly those prior to the twentieth century, they are rarely from the working classes.

This book is about women, mostly working class, who decided to reject the dictates of society that controlled their movements and their lives by doing one thing – changing their clothes.

I came across some of these women while writing *Forbidden Lives: LGBT stories from Wales*, the first completely historical work looking at Welsh sexual orientation and gender identity. Part of the research for that book consisted of searching for unpublished material and I was able to amass an extensive collection on cross-dressing women.

However, there are few convenient words and phrases one can use when researching the stories of those who changed their clothes. In order to locate these people in the historical record, it became necessary to expand on the traditional idea of a set word/phrase glossary by including a more 'pick-and-mix' selection technique that combines words and phrases in a variety of ways. This more accurately reflects the way journalists and authors write as they often avoid set glossary words and phrases in order to present a more individual style of writing. This new type of pick-and-mix keyword/s was published as part of a research guide funded by the Welsh Government and published by Glamorgan Archives. It can be downloaded freely from the latter's site under the name of *Queering Glamorgan*.[1] I later expanded this work into a book, *A Practical Guide to Searching LGBTQIA Historical Archives* (Routledge) and anyone who wishes to research the stories in this book, or look for new ones, can use the methodologies outlined in those publications. Although based on LGBT+ research, the principles apply to any subject.

Using this system of research, I was able to uncover in excess of 3,000 stories of which circa 80 per cent were unpublished outside their original source. I could have continued, as there are so many more stories in the record, but I had the material needed to compile this book.

What became apparent during the search for stories about women who were wearing men's clothes was just how many of them were doing so. I could easily have continued the research into thousands more records in English alone. Also, my main research parameters are the nineteenth century to the First World War in the UK. Taking into account similar results in other languages and other time periods, the total number of women cross-dressing is incalculable – mainly because we are restricted to those women we know about – many thousands more will never have been caught or talked about publicly. Also, my research considers women wearing a westernised concept of male attire – women across the world wore clothing ascribed to males but descriptions and names do not always conform to those used in the west.

The vast majority of women who are included in this research have come to light from newspapers. Many are matchstick-like stories that flare up only to quickly die out and it can be very frustrating not being able to discover what happened to certain individuals. Perhaps local researchers can pick up some of these stories and find out what happened to those women after reporters lost interest in them.

One thing that needed to be considered when writing up these stories is what to call the women. The most common description in the original articles is 'in male attire'. However, I also make use of three modern terms: cross-dressing, cross-working, and cross-living. While these terms were not used during the period covered, they do convey an idea of what is happening. Cross-dressing is used predominantly for those women who wore male attire for a specific time; cross-working for women who worked as men; and cross-living for those who lived either a short or extended period as a man and was identified by others as a man. These terms give a more neutral image and are preferable to others such as transvestite, which conjurors up specific, modern images.

When writing about women who cross-lived, even if only for a few days, it can be difficult to decide which pronoun to use – she or he. Usually, there is not enough information in the record to make categorical statements as to gender identity (what we would today call trans) and for those who have been identified as such, there is a separate chapter in this book. When women were written about in the press, some journalists insisted on retaining feminine pronouns throughout the story while others would use a combination of both – male pronouns when discussed as a man and female when discussed as a woman. In addition, phrases such as 'woman-man' and 'man-woman' were frequently used. Some journalists, such as one on the Australian paper *Empire*, stated from the outset that he would 'speak of her in the masculine gender.' In this book, when the subject appears as female, the pronoun used is 'she' and when appearing as male, it is 'he'. For those individuals who conform closely to those we would now refer to as trans, transmasculine or transmale, the pronoun 'they' or 'them' will be used.

Terminology for sexual orientation is kept to a minimum as often there is not enough evidence to make definitive statements and when a woman living as a male co-habits with another woman, the sexual orientation could be either homosexual or heterosexual.

Wording plays an important part in how cross-dressing women were perceived. 'Masquerade' and 'disguise' were popular expressions, emphasising a pretence. Almost all terminology used was designed to separate the women from 'real life' and headlines would include words such as 'amazing', 'discovery' and 'grotesque'; during the early part of the nineteenth century, it was not uncommon to place the words 'male attire' in italics to separate it from the rest of the text. 'Creature' and 'it' were also used.

Sometimes, descriptions of the male clothes or appearance were included, often in reductive terms designed to trivialise, mock or imply a temporary aberration. Clothes were frequently described as 'costume', 'garb' or 'toggery', and they were 'donned' rather than worn. This both downplayed the threat of women appropriating male dominance while emphasising the absurdity and theatrical notion of a woman who chose to dress as a man. Phrases such as 'pretty in her male attire' were not uncommon and trousers are often referred to as 'unmentionables' in order to draw a thin veil of respectability.

Given the enormous number of women who appeared in the press, a shared language developed, the most common being the excuse 'it was just a lark' and many of the stories have frequently repeated themes. Running from or to a man is common but rarely were these stories actually checked, so we cannot separate truth from shared stories and language. Humour is a dominant theme. Despite many of the stories originating from court proceedings, the woman's appearance or version of events often evoked laughter during her hearing. This was often emphasised by journalists as if none of it should be taken too seriously.

By making light of the subject, a veil could be drawn over the fact that these women were able to pass as men simply by learning to wear the clothes, how to walk, how to hold themselves, lower their voice and develop the necessary muscles through manual work. The question of how easily the genders could be blurred was too risky a subject to tackle face on. How could men maintain their dominant role when a woman could learn how to be a man? It questioned the biblical notion that man was a superior being and ran too close to Darwinism and other scientific discoveries that were beginning to question the biblical explanation of life.

As most of the cases are recorded in newspapers and court records, it is almost always a male, heterosexual voice we are hearing. The descriptions of the women, their behaviour, the interpretation of what they said and the choice of what to include of the woman's own words, are all male. Female voices are rarely heard and the excuses they provide for why they cross-dressed cannot always be relied on as these were cribbed from the newspapers, according to how leniently each excuse was dealt with. All the cases say more about the male view and opinion than that of the women. Only towards the end of the nineteenth century, when the New Woman began to wear rational dress, do we start to regularly hear women's voices.

For most of history, man saw himself as the superior partner and was described with words implying strength, intelligence and dominance. Women were described as weak, overly passionate and unable to control their feelings. Their perceived weakness was used to justify their dominance by men. If they were capable of intelligent thought, they were given the back-handed compliment of having a 'masculine mind.' Equally for a man to wear women's clothing was to reduce him to a weak state. It was understandable for a woman to want to raise herself to man's high status, but not for a man to reduce himself to a weaker one.

While the myriad examples of cross-dressing in literature are outside the scope of this book, it is worth quoting Virginia Woolf from *Orlando* (1928), even though it falls outside the dates covered in this work:

> Different though the sexes are, they intermix. In every human being a vacillation from one sex to the other takes place, and often it is only the clothes that keep the male or female likeness, while underneath the sex is the very opposite of what it is above. Of the complications and confusions which this result everyone has had experience.

Those writing about cross-dressing constantly emphasised femininity and the fact that the women were eventually discovered. Nothing could be allowed to creep in to question the biologically thin line between male and female. In most real-life accounts, as well as the plethora of plays and books featuring women cross-dressing, there was in the end a restoration of the women's subordinate position and heterosexual happiness. When back in female clothing, women were described as in 'proper attire'.

The stories in this book are just the tip of the iceberg, not only in numbers (about 10 per cent of the 3,000 stories are included) but also in terms of the narratives – some accounts were extensive and fascinated the public for weeks, and they deserve another book to themselves.

I would like to see a reconsideration of nineteenth-century women's lives and an acceptance that many did not conform to the standard idea of womanhood; by crossing boundaries, they found a much greater freedom than social dictates allowed. It is also hoped that humanity can be viewed outside the binary tradition.

While there are many, many books on cross-dressing from a transgender perspective, there is little with regard to cis-gender (those who are not transgender), heterosexual or homosexual women. While some stories appear in books on lesbianism, it only serves to separate those women from the main body who regularly cross-dressed. This book aims to put all these women together to show that they cannot be seen as separate but as something which was common throughout society.

Cross-dressing was, in a sense, escaping from men's control, which is the reason it was received in so many different ways by the men who controlled the police force and the courts. Some could not understand why women would want to escape protective custody into a world of danger, while others were outraged that they should be so ungrateful. Occasionally, there was a glimmer of understanding, or acknowledgement, when men realised how badly women could be treated and sympathised with their desire to escape. Sometimes there was even admiration for the 'plucky little woman' who was willing to be 'shameful' in order to protect her family or escape domestic violence.

Here, then, are hundreds of plucky women who refused to conform.

Chapter 1

To See Lovely Things

The nineteenth century saw a great rise in the number of women travellers – some accompanying husbands or other male family members; others wishing to experience new places or become missionaries; some simply to escape the stifling oppression of their homes. For wealthier women it could be an escape from boredom, as Isabella Bird complained, 'nothing new, nothing exciting, but the same drudgery day in, day out'.[1]

Most women who travelled were accompanied by men, to avoid assaults or social condemnation. The attitude to their dependent roles as wives, daughters and sisters was compounded by the fact that any work undertaken on their travels, either scientifically or expeditionary, was often not taken seriously and either attributed to the man or simply ignored. A number of women did travel alone and often wrote up their exploits, but they were in the minority and most continued to wear female attire. Gertrude Bell, the famous explorer, wore silk petticoats – albeit with a pistol strapped to her thigh. Some adapted native costumes: Isabella Bird wore female Manchurian clothing in China and unlike many women who continued to ride side-saddle, she rode astride like a man – although she threatened to sue *The Times* if it published the fact.

Isabella was right to be worried, for the press could be scathing of women explorers who chose to wear male attire, questioning their femininity and attempting to put them aside in a category of 'unnatural'. Frenchwoman Jeanne Geneviève Garnerin (1775–1847), described as the first solo woman balloonist and the first woman to make a parachute jump, suffered this kind of abuse. While there is not much evidence to support her wearing men's clothes on a regular basis, she certainly did in 1802, when the *Bury and Norwich Post* reported that in France, she 'went about that place in *male attire*. So much for female delicacy!' The offensiveness being so great it required the clothing to be described in italics. The *Post's* horror can be clearly seen when they go on to compare Jeanne's unseemliness to that of fifty women in Pudukkottai, East Indies who chose to burn to death as they 'preferred death to an exposure of their persons to the sight of man.'[2]

Equally controversial was Frenchwoman Jane Dieulafoy (1851–1916), a highly regarded archaeologist and one of the few women who have been acknowledged as receiving the title of Chevalier of the *Légion d'Honneur*. When her husband Marcel was called to war, she dressed in a soldier's uniform and served alongside him. Throughout her life she dressed as a male and appeared so convincing that many did not recognise her as a woman. Images of her with close-cropped hair, tight collars and a man's jacket give her an androgynous appearance. Jane had very strong views on the attire assigned to women and declared that 'women's dress has done more to hamper women's energy and brains than all the scolding's administered to independent women by men from the time of Isaiah the prophet to the present day.'³

Not all approved of her choice. After causing a sensation when appearing at the theatre, one unnamed journalist in the *Belfast News-Letter* sniped, 'That Mdme. Dieulafoy found a rough tourist suit very convenient in the interior of Asia and Africa is justly held to be no reason why she should don a dress coat at the Opera Comique.'⁴

At the end of the article, the journalist complained that the number of women wearing men's clothes had risen, contrary to the law, but he was wrong – it had been never illegal in the UK for women to be in male attire. That was not the case in many European countries, however, particularly France, and it could have been this that confused him. The European law did have an impact on some British female travellers, such as in 1834 when a 'trousered' woman was detained at Calais and forced to apply for permission to continue her journey – with the police at her intended destination being 'informed' of her arrival.⁵

Jane Dieulafoy had received permission from the French authorities to wear men's clothes and would often buy ready-made suits to save time. She said she wore them for convenience but there seems more to her desire to cross-dress than that. She wrote fiction and two of her novels, *Volontaire* (1892) and *Frère Pélage* (1894), include cross-dressing characters and both works are now considered early trans novels. In *Frère Pélage* a woman disguises herself as a monk, an idea which may have been inspired by Pelagia of Antioch from the fourth or fifth century who, having become religious, took to a cave on the Mount of Olives and remained there dressed in a monk's habit. Her story was apparently an inspiration for Marina the Monk in the fifth century who lived undetected for ten years.

A similar dedication to wearing male attire outside the bounds of 'convenience' was shown by Austrian Ida Laura Pfeiffer (1797–1858), one of the earliest popular travel writers. The only daughter of six children, she was bold, enjoyed sport and exercise and 'loved to dress like her brothers'. Indeed, her cross-dressing was attributed to her growing up with all boys.

She was 10 when her father died and her mother 'could not understand why her daughter should prefer … the masculine trousers to the feminine petticoat' so put an end to her unconventional ways. After the death of her husband in 1838, Ida began to travel and her first book, *Reise einer Wienerin in das Heilige Land* (A Vienna woman's trip to the Holy Land) appeared in 1843, earning her enough money to carry on a roving life.

Most women travellers dressed in female attire, however, there were those who attempted to both dress and pass as men – such as two other Frenchwomen, Jeanne Baret (1740–1807), the first woman to circumnavigate the globe, and Rose de Freycinet (1794–1832), the first woman to record her experiences.

In 1766, the naturalist Philibert Commerçon was invited onto an expedition and, as no women were allowed on board a ship, his lover Jeanne Baret dressed as a man to be with him. Due to the large amount of equipment Commerçon took on board, he and his 'assistant' were given a cabin to themselves, helping Jeanne to keep up her disguise. Commerçon suffered from a bad leg and so it was Jeanne who did a great deal of the work, not just collecting specimens but cataloguing them; this left French admiral and explorer, Louis Antoine de Bougainville to describe her as an expert botanist, for which she received little recognition until her first biography in 2002.

Despite trying to pass as a man, Jeanne's transvestitism was temporary and did not appear to fool many people. The same can also be said of Rose de Freycinet, who went to sea as a man. Rose accompanied her husband who had been given command of an expeditionary ship and the crew became very quickly aware of her sex, as did the Ministry for the Navy. Reaching Gibraltar, Rose maintained the masquerade at a dinner, the French Consul describing her as 'dressed as a man in a blue frock-coat with trousers to match.' Obviously, the disguise was not particularly convincing. Rose kept a diary detailing places, people and events, the first woman to do so, and it remains an important anthropological resource.

When women did travel on land, most of them upheld Western dress traditions and would wander about hot countries in voluminous suffocating dresses. A number did wear native attire such as Alexandrine Tinné, a Dutch explorer and the first woman to attempt to cross the Sahara. When she was young her 'earliest developed tastes were those of an Amazon'[6] and on the death of her father, she became the richest woman in Holland allowing her freedom to travel. She never married but spent her time exploring the Nile having 'adopted the Egyptian dress' but there are few images of her wearing this. It is worth bearing in mind that photographs and sketches of female travellers may seem to conform to dress conventions, but behind the lens they could and would dress more comfortably.

Isobel Burton, wife of the explorer Richard Burton, admitted they lived two lives:

> we were always thoroughly English in our Consulate, and endeavoured to set an example of the way in which England should be represented abroad, and in our official life we strictly conformed to English customs and conventions; but when we were off duty, so to speak, we used to live a great deal as natives, and so obtained experience of the inner Eastern life … I always wore the men's dress in our expeditions in the desert and up the country. By that I mean the dress of Arab men. This is not so dreadful as Mrs. Grundy may suppose, as it was all drapery, and does not show the figure.[7]

When female explorers cross-dressed, or adopted local attire, they rarely tried to appear as men. For example, in certain countries they still followed the requirement to veil their faces and there are images of Alexandrine Tinné doing so. Pioneering archaeologist Lady Hester Stanhope's was said to be quite 'mannish' and was subjected to gossip as a result. In the Middle East, she wore Turkish male clothing and later dressed as a Bedouin; but in 1889 as she approached Jerusalem, she was advised 'by her native escorts to veil her face in conformity with Turkish usage, since in spite of her masculine attire, it was known that she was a woman.'[8]

Conversely, when women from Eastern countries arrived in Europe, their dress often created a sensation. The *Birmingham Daily Post* in 1889 described how two of the Shah's wives, visiting Berlin, were dressed in 'men's clothes' – 'long black tunics, baggy pantaloons and loose cloaks so that they looked like boys.'[9] Three Chinese women arrived in New Zealand (apparently the first to do so) described as 'disguised in male attire'. But it was evident to a 'close observer' that their voices and general demeanour provided unmistakable evidence of their 'real sex.'[10] If their 'real sex' was evident were they really *disguised*, or simply wearing the loose pantaloons oriental women were known to wear?

In 1888, a journalist mused on the social demands that clothing places on people whilst describing a trip in Japan:

> As we got further from the ordinary roads of travel, dress ceased almost entirely to differentiate sex: men and women, boys and girls, alike wore the blouse and tight trousers of rough blue cotton. It would seem, therefore, that civilization emphasizes sex – a nut perhaps for some of our more radical reformers to crack. Given unceasing and wholly unimaginative labour for both, and the sentimental distinctions between man and woman are obliterated. "Segregation is asexual," remarked our professor sententiously.[11]

Despite his piece, few other writers considered how dress differentiates sex; instead, women were generally seen as sensationally different for wearing what was considered exclusively male attire. Bifurcated lower garments, no matter how 'baggy' they appeared, were considered trousers and to many Western societies, which followed a strict moral code governed by biblical rules, trousers were only for men.

Society's reaction then would be comparable to a man wearing a dress today. When David Beckham wore a sarong in 1998, he was universally mocked. In 2017, a story about boys from Isca Academy in Exeter made international headlines when they defied a ban on shorts, even in a heatwave, and opted for skirts instead.[12] In the same month, French bus drivers wore skirts in defiance of their no shorts rule during 30°C heat. The hundreds of social comments around these stories were overwhelmingly positive but only because they challenged what was seen as a ridiculous rule – the boys and men were seen as champions of common sense, not as champions for the right of males to wear female clothes. The handful of comments advocating that boys and men should be allowed to do so permanently were generally ignored.

Throughout the nineteenth century, the reports of women wearing trousers were, as with David Beckham, mocked or disapproved of. By the end of the century, the media, although accustomed to women wearing trousers, could still range in its commentary from criticism, through resignation, to complimentary.

Ménie Muriel Dowie (1867–1945) rode through the Carpathian Mountains alone and described her travels in a number of popular books. Her *Women Adventurers* (1893) covers well-known cross-dressing individuals and she defined the woman adventurer as:

not a woman who has achieved some heroic deed (whether in men's clothes or not), nor yet the woman who has yielded to some strange freak and left the beaten track for a little time; far from this, she is the woman with one inherent, dominating passion for adventures, for change, for surprise; the woman who keenly loves to be overtaken by unexpected situations.

There were those who were not always convinced about female adventurers. 'Cosmos', writing in the *South Wales Daily News* in 1891, claimed that Ménie Dowie had visited places with plenty of good hotels and an abundance of tourists. 'She would,' wrote Cosmos, 'have encountered more danger in the Essex salt marshes, where she would have been apprehended for masquerading in masculine attire.'[13]

Perhaps women felt that they could not achieve anything in their native country, and needed to travel elsewhere. When Minnie Hodges was arrested in New York, she told the court she was going to the diamond fields in Brazil to make her fortune. 'Men seem to think that girls can't do anything,' she said, adding, 'and they can't do much in this country.'[14]

As the number of women travellers grew, their desire to visit places normally reserved for men increased – as did their desire to ditch their chaperones. Even visiting museums or galleries in Britain required supervision. Gertrude Bell wanted to visit the National Gallery 'but you see there is no one to take me. If I were a boy, I should go to that incomparable place every week, but being a girl to see lovely things is denied me!'[15]

It wasn't just 'lovely things' that women wanted to see but also the wonderful and strange. In 1830, an Egyptian fete celebrating the circumcision of three princes was attended by most of the European ladies dressed in male attire.[16] A year later, two women in male clothing entered King's College, London to view the corpse of John Bishop, the hanged body snatcher. They were promptly arrested and detained 'for a time.'[17]

Some newspapers included details from a more distant past, such as a story from 1212 about a shepherd boy called Etienne from France. He had been preaching in what was later to be called the Children's Crusade, encouraging shepherd boys to join him on a pilgrimage to the Holy Lands. When 10,000 boys turned out to hear him speak, a number of cross-dressing females joined them.[18]

Other attractions were less unusual. In 1833, a disguised woman entered a London gaming-house and 'was speedily cheated by the sharpers out of

£1,500.'[19] And a report in 1839 from a Paris gambling house found that eighteen women had tried to gain admittance dressed as men, including 'an old gentleman, with a snow-white wig, spectacles over his nose, and his decayed frame propped by a gold-headed cane,' who turned out to be a very young and pretty woman.[20]

Such examples show that women were often easily spotted and that establishments had people on the lookout for them. For those who donned men's clothes on a temporary basis, there was always the problem of being unable to replicate the way a man held himself, walked or talked – making the women easily identifiable.

Many cross-dressers only came to light through sharp-eyed policemen or security guards. At an 1847 court trial in Berlin, women were disguising themselves to get into the public gallery and the police adopted stringent measures to prevent other women from gratifying their curiosity in watching trials to which they were normally banned.[21] Similarly, Paris police took measures in 1856 to expel women from the Bourse (stock exchange) as they had been in the habit of going there in male attire.[22]

It wasn't just the police who were on the lookout, churches also had to be alert to women encroaching their preserves. In 1860, monks in the French monastery at Grand Chartreuse were 'horribly scandalised' to find that a woman had spent the night there, against all regulations. Mrs Henry Wood, wife of the conductor, was smuggled in dressed as a monk although she later claimed she only wore the robes to keep out the cold.[23] Another gained admittance to the same monastery and was shown around by a monk – unfortunately, she forgot herself and asked where her husband was.[24]

Some religious houses had extreme rules. Mount Athos in Greece has a prohibition against any woman, or indeed the female of any animal species, from entering: a ban that has acted like a magnet to some. In the early twentieth century, an American student dressed as a male tourist and gained entry but when a suspicious friar called out to be careful as she crossed a muddy street, she instinctively lifted her skirts.[25] Maryse Choisy disguised herself as a sailor and remained for a month, writing up her exploits in *Un mois chez les hommes* (A Month With Men).

Mount Athos continued to be a challenge for women and a number have succeeded in gaining entry, including Maria Poimenidou. In 1953, Maria stayed there for three days and as a result, the Greek government passed a law prohibiting women from entering the monastery – with a maximum penalty of twelve months' imprisonment for those who break it. Even today, women are not allowed within 500 yards of the coast and it is the largest area in the world from which women are banned. In 2017, the Orthodox monks were concerned about new gender recognition laws allowing Greeks over the age of fifteen to change their birth-assigned gender through a simple court ruling, without proving they had undergone gender reassignment surgery. The monks feared that women would simply declare themselves men in order to gain access but at the time of writing, none appear to have done so. In 2019, a female skeleton was discovered during excavations of graves on Mount Athos, which certainly raises some questions, but to date it is unclear who this woman was, or how she came to be in the graveyard.

There are other accounts of women passing as monks. In 1890, a handsome, young applicant obtained the permission of the abbot to enter a Russian monastery, across whose threshold no female had ever passed – or so they believed. The young man soon became a great favourite with the monks but just as he was about to take his vows, it was discovered the novice was a young woman and she was immediately expelled.[26]

In the UK, women were also attempting to gain admittance to religious institutions. As far back as 1471, Matilda Burgin and Margaret Ussher donned men's clothes in an attempt to approach the shrine of St Cuthbert in Durham Cathedral 'knowing this to be prohibited to all women whatsoever.' The sentence was, 'each of them shall go before the procession on three feast days round the Church of St Nicholas and on three other round the Church of All Saints, Newcastle, in the same male attire.' They were also to be publicly admonished in those churches, lest others 'should dare to break forth into such audacity of evil doing.' St Cuthbert is said (according to Simeon) to have disliked women and before the Reformation, they were not allowed any further into Durham Cathedral than the Galilee porch.[27]

There are occasional reports of women being punished by making them parade in male attire. For example, in Australia in 1855, 23-year-old Jane Williams was arrested when a crowd of men gathered in 'admiration of the danseuse, who appeared as a fisherman, and was attired in white ducks and shirt, black neckerchief with sailor-tie, and a red woollen short or jumper over all.' Having given no excuse as to why she had done this, the magistrate suggested that she should be punished by being exhibited on the police court balcony for an hour, or 'promenaded in Collins Street for the delight of her Majesty's lieges.' In the end, she was simply cautioned and released.[28]

Few examples exist of non-Western women cross-dressing to gain entry to restricted places. One is an account by Meleck-Hanum, who fell in love with H. H. Kibritzli-Mehemet-Pasha and agreed to marry him – despite her horror of having to join his harem. In her 1887 autobiography, *Thirty Years in the Harem*, she details the life of the women showing how much more freedom they enjoyed than their Western counterparts. 'They go out a great deal,' she wrote, 'and sometimes visit the mosques in male attire.'[29]

Occasionally, women did cross-dress for a specific purpose with the full knowledge of others, even men, but only in situations where female attire would have been impractical. In Australia, the first women to walk through a deep mine was in Fergusson's Shaft at the Moonta mines in 1873. The Adelaide *Evening Journal* reported that two women who had gained permission to go underground, 'habited themselves in male attire with miners' hats and probably candles complete, descended the shaft.' But still the attitude that females were weak beings crept into their report as they proudly noted the women showed wonderful presence of mind in going down the ladders. Later, the miners claimed they were unaware of their presence, supposing the youthful forms to be those of some boy visitors.[30]

For many young women, dressing as a boy gave a very androgynous appearance and they could be accepted with just a glance. For other women, who had cross-lived for some time, even if appearing quite masculine, suspicions gathered about them, such as the unnamed individual in Aberdeen who was a well-known businessman but about whom 'a sensation has been caused by whisperings' that he was a woman. After being seen visiting a 1902 Aberdeen Art Exhibition, he was described as being 'dressed faultlessly in every detail', the concealment helped along by 'a deep voice and a decidedly manly appearance. She has, in fact, grown a slight moustache, and is a regular attendant at the hairdressers.'[31]

Perhaps because he was a well-known businessman, the newspaper didn't want to name him in case of potential law suits. Not naming individuals is common in the reports of cross-dressing and cross-living, particularly in the first half of the nineteenth century when there were genuine concerns of bringing shame upon not just the individual concerned, but their family. However, as the number of newspapers rose sharply in the second half of the century, and competition became fierce, such consideration faded when it was realised that sensationalism brought in readers. Often newspapers justified their decision to name an individual because they were in the criminal record or when a story was seen as 'romantic' and would garner public sympathy.

For some women, gaining admission had a much more serious purpose than to see 'lovely things'. Despite being barred from voting and taking any significant part in politics, some women still attempted (and others probably succeeded) to force their way in. And what better than the apex of political life – the House of Commons itself. The Strangers' Gallery, from which the proceedings in Parliament could be watched, was barred to women yet the *Liverpool Mercury* in 1820 noted that 'the curiosity of many ladies' had frequently 'induced them to gain access to the gallery in male disguise.'[32] In 1802, Elizabeth Ann Sheridan, wife of the playwright Richard Brinsley Sheridan, was said to have gained entry to the gallery in male attire in order to hear her husband speak.[33] Scotswoman Jane, Duchess of Gordon, who raised the Gordon Highlanders regiment at the time of the French Revolution, was known to ride around in military-style clothing, even being painted in 'uniform'. In 1836, she wished to hear William Pitt the Younger speak and so went to the Strangers' Gallery dressed as a man. When it became known she was present, the Sergeant-at-Arms pointed out that females were not allowed in but Jane was not to be beaten. 'Pray Mr Sergeant,' she asked, 'is there any order that ladies who have once got into the gallery, shall be turned out?' This stumped the Sergeant and he made a dignified retreat.[34]

Jane's sister was Lady Wallace, described as 'a woman so eccentric and so entirely void of feminine delicacy that she was shunned even by the society of those indelicate times.' After a separation from her husband, she developed some extraordinary peculiarities and would constantly dress in male costume; she was even 'known to push her way into the Strangers Gallery in the House of Commons during important debates while clothed in that indecorous fashion.'[35]

Similarly, elections proved too tempting for some women. In 1853 in Cincinnati, a woman passed herself off as a man and voted. When she was caught, she was sentenced to 20 days' imprisonment on bread and water.[36] In 1897, a woman doctor, Mrs Andrew Bird, went to vote for her friend who was standing for a position on a London school board. However, on a previous occasion, her name had been erroneously recorded as Dr Andrew Bird and the presiding officer refused to give her a paper. 'I suppose that if I had come in male attire no question would be raised?' asked Mrs Bird. 'None at all,' said the officer. Mrs Bird hurried home, changed into men's clothing and went back to the polling station. However, things did not work out as planned and she was spotted and sent home. This time, she collected her own documentation and birth certificate and managed to vote.[37] In 1908, one woman was caught impersonating her dead husband.[38] There were probably many, many more who simply got away with it.

Women, throughout the centuries, were escaping restrictions on their lives and cross-dressing in order to get out and about. For travellers, wearing of clothes normally forbidden to them was accepted as a necessary evil – but for some, their inexperience often left them exposed. Failing to accurately replicate a man's movements meant they were quickly spotted but it is precisely these women who have left us with an extensive record of how they circumnavigated societal restrictions. Given the thousands of records recovered it begs the question: how many more were there that were never caught?

Chapter 2

Individuals Not Distinguished

Improvements in transport in the nineteenth century meant people were travelling in far greater numbers, not just within the UK but internationally. A curious entry in the *North Wales Chronicle* regarding emigration figures for the year 1857 recorded 120,279 males and 89,202 females but 3,394 individuals as 'not distinguished.'[1]

By the late nineteenth century, more stringent methods were being put into place to check the health of immigrants, so those trying to disguise themselves were quickly found. This didn't stop people trying; Russian David Kovatz arrived in America in 1909 and was taken to Ellis Island where he was found to be a woman. 'David' had assumed male attire in the hope of entering the country more easily but was deported as officials felt they were likely to become a public charge.[2]

Although foreign travel was not readily available to those of low income, ordinary people were now moving more freely around their own country – but for single women, it still remained almost impossible to travel alone. A number resorted to cross-dressing and when caught, one of the most prevalent explanations was that they did so for 'freedom' – not only to go where they wanted but to be treated respectfully and not worry about men's advances. Women travelled for necessity or fun; some were suffering from mental health problems and their reasons could be more complex. Women could also be influenced by what they were reading – the number of novels authored by, or about, women had soared throughout the nineteenth century and as with newspapers, the number of cross-dressing women featured had risen exponentially.

This is not to say women did not travel before the advent of trains: women would have taken coaches or ridden on horseback but there is less direct evidence for these journeys. One example can be found in Victor Hugo's social commentary on Britain, *L'Homme qui rit* (The man who laughs), written in 1869. One of his characters is the spoiled aristocrat, Duchess Josiane, whom Hugo describes as going to a boxing match dressed as a man. He notes that it 'was then the fashion in England' for women to wear men's clothes and that out of six passengers on the Windsor coach, it was seldom that one or two were not women dressed as men. It was, he said, 'a sign of belonging to the upper classes.'[3]

Railways had expanded rapidly since Trevithick's first train puffed into life in Wales in 1804. From 98 miles of track in 1830 to over 10,000 miles in the 1860s, railways connected significant centres throughout the UK, providing new opportunities for travel. The public took to the rails with great enthusiasm, particularly those of the lower classes who were able to travel much further than previously possible – and women could travel in disguise.

Early carriages were as crowded as cattle trucks and the mass of bodies pushed together would have sheltered those in disguise. While many relied on cutting their hair short, or hiding it underneath a cap or hat and wearing men's clothes, others went a little further in their travelling attire.

In 1876, a man travelling from Stafford to Rugby called the attention of a guard to someone in his compartment in the 'garb of a gentleman', whom he was convinced was a lady. The guard, on addressing the 'gentleman', was answered in a 'very musical voice' and the person's clothes did not appear to be a good fit. The two men tried to catch the 'gentleman' out by asking a series of questions, when suddenly, as the train took a sharp curve, the carriage jerked and the man's moustache fell off. This seemed to confuse him greatly but he stuck it back on again, to the amusement of the other two. It was later discovered that the 'man' had taken a first-class ticket from Liverpool to Euston and when travelling through Stafford, some people met him and some monetary transaction passed between them. He then left the train at Willesden and nothing more was known of the mysterious woman.[4]

She wasn't the only one to use such a disguise. In 1904, Mabel Truelove, who had a record of sixty convictions for riding the railways without paying, decided to alter her luck by dressing as a man – complete with 'a fierce-looking moustache' which unfortunately fell off. Mabel explained to the guard that 'she found it impossible to obtain employment as a woman, and so she was going to try what she could do as a man.' She appealed to the guard to give her a job as a ticket-collector, apparently on the principle of 'set a thief to catch a thief.' In court, Mabel expressed surprise that her disguise should have been detected and she asked to be sent home; instead, she went to Lincoln Gaol for a month.[5] In the same year in Leicester, Mary Collett was arrested for travelling without a ticket. She was well disguised, and with her 'artificial hirsute adornment' made a capital 'man'.[6] One Australian newspaper even joked, rather inappropriately, that a Brisbane woman, clad in male attire and wearing a false moustache, had been sent to the lunatic asylum, quite rightly as women 'shouldn't put on (h)airs!'[7]

There were those who could not afford the few pence to buy a moustache. Sally Brown, who appeared before London magistrates in 1892 for walking around in male attire, had used soot to create side whiskers and a curly moustache.[8]

It was not only women who were cross-dressing. Men were doing so and while newspaper reports are not as numerous, they were still appearing quite regularly – and those in authority looking out for suspicious people could make mistakes. Dr Katherine Freytag, a medical assistant at Bonn University, was on a train from Cologne to Hamburg in 1906 when she was arrested for being a man in female clothes. Katherine insisted the police call Bonn University to verify her identity but what she asked the journalist, would have happened if she had not been able to do so? There would probably have been an arrest, an embarrassing interview, or worse, an intrusive body search. Another instance occurred in the same year when Dr Anita Augspurg, the well-known leader of the German women's rights movement, was charged with being a man in woman's clothes – simply because she wore her hair short.[9]

Wearing male attire gave women a mental freedom they could not always get at home. As 'men', they were able to make their own decisions and they were seen as individuals – not a dependent appendage to a male. And they were treated with respect. Very rarely in newspaper reports are we allowed a glimpse into the minds of those who cross-dressed, as they were extremely aware of the shame and disgrace that could be brought down on their families. Aside from quick explanations, ranging from 'a lark' or escaping cruel parents or husbands, few women spoke of what wearing the dress meant to them. To have done so would have been to glorify something that was socially unacceptable and would have brought accusations of usurping male authority. Some women (it was claimed, usually by men), were suffering from mental health issues.

In 1890 in Bath, Nelly Stone was arrested for attempting to defraud the railway company by travelling from Bristol to Weston without a ticket. A guard had discovered Nelly hiding under a seat after apparently wandering about the country for some time wearing male attire – supposedly for protection. Nelly's brother told the court she had left her home at Plymouth but did not know why, although he thought wild things had got into her head through reading trashy novels. The railway company did not press the matter providing her brother took charge of her.[10]

Reading 'trashy novels' was often given as an excuse by women who decided to cross-dress but rarely was it mentioned that newspapers could also have given them the same idea. Many of the articles appearing in the press included prominent headlines of a woman, or girl, in 'male attire', in 'men's clothes' and suchlike, and these were beacons to those considering the idea. One of the most notable features of arrests is the terminology women used, such as 'I did it for a lark'. Even women who were arrested for the first time and who had no record of leaving home would use the same phrases, indicating they must have learnt them from somewhere.

In 1900, Ethel Price, the daughter of a Birmingham Baptist minister, decided to go to France in order, so she claimed, to perfect her French. She walked to the station with her mother, who did not suspect that underneath a long cloak, Ethel was wearing male attire. But in London, Ethel was arrested and put on trial at Marylebone Police Court. Ethel was dismissed with a warning and as an explanation for his daughter's 'mad freak', Dr Price said, 'She is a perfect bookworm, and I find that she got these ideas from reading the works of an authoress who does that kind of thing.'[11]

Paul Bausor, a well-known Cambridge architect, was at a loss when his troubled daughter Winifred appeared in court for smashing windows in 1910 while dressed in male attire. She read a lot of trashy literature, said her father, detective stories, and so on. The magistrate suggested she should be sent away to an asylum.[12]

Other cases claimed that the women were mentally unstable, regardless of whether that was true or not. During the nineteenth century, women could be locked into asylums for any number of reasons and often had little say in the matter. Postnatal depression, alcoholism, dementia, suicidal thoughts, or a variety of social transgressions, including dressing in male attire, could mean a woman being confined to an asylum or prison.

Sometimes, it was not the woman herself who was considered mad but those who had authority over her. A curious case occurred in 1904 when Beatrice Holland, described as a secretary, was travelling around with Frances Woolf Murray. Beatrice was charged with being a suspected person found wearing male attire and Murray, who described himself as an Indian civil servant, was charged with being a suspected person in her company. The girl wore a suit of black-grey tweed, a golf cap, fancy tie and patent leather shoes. The policeman had stopped them just after 10.00 pm as they left the Russell Hotel, telling Beatrice that he suspected her of being a woman. Murray admonished him loudly, 'What about it? What is it to you? That's my servant, and I can do as I like with her.'

At the court, a previous servant named Alice Butler appeared as a witness to state that she had been engaged by Murray but because she refused to go with him dressed as a boy, he tore her skirts off and endeavoured to strangle her. She quit his service. When she saw Murray and Beatrice in an omnibus, it was she who gave information to the police which led to their arrest.

In court, Murray was reluctant to explain why he had dressed Beatrice in male clothes but the magistrate insisted. Murray explained that he had been a judge in India for twenty-one years and that he had been staying at the Arundel Hotel in the Strand. 'I have inquired of the police in that neighbourhood as to whether I am allowed to so dress my servant,' he said, 'I have my own object in doing what I have done.' He went on to give a bizarre explanation, saying he was carrying out a study on the opinion of the lower classes about tax reforms but people might recognise him as a gentleman and not talk to him. He decided to use a servant to undertake the research but would have to pay higher taxes to employ a man, adding that he rarely lost his temper with a woman.

The magistrate was not convinced and directed Murray to be medically examined. He was later found to be 'of unsound mind and Beatrice was dismissed.'[13] There is the possibility that Murray was a homosexual and employed female servants dressed in male attire who pretended to be males. Homosexuality in 1904 could result in years in jail whereas sex with a female servant would usually carry no penalty.

Of all the stories uncovered about women travelling in male attire, not many include those of tramps or individuals who lived on the road, travelling from place to place. Male and female tramps were numerous, but few women were caught cross-dressing despite the fact that in all probability the number was high.

In 1889 in Cahir, Ireland, a youthful street singer known as John Rimmey was refused alms and proceeded to smash windows. When arrested and charged, he was found to be a woman called Binny Rover. She explained that she had come to Ireland some months ago and managed to live by tramping about the country, singing in the streets, and begging. She was sentenced to a month's imprisonment in the female prison at Limerick.[14]

In 1907, 17-year-old Mary Grubsy, whose hair had been closely cropped, was charged with begging alongside an elderly and dejected-looking tramp at Lincoln. When she was searched at the police station, a pair of scissors and bunches of hair were found in her pockets. She explained that she had come from Mansfield, where she had been in service, and had stolen a suit of her master's clothes. She put them on when she got into the country, had met the elderly man and they had been on a 'begging tramp'. The man was sent to gaol for three weeks, and Mary, who cried bitterly, was remanded for further inquiries.[15]

In 1897 in Pennsylvania, Annie Spence was killed on the railway. She had told family she wanted to see the world, so she dressed as a man and tramped around the USA. Unusually, she kept a diary and the *Chester Times* (Pennsylvania) printed several extracts describing her few days as a tramp.

In 1863, an unnamed young woman, 'very decently dressed in male attire' appeared at Coventry Police Court. She had called at the police station the previous night and asked for an order for admission into the tramps' ward at the workhouse, but the officer on duty quickly realised she was female. She said she came from Birmingham and expressed the greatest anxiety about her name being made public but made no statement as to the reason for her actions. Her hair was closely cut and her ensemble was that of a very prepossessing young man. Mr Norris, the chief constable, treated her kindly, made sure some 'decent clothes' were procured for her and sent her home.[16]

Quite often, the only reason women were discovered was through being arrested, particularly if they were given health checks or forced to take a bath. In 1879 in Australia, George, or James, Gould, who was around 15 years old, was found on board the ship *Vernon*, a training ship where young people were sent for correction. He had been arrested for vagrancy and sent to the *Vernon* but while being checked for lice and having a haircut, it was discovered that George was a girl. Her mother, she said, had died eight years ago but before passing away, she had made her daughter a suit of boy's clothes believing she would fare better in the world and George had been in male attire ever since.[17] George first found employment looking after sheep and cattle but was not given any wages even though, as she said, 'she could beat any one of 'em on horseback.' She left and got a job as a 'boots' (a boot cleaner) in a hotel, succeeding until the hotel shut down. Out of work and so despondent that 'she didn't care a bit whether she died or lived,' George travelled first to Sydney. Unable to find work, she wandered around the country, almost starving until the police picked her up. She was looked after by the matron,

Mrs Walker, and there were rumours that Lady Parker was going to adopt her.[18] However, details later came out that George had constructed this romantic 'plucky young girl' story, probably in the hope of eliciting sympathy and lenient treatment at the court. This was perhaps inspired by the large numbers of these types of stories featured in the media; even at fifteen, she may well have been aware of how to use the phenomenon of cross-dressing to her advantage. In truth, 'George' had been employed as a female servant, apparently stole jewellery and money, and was simply on the run using male clothing as a disguise.

There was not always the need for women to travel in complete male attire. A disguise could be engineered from using voluminous clothing, such as in Edinburgh in the middle of the eighteenth century when 'ladies walked in the streets their favourite attire was a large plaid, which was gracefully disposed over the head like a Spanish mantilla, so that it formed a more complete disguise than even a mask.' Edinburgh at this time 'abounded with little dark cellars, which were used as vulgar hostelries, and in these subterranean dens fashionable parties of both sexes assembled for the purposes of feasting and revelry.' To access these parties, women would dress in large cloaks or occasionally in male attire as Anne, the eldest daughter of Lord Royston, did. A lady of wit, beauty, and accomplishments, she used to 'disguise herself in male attire and scour the streets at midnight in quest of adventures like a regular Mohock.'[19] This was a strange comparison as Mohocks were a gang of well-born criminals who, in the early eighteenth century, travelled in gangs terrorising Londoners by disfiguring male victims and sexually assaulting female ones.

Large cloaks could conceal a person so why would women deliberately wear male attire, knowing that it was against biblical and societal strictures? Any attempt would take a certain amount of courage (or inebriation) to risk such social condemnation. But the idea of women disguising themselves had become so commonplace that by the early twentieth century, even the press was reminding the public to consider this. In 1903, when Miss Hickman, a 'lady doctor', went missing, photographs and descriptions were circulated in the *Sketch* pointing out that it was too readily assumed that she would be in female attire. 'Why,' they wrote:

> should she not have adopted man's clothes as a form of disguise? It is known that she has always been an exceedingly active and athletic girl, and for that reason male attire would probably sit more easily on her

than in the case of most women. The fact that she left behind her at the hospital her mackintosh and other articles of clothing certainly gives colour to this theory. Detectives, policemen, and the general public alike all seem to assume too readily that wherever Miss Hickman is hiding she still looks exactly like her photograph.[20]

For the first half of the nineteenth century, the press did not identify arrested women in order to avoid bringing shame upon them and their families. This, however, only applied to those individuals seen as worthy of such respect, such as the 'plucky' girl, a 'romantic' cause or other story which moved the reading public. Even if they had appeared in court and been fined, the press often kept quiet about real identities, although a number would freely use the women's male aliases. However, this consideration did not apply to women who were convicted of offences deemed socially unacceptable. This can be seen from a case in 1856, regarding two young women wearing militia uniforms. It was covered quite extensively, not because of the arrest, but because of a row between court officials and the editor of the *Belfast Daily Mercury*. It originated when the editor had complained about 'the Indecent Exhibition in the Belfast Police Court', when girls were allowed to appear in court still dressed in male attire. The magistrate, who noted the girls had been arrested because 'assuming of male attire by females is contrary to the Town Improvement Act (laughter in court)' added, 'I cannot understand how any person can charge me with having treated a female inconsiderately or cruelly … I could not but pity those unfortunate females.' The defending solicitor, Mr Seeds, commented, 'if you go to the theatre, you may see ladies dressed in male attire, and there is no talk about it.'[21]

In many cases, journalists would often tie themselves in knots switching back and forth between pronouns when describing an individual's life. They would frequently use 'it' – a term which further distanced the women from normal society. In 1828, writers at *The Morning Chronicle* were obviously enjoying themselves as they lavishly described Juliana Blake, an Irishwoman from Galway, but arrested in London. It is most proper they wrote, that 'its' dress should be described:

> On the head was a genuine beaver, of the complete Anglesey cut; the coat was blue – a deep, deep blue; but for the honour and taste of the wearer it should be stated that there were no brass buttons about it. The vest white marseilles, and the – the "*subligacula*" or *unmentionables* were of pure white duck, somewhat too copiously adorned with gutter,

and the boots were like the hat, called after a hare of Waterloo. Thus *martially* arrayed from head to foot – the individual was led into the Board-room – *it* was desired to take off *its* hat in the presence of the Magistrates – *it* refused – the hat at length was removed by the rude hands of a policeman – when, you Gods! what a discovery – as a poet or love-sick peace-officer would say – "her hair fell in golden and luxuriant ringlets around her shoulders; and her sweet face covered with blushes, as it peered over the collar of her blue coat, looked as bright and lovely as the morning star glowing over the waters of the Mediterranean."

This rather romantic image was somewhat destroyed when looking more closely at her hair which, rather than 'golden and luxuriant ringlets', was a 'regular crop' standing up 'like quills upon the fretful porcupine'. Aware of her appearance, the first words Juliana uttered were, 'Please your Honour, they sawed off all my hair.' 'They', whom she did not identify, had apparently sold her hair for two-and-sixpence. When the magistrate asked where she had been the previous night, she replied, 'Where, but in my own virgin virtuous bed.' Unamused, the magistrate ordered her to be removed with the police officer adding, 'Please your Worship, she is dead drunk.'

'Drunk! (said the lady) no, your honour, I am not drunk. I am only in *spirits*; and now, you *ruffian*, you who say I am drunk, I will give you a question, I bet you a shilling you don't answer. Supposing I was drunk, why should I be like a good masquerader? Answer me that, you nincompoop. *D'ye give it up?* Because I would be double disguised – first, disguised in man's clothes, and next *disguised in liquor*. You see, your Worship, I am not drunk, only a (hiccup) *little in spirits*.'

It later turned out that Juliana had shared her 'virtuous' bed with 'a tender-hearted linen-draper, whom she had left in the arms of Morpheus, while she marched forth in male attire, *a la Vestris*, for the admiration of the men, the envy of the women, and the glorification of this sweet little city, which she honours by her residence and adorns with her presence.'[22]

Aware that being identified could bring shame, some women took steps to avoid identification, such as the use of aliases. With no knowledge of their real name, or where they came from, it was often impossible for the police to discover their actual identities. Others would invent stories, such as an unnamed 17-year-old girl from Dumbarton, Scotland who had been found in an almost nude condition on the shore of the Clyde some miles from her home, with her hair cropped short. She insisted that she had been carried off from her home in the early morning by two men who ordered her to change clothes. The police, dubious of this story, pressed for more details which became more and more convoluted, describing at one point the number and variety of scissors her kidnappers carried in their pockets. Finally, she revealed the real story: her parents had been urging her to get work and so she determined to try 'a man's job'. She had taken her brother's suit and a pair of scissors and in an outhouse, she had cut her hair before tramping around the country looking for work. She tried the Bowling shipyard first but at the gate, her courage failed and she retraced her steps towards Dumbarton. Halfway home, she became ashamed of her hair and 'mannish raiment' so discarded the suit with the exception of the tattered shirt in which she was found. The reason she had come up with the kidnap story was that, as she wandered about, two show attendants had joked about her appearance, which made her feel ashamed.[23]

As rational dress began to become popular and women travelled more, particularly on bicycles, more and more began to wear trousers. Even so, images of these women are rarely seen. One story from 1897 sums this up when Ellen Penrose, 'shocked the good people of Coney Island, USA by parading about the streets in male attire' and was brought before a court. Her lawyer denied that Ellen had any intention of violating the law and asked that the charge of disorderly conduct be dismissed. The judge refused and set a date for the hearing. When she was asked why she 'came to be dressed in such an odd costume' she 'naively' remarked that she thought she had as much right to wear 'knickers' and a cutaway costume as any of the other numerous bicyclists that were seen day after day on the Coney Island cycle paths. She also admitted that Ellen L. Penrose was not her right name, but refused to tell them her name, or where she lived.[24]

Few female explorers and travellers intended to pass as men, and those who tried to gain admission to view sights, events or to vote only did so for a short period. This raised certain issues, as many of the women or girls were not accustomed to appearing as men. They could not replicate the way men walked or held themselves, their voices were higher and their hands and feet smaller. For those women who cross-dressed for short periods of time, it often placed them in dangerous situations. Most sensibly stayed in busy areas where they could blend in, for crowds provided a level of safety but if discovered, they could quickly be subjected to violent treatment and often needed others, or the police, to rescue them. Any idea that women should be protected was quickly discarded when they were seen to be deliberately flouting societal and religious rules. When discovered, women could be subjected to having their clothes pulled off, spat at, or hit, which demonstrates the bravery of those who chose to undertake this path.

The majority of women who cross-dressed in order to travel only appear once in the historical record. Was it the publicity and shame that led the women never to don male clothes again? Or did they learn to disguise themselves better? Use more aliases? Whatever the reason for the sole appearances, it will be difficult to discover more.

Chapter 3

It Was Just a Lark

The earliest writings in history describe people who have reversed gender. Some of the oldest myths, legends and traditions include gender switching, or describe a 'third' sex. Androgyny, particularly in gods, exists in many religious traditions around the world, demonstrating that gods transcended sexual categories. However, colonial regimes destroyed many indigenous imageries and enforced Western notions of binary genders.

The custom of mummering or janneying in Newfoundland, Ireland and the UK included 'an exchange of garments between men and women, who, thus attired in the habiliments of their opposite sex, went from house to house making merry.'[1] One of the reasons mummering died out was the link to violence – in Newfoundland, Isaac Mercer was allegedly murdered by mummers, resulting in an 1861 Act making it illegal in Canada to wear a disguise in public – thereby reinforcing the connection of cross-dressing with nefarious purposes.

Cross-dressing during these traditional entertainments was usually with the full knowledge of all concerned but women often took advantage of these high days and holidays to try out their disguises. In crowds, there is a large variety of body types and with just a few adjustments, a basic disguise could pass unnoticed. Another factor which aided them is 'selective attention'. This happens when so much is going on that the observer's attention is fixed on what they are most interested in – missing the less obvious. A modern example of this is the 'invisible gorilla' test (which anyone can try online), which gives viewers certain tasks that are so absorbing they fail to notice a man in a gorilla suit walking across the screen. Such studies in selective or inattention blindness show just how much human beings fail to observe, which is why eyewitness testimony in courts can sometimes be unreliable. Despite wide coverage of cross-dressing women in the press, they were often rendered invisible by such inattention blindness.

Women, however, did not rely on celebratory days to cross-dress – any party would do. The eighteenth century was the great age of 'travesti' when just about everyone was masquerading. Parties, balls, festivals and entertainments galore appeared all over the country in a myriad variety of locations such as assembly-rooms, theatres, brothels, private residences and public gardens.

One place famous for its parties and entertainments was London's notorious Vauxhall Gardens. People flocked there and women cross-dressed for a lark, or because they had no chaperone to accompany them. In 1829, domestic servants Ann Thorogood and Elizabeth Sheppard, having no man to take them, appropriated the clothes of their young master but got overexcited and were ringing door bells until a policeman caught them. Having lost their position as servants, the magistrate thought that was punishment enough and discharged them.[2]

So prevalent was cross-dressing at Vauxhall Gardens that in 1859, some advertisements warned that 'no Lady will be admitted in Male Attire.'[3] The gardens were shut that same year.

Entertainments did not necessarily rely on specific locations and parties could be held anywhere. One of the most popular was the *bal masqué* (masque ball) where people would dress, often in outlandish costumes and masks, to disguise their identity. There was a vogue for these balls in Russia, which the famous Chevalier d'Éon, a man who claimed to be a biological woman, attended. Italy, France and Britain were particularly fond of them and Horace Walpole, the politician and writer, had 'a large trunk of dresses' available so he could attend regularly. The aristocracy in several European countries attended masques regularly and would have been very familiar with cross-dressing – but it wasn't just the rich. Mary Clermont, a London woman, was charged in 1871 with loitering dressed in male attire supposedly for unlawful purposes. She claimed she was going to a *bal masqué* but, because she was a suspected prostitute, she was fined 20 shillings.[4]

Many stories about cross-dressing women have the feel of fiction. A story, purporting to be true, appeared in the *Illustrated Police News* in 1872 entitled 'Strange discovery – a woman in male attire'. A young man was taken ill and removed to another room where his tie was loosened. As the men were unbuttoning his waistcoat, it was suddenly realised 'he' was a woman. The accompanying illustration, on the front page no less, added a lascivious sensationalism by showing her exposed breasts.[5]

By the mid-nineteenth century, the masque ball as such died out but resurfaced in various guises, including fancy dress parties still enjoyed today. In 1917, a pamphlet by the Juvenile Protective Association of Chicago condemned these entertainments and their indecent dress. 'The greatest dangers,' they wrote, 'are to be found in connection with masquerade and fancy dress balls, where the costumes often permit the most indecent dressing, many girls attending in male attire.'[6]

Masque balls were, and continue to be, enjoyable but for women, there was a freedom that went beyond the removal of constraining, heavy dresses – the freedom of simply being oneself. Harriette Wilson, a famous courtesan, wrote in her 1825 memoirs, 'I love a masquerade, because a female can never enjoy the same liberty anywhere else.'[7]

Women would not have been allowed to attend parties without being accompanied by a man, as to do so would have risked the accusation they were either looking for casual sex, or were whores. However, to go dressed as men would require courage, particularly if going alone and most women would have known there were dangers of arrest.

The women would either have had to buy the outfits or borrow them – but purchases would require a disposable income, which excluded many working-class women. The clothing would also have to be stored at home, as Walpole did with his costumes, requiring secrecy or collusion with someone else. Secrecy required the woman to get dressed, leave the house and either walk or take a cab to the venue, which would put her at risk of arrest. Or the clothes had to be borrowed from a male family member or friend – with or without their knowledge. All of this would have required great courage or daring, which could be ruined by drink.

In 1854, Rose Graham went to a London masquerade attired in 'youth's clothes, *a la Greque*' (Greek style). She was later put into a cab but when it became apparent that she did not know where she was staying, the cabbie handed her over to a policeman. A large crowd followed her to the police station with Rose evidently enjoying the 'spree'. In court, she was 'an object of much curiosity' and claimed she had done it 'just for a bit of a change, as everything in town was so dull.' The magistrate was not amused and lectured her: 'Appearing in the streets in man's apparel is an offence in itself,' – he meant morally, as it was never a criminal offence – 'and had,' he continued, 'been looked upon as such in the Holy Scriptures. In the 22nd chapter of Deuteronomy 5th verse it is stated that "a woman shall not wear that which pertaineth to a man, neither shall a man put on women's garments, for all that do so are abomination unto the Lord thy God".' The *Morning Post* added its own condemnation, 'such an offence … could not be looked upon as a frolic, but as an act of rebellion against God.' Rose was ordered to pay the cabbie and dismissed. Outside she jumped into a cab 'amid loud hurras', and cries of 'Bravo, you lovely Greek' from the crowd.[8]

Undoubtedly, one of the great attractions of the balls was the ability to appear anonymous, making people more daring, more inebriated, and more promiscuous. Writers highlighted the seductive nature of balls and artists produced numerous engravings – all of which increased the sensationalism of masques. Going in 'disguise' took away personal constraints and emboldened people. They might talk in a more seductive, sexualised way, or act more adventurously. For the wearer, the sensation of being in a new costume could provide an exotic and erotic feeling. For those whose disguise was never intended to mask the fact they were a woman, the tighter trousers could give an impression of nakedness and snug waistcoats emphasised the bosom. There was also the possibility of enabling homosexual expression due to the 'fictional' setting.

Many of the large masque balls were in well-advertised and prominent locations, and people wrote about them, but these were primarily attended by wealthier people. For the working classes, similar entertainments were more known through the criminal record. In 1829, there was a complaint about a 'Cock and Hen Club' party in London that included women dressed as men. They, thought the judge, proved what 'sort of individuals resorted to the room.'[9] In 1834, William Bowles, a London landlord, let a room for a masquerade and the subsequent court case considered it a riot, with 'females, attired in men's apparel.'[10]

Naturally, all these types of events came under attack from moralists and religious organisations. This backlash was part of a trend against what were seen as increasingly lax sexual morals and a prevalence for cross-dressing. Gender blending was common in the eighteenth century and commentary from many writers drew attention to the fact that it was becoming difficult to tell men and women apart. Men, went the argument, were becoming too feminine and women too masculine, and moralistic crusaders pushed for more rigidly enforced gender barriers. Once these gender barriers were in place, moralists could use arguments, like those against masques, to deny female emancipation and use them as verbal weapons to curb women's freedoms.

To counter public disapproval, women relied heavily on the excuse that it was all a 'lark'. In this, they were inadvertently aided by the courts, the press and others who portrayed the women in a humorous, patronising way. The women were often described as 'acting' or 'pretending', downplaying their behaviour in order to dismiss it. Mocking the woman is also a recurring theme, turning the event into a comic or theatrical appearance and when men of authority, such as court officers and the police, expressed confusion about gender, it was all part of the amusement. In many articles, the description of the woman is often accompanied by (laughter) in brackets to emphasise to the reader that this was not being taken seriously.

Great hilarity was caused at a court in Glasgow in 1854 by a man and wife who came dressed in each other's apparel. This was reflected in the newspaper article entitled 'A comical couple at the police court.' John Blyth and Elizabeth McInnes were described as having a 'grotesque appearance' and a 'comical expression of face' and their predicament only seemed to 'increase the merriment which prevailed in the court.' The Bailie ordered them to leave and be properly attired before he would hear the case. When they returned, John explained that he and his wife had been drinking but decided, for 'a lark', that they should try on each other's clothes. The Bailie told Elizabeth, 'I will allow you to go with the caution that if ever you wear the breeks again, don't come here with them; (laughter) – for depend upon it, if you do I'll make you take them off quicker than you put them on (great laughter).'[11]

Sending the couple out to change was not unusual; indeed, many men would refuse to hear a case until the woman was 'properly' attired. In Sydney in 1837, the case of Ann Martin put the magistrate's feelings 'to the blush' so that he refused to hear it until she appeared 'in *propria persona*.'[12]

The portrayal of these arrests in the media emphasised the 'silly little woman' theme, particularly if they were one-off occurrences – but men who cross-dressed were rarely treated with humour.

Some articles described cross-dressing as just an 'adventure' or 'mad cap' and the like. When Irene Burston left her home in 1899, her story was headlined as 'Girl's Mad Cap Adventure as a Boy'. Irene abandoned her clothes near a pond, so local police dragged the pool, believing that she had committed suicide. In fact, Irene had travelled to Yeovil and then back to Langport under the name of Sydney Morris. She took a room and during her stay, she even engaged in a 'mild flirtation' with the landlady's daughter. However, people became suspicious, especially as Sydney resembled descriptions of the missing girl.[13] What is unusual about this story is that Irene had been born at Langport and why she would have returned to an area where she was known is a mystery. Similarly, Edith Philips remained in her local village as a miner's assistant while the police dredged the canal, believing she had drowned.[14] However, those who did remain in their local area were a minority.

The newspaper article treated Irene's jaunt as a 'mad cap adventure' and even her 'mild flirtation' with the landlady's daughter did not elicit any further comment. The possibilities of there being anything more to this attraction than the upholding of the disguise was not considered. Indeed, the very fact that it is mentioned at all is merely to stress the lengths that Irene, and women like her, would go to maintain the masquerade.

The lark excuse was used for numerous reasons, particularly if some women wanted to taste activities normally denied them, such as smoking. In Paris in 1863, a 20-year-old woman was arrested because, she said, she simply wanted to walk the streets unmolested whilst she smoked her cigar, which, as a woman, the 'gay youths of Paris' would not let her do. The court was not impressed and she was sentenced to imprisonment, during which period it was said, 'she can reflect on the evils of having a passion for tobacco.'[15] Similarly, Georgina Goodall was charged with being disorderly in 1887 in London. She was carrying a pipe in her hand and stopping every man she met asking for tobacco. She was talking to a flower woman who, on recognising her, said, 'You'd better go home, or you'll be run in,' but Georgina laughed because it was all for a 'spree'. The magistrate was not amused and she was ordered to pay £5 surety for three months, or face 14 days' imprisonment.'[16]

Drink is a common feature of many stories. Women may have needed courage to go into the streets in a manner considered unacceptable, and alcohol often gave them the nerve to try. In 1855, Ann Williams, a good-looking girl of 'light fame' (prostitute), was charged with promenading in Cardiff habited in the garb of a sailor. Her excuse was that she had wanted a glass of grog. She was taken into custody, as it was 'desirable to put a stop to these antics, owing to the constant usurpation of the masculine prerogative by the members of the frail sisterhood.' The girl's appearance seemed to afford much amusement to court spectators and she was committed to prison for fourteen days.[17]

An old woman, Mary Rice or 'Lattie', and a middle-aged woman called Margaret Graham were charged at Glasgow court in 1894 with being disorderly. Mary said they had not intended to annoy anyone and were simply looking for her daughter, and that Margaret had dressed as a man 'for a lark'. They were singing and dancing down the street followed by several lads. The magistrate asked Margaret if she thought she 'honoured your marriage lines by your conduct,' and she replied, 'Well, if it hidna been for drink, I widna hae been here.' They were fined a guinea each or fourteen days' imprisonment.[18]

Other popular excuses which women used for their 'lark' were birthday celebrations. Matilda Stevens and Mary Nolan were charged at Thames Police Court but Matilda claimed she had done nothing wrong. It was her birthday and she had done it for a joke.[19] In Stepney in 1900, Rosetta Manning had said that, as it was her boy's birthday, she put on the things for a joke but assured the magistrate 'most' of her own clothing was underneath the male attire. She was bound over to keep the peace.[20]

Or women did it for a dare. In 1890, Jane Russell, described as a 41-year-old married woman, of South Croydon, was charged with being dressed in male attire and 'thereby causing a crowd to assemble.' A friend had dared her to masquerade, so she went shopping, apparently with the knowledge of her husband.[21] Similarly, in 1891, in the Westminster Police Court, Sarah Brown, 'a buxom little woman', was charged with being dressed in male attire and behaving in a disorderly manner while being followed by a disorderly mob. She wore a baggy pair of trousers, a jacket, and a large billycock hat, and her face had been blackened with soot to represent side whiskers and a moustache. Sarah said that she had put on her brother-in-law's clothes for a 'game' and to win a bet – and did not see 'anything very dreadful' in it. The magistrate called her behaviour foolish but Sarah disagreed, adding, 'I did it for mere devilment, and there will be a good deal more harm done to-day than I have been guilty of. I have never hurt anyone.' She was bound over for two months and, still laughing, left court.[22]

Some 'larks' could have had serious consequences if it was not for the understanding nature of the magistrate. In 1843, Eliza Harris dressed as a man and went into a London street, accompanied by her husband, where she tried to kiss another woman. The woman's horrified husband attacked Eliza and then sued for assault. After promising to 'never put on the disguise of a man again as long as I live, if you will look over it this time', Eliza was discharged with a caution – but if found guilty, she could have faced a hefty fine or even imprisonment;[23] this happened with Harriet Wilson in 1844, who was also charged with assaulting a woman. Harriet, with her husband, had entered a bar and 'chucked the landlady under the chin', asking how she was. The woman, shocked with what she perceived as a man's familiarity, told him he had better offer his attentions to somebody else but Mary persisted and a scuffle broke out. In court, she was fined 10 shillings for assault.[24]

Some magistrates did not appreciate 'the lark' at all. In a court in Roma, Southern Australia, in 1885, one complained, 'We have been told that some women were walking about the streets of Roma on New Year's Eve in male attire. If this be true, and anyone knows the parties summonses should be issued and the offenders severely punished. Jokes of this kind are serious offences, and an immediate check should be put on such impudent immodesty.'[25]

Working-class people rarely had many clothes, and if a woman was walking about the streets in male attire, it usually meant it had been taken from a man – which often left him housebound until the woman returned. If she was arrested, this could take some time. Eliza Fox and Mary Jane Sherlock were detained in 1898 when they had pushed their luck by cheekily going up to a policeman and asking if he knew where they could find lodgings. The men to whom the clothes belonged had to wait until the women were discharged.[26]

As the century ended, and with the rise of the New Woman who favoured bloomers and other bifurcated garments, there were more instances of cross-dressing. When an unnamed woman in Whitechapel was charged, she protested it was just a 'lark' and was discharged. However, as she stepped from the dock, she dropped the skirt she was wearing and strode off as 'the New Woman, indeed, decked out in all the glory of bright-checked "bloomers".'[27]

Some even tried to claim that what they were wearing wasn't really male attire at all. A woman in West Ham in 1896, who dressed for a 'bit of fun', claimed that because 'she had her own underclothing on,' she was not dressed as a man; she too was discharged.[28]

Despite the fact that women were not severely punished for cross-dressing, there were dangers in undertaking such behaviour. Most who dressed for a quick 'lark' did not pass well and were easily recognised as women, resulting in crowds following them – crowds that could turn violent very quickly. They would jeer, spit, and some turned to physical violence, driven by the disapproval of seeing social mores transgressed.

In 1877, Louisa Jones and Thomas Saunders were charged at Brentford, the former with creating a disturbance by walking about in male attire and the latter with attempting to rescue her from the police. Louisa had been followed by a jeering crowd so they took refuge in the Bell pub. A policeman followed them in and roughly handled her – Louisa's nose was bleeding and she was in a dishevelled state, caused by the mob, the policeman or both. When Thomas tried to save her from the policeman, he too was arrested.

In court, Louisa explained that Thomas had been abroad for a considerable length of time and so she had dressed herself in a man's clothes in order to test his recollection of her. They were fined 40 shillings each or a month's imprisonment.[29]

Impromptu punishment from crowds often happened. In 1877, a girl in Geelong, Australia, had left a shop where she had bought some fruit, only to be surrounded by a 'tribe of young urchins who pounced upon her.' Her hair, which was fastened at the back, fell down, and hung dishevelled about her shoulders' – she did the foolish act, she said, for a joke.[30]

Sometimes, crowds followed a woman because she was behaving in a way deliberately designed to attract attention – such as prostitutes – or simply because they were so drunk. Jessie Clark was arrested in 1850 in Newcastle for being drunk and disorderly but as it was her first offence she was discharged; however, the officer had to escort her home 'to protect her from the mob.'[31] Susan Grimes, a 'tall strapping wench' in 1851 was charged with behaving in a riotous manner in the public street at Portsmouth. She had dressed herself partly in soldier's clothes and was driving about in a donkey cart, with 'a rabble attending her.'[32] In 1860, Emily Franklin of London was spotted by a policeman and arrested as a great crowd had collected around her; Emily 'left the court in a cab amidst the salutes of a large assembly of people.'[33]

In 1871, there was a cross-dressing case that caused a media frenzy. Two men called Boulton and Park were caught wearing women's clothing and put on trial. The case generated similar stories, including one from Southport when 'quite a commotion' was caused by the appearance of individuals who were taken for women in men's clothes. The head-constable had to smuggle them out by cab[34], showing that men could also be suspected of being women in male attire.

By the late 1880s, the press was complaining about the large increase in cases: 'This dressing up in men's costume is apparently getting quite a mania with a section of the London female population. The police have had a large number of such cases reported to them of late, and they report that the eccentricity is decidedly on the increase.' They cited the case of two factory girls who had been caught 'near to the scene of the latest Whitechapel murder'.[35] It did not seem to occur to the writer that it may have been precisely because of the Jack the Ripper scare, which was happening at the same time, that more women were going about disguised as men.

This large number of cases posed a problem for the courts in deciding what charges could be brought against the women. The most common were drunk, disorderly, or both. Susannah Long of Paddington was charged in 1872 with being disorderly and causing an enormous crowd, of between five to six hundred people around her, some behaving in a disorderly manner and causing an obstruction of the road. Susannah said her sister-in-law had dared her and she had foolishly put on her brother's clothes – but only for a joke. The magistrate said her conduct had been excessively foolish, and she would have to pay a fine of 5 shillings or be imprisoned for seven days.[36]

However, some magistrates thought it all a waste of time, such as in a case from 1872 in London, where a young woman giving the name of Charles Mao was charged with causing a crowd to assemble. The magistrate was at a loss to know what offence had been committed as Charles had not been disorderly – a crowd had followed her but the magistrate did not think that it was her fault so he discharged her.[37] Similarly, Louisa Halfearines in London was charged with assuming male attire for the supposed purpose of committing a felony. Her hair had been fastened on the top of the head so as to give a manly appearance when her hat was on and she wore a fake moustache. The magistrate said that the prisoner had not committed any offence and if she chose to be 'goose enough to expose herself in male attire, she must take the risk.'[38]

Some men could also be violent towards cross-dressing women but received lesser sentences because of the women's own behaviour. At Newport, Rhoda Smith had attired herself 'for fun' on Whit Monday. She was invited into a house but as soon as she entered the kitchen, two men set upon her and tore off the male apparel, stripping her naked. The men were sentenced to two months' imprisonment and told that 'but for the conduct of the woman they would have had six months.'

In a similar case of men taking offence to a woman wearing male attire, it was the husband who suffered. One night in Wolverhampton in 1881, William Pennell was beaten by William George Porter following an incident two weeks before when Pennell's wife, Florence, a former actress, had dressed in men's clothes. She had apparently done this with his approval to go across the street to buy beer. While no explanation for the assault was given, the length of time the report spent describing Florence's cross-dressing seems to indicate that the men had taken offence at her doing so.[39]

Some larks had tragic outcomes. In 1876 in Australia, Miss Boyd, Miss Taif and several other young girls were bathing when one of them, for a 'freak', dressed herself in male attire. As soon as Miss Boyd saw the 'man', she leapt into the sea, her little dog jumping in after her. A man tried to rescue her but seeing several sharks, he beat a hasty retreat. Drags were used and the little dog's body was recovered but not Miss Boyd – it was believed she had been devoured by sharks.[40]

Most 'larks' carried out by women have only become known through the newspaper reports and court records. Despite many women having their charge dismissed, there were still many whose punishments included bringing shame on her or her family, fines, beaten by mobs, even causing a death, showing that pretending to be a man was not always an easy thing to do.

Chapter 4

Family Life

When women and girls were discovered cross-dressing, the general response from authorities and the public depended on the type of explanation they provided. There were many ways to elicit sympathy, ranging from dressing for 'the lark'; becoming a patriotic sailor or soldier; earning money to keep a family; or even running away from a cruel father. These reasons often secured a more lenient sentence or dismissal, and if the explanation confirmed the subordinate situation of women, accompanied by crying while dressed in 'proper attire', they were generally treated with sympathy and understanding.

Many women used a small set of explanations, perhaps gleaned from newspaper reports. There was so much coverage of cross-dressing to read, and for the illiterate, there was usually someone to read them aloud, so these excuses appeared regularly. This is not to say that women who used stock answers were lying but due to the prevalence of similar answers, often with no corroborating evidence, we cannot always take their claims at face value.

A woman's first experience of the dominance of men was usually from her father. While there are numerous cases citing a father's harshness, there are few about mothers, although miner's assistant Edith Phillips did claim she left home because her mother beat her.[1] However, claims of parental cruelty were rarely followed up, so some could use the excuse to their advantage, as Maud Grace Boardman did in 1910. Charged at Marylebone with wandering, she claimed she could not agree with her father at home and had adopted male dress for the purpose of running away. In truth, she had run away because she was wanted in Lancashire on a charge of stealing £6 and a silver watch.[2]

Occasionally, there was proof of cruelty, sometimes from the father himself. In 1871 in Australia, 'a disconsolate father' was searching for his missing daughter; when she was found disguised in male attire, she refused to return with him and only after giving a solemn promise not to beat her again did she relent.[3]

More often than not, it was less about cruelty and more about caring fathers trying to prevent their daughters' 'ruin'. In Cincinnati in 1849, a father discovered his daughter had arranged to marry without his permission and was preparing to meet her lover in Covington. He asked her to lunch, intending to then follow her and prevent the elopement but was taken aback when she asked him to meet her at Covington. Waiting for her to arrive, he realised he had been duped and so headed for the ferry where he stood watching passengers embark. Before long, 'a ragged cripple, limping naturally, and staring about as though he had never seen a boat before', accompanied by a young-looking boy boarded and disembarked on the other side. Remaining on board, the father continued his search until she finally turned up, confessing that she had been the boy and had since been married. In the spirit of the best romantic stories, the father accepted the inevitable and blessed them both.[4]

It was not always the case that family members would chase after the women themselves; sometimes they sent a servant or the police. In 1827, G. Russell, Cheltenham's chief police officer, was sent to the house of a lady whose daughter was missing. There is no mention of a father, or any other male family member, so officer Russell set off in hot pursuit, eventually tracking the daughter down to Gloucester's Golden Heart hotel, a destination apparently a 'happy omen for those fair runaways who are ready to sacrifice "all for love".' The story then turns into something of a farce. Bursting in on a chamber, he startled another woman who 'uttered sundry exclamations of terror and alarm' and a chambermaid, hearing the screams, rushed up the stairs. On learning why Russell was there, she told him of a young gentleman who had arrived that evening and *'who wore earrings.'* The maid had mentioned this oddity to her mistress but she dismissed it as the latest fashion imported from the Continent. The chambermaid took Russell to the gentleman's room, which seemed at first to be empty, until Russell noticed a pair of 'delicate feet' protruding from under the couch and ordered her out. Unable to find the man who had aided the girl, Russell then returned her to her mother, despite her reluctance.[5]

Another case from 1864 saw a private detective chasing the woman. The daughter of a French baron had formed an 'intimacy' with an Englishman who lived in the West Country and had left her Paris home. It was midwinter and the unnamed woman took a journey of some hundreds of miles to a foreign country, which must have required great courage. Ignatius Paul Pollaky, the first and most famous private detective in Britain, was sent to find her but as with many of these cases, the outcome is as yet unknown.[6]

From 1275, the age of consent for sex was 12, rising to 13 in 1875 and 16 in 1885, where it remains to this day. When we read reports of couples with large age differences, it can make uncomfortable reading but such differences were not uncommon prior to the twentieth century. In 1805, a man aged between 40 and 50, and his 'son' who appeared to be about 14, had lodged at a linen-draper's in Covent-garden. It soon became apparent that the youth was female and so she was taken into custody. Ann Edgley had left her father, a farmer in Devonshire, about three years earlier and for the last four months had been in Germany with her companion, an Irishman.[7]

One difficulty with a number of these stories is that the media often uses the word 'young', making it difficult to judge an accurate age. Certainly, the younger a person is, the easier it is to appear androgynous. Also, the word 'girl' is often used for women and this can make it harder to assess age. Even today, such belittling language is still used to describe grown women – in sport and elsewhere. When American actor Mayim Bialik (Amy from *The Big Bang Theory*) joined the argument, she posted a video blog in 2017 that was watched over 2.5 million times:

> When we use words to describe adult women that are typically used to describe children, it changes the way we view women. Even unconsciously, so that we don't equate them with adult men. In fact, it implies they are inferior to men … You would never say to someone, 'Go ask that boy behind the bank counter if the notary is here today.' We never call men boys because it's demeaning and emasculating.

The nineteenth century usage of the word 'girl' was intended specifically to emphasise women's inferiority to men.

Women and girls would have needed money to leave home alone and many stories include details of thefts, but if women had no practical knowledge of the wider world, things could go badly wrong when they tried to steal. In 1837 in Hendred, Oxfordshire, a man was offering for sale some waistcoat pieces, a watch and several books but shoppers were immediately suspicious because the prices were so low. It transpired that the woman had stolen them from her father to 'gratify her penchant for a roving life' but she was sent back to 'her injured parent.'[8]

Thomas W—, who was walking about the streets of Kirkgate, Wakefield carrying a bundle, had stolen two of her father's suits and some money. The father arrived and the daughter was reprimanded.[9] In 1881, Sarah Jones, aged 11, had lived with her aunt and uncle in Marylebone for seven years before being charged with stealing five shillings, with which she had purchased two suits of boys' clothing. Sarah went to Taplow intending to apply to a boys' school as she had seen an advertisement and had written to the master, pretending she was a lady who wished to send them an orphan boy. After she had been caught, authorities asked her father to reason with her but all he could get out of her was that she wished to leave her aunt. The magistrate relented to the father's pleas and she was 'taken away by her friends.'[10]

Another way for a woman to raise some money was to sell her hair, which would have had to be cut off in any case if she wanted an effective disguise. An unnamed 16-year-old girl in 1900 suddenly left home at Radstock. As she was believed to be heading for Bournemouth, a telegram was sent asking the police to pick her up. Journalists reporting the story tripped over pronouns and switched between 'he', 'she' or 'he/she'. The girl carried with her a box containing her cropped hair, possibly intending to sell it. Her father came to collect her and the only explanation she gave was that she wanted to go off to South Africa as a nurse, to which her friends objected.[11]

Reading trashy literature is a theme which regularly arises, for in the second half of the nineteenth century, there were countless romantic novels and detective stories featuring cross-dressing women. Reading was usually blamed in cases involving teenage girls or young women, such as Blanche Larne, a 16-year-old from Rouen, France who ran away from her boarding school in 1905. She had apparently been reading the 'penny dreadful' novels and wanted to experience 'real life'. She was sent back to her family.[12]

Only occasionally is it mentioned that the media influenced women. Miss Taylor, trying to walk to her uncle in Sussex, was inspired, according to her mother, by the media coverage of a female convict escaping from Tothill Fields prison in male attire, in which the girl had showed much interest.[13]

There were also young women who ran away from other places, such as boarding schools. In 1904, a Sydney girl ran away from her school because she disliked the discipline and close confinement. Having changed her clothes and taken a hotel room, with 'unbounded confidence she took her meals at the general dining-table, and after dinner sauntered round "the block" and paid a visit to the theatre.' However, the hotel manager became suspicious and called the police, who shipped her back to her father.[14]

15-year-old Agnes Wigtman of Glasgow had been at boarding school at Arbuthnot for five years but ran away in 1908. Returning home, she stole money from a relative, used it to purchase boy's clothing and went to a hairdresser where she was discovered because despite a 'decidedly masculine' appearance her voice betrayed her sex.'[15]

Parents want to protect their children and some thought they had little choice but to bring up their girls in the opposite gender. A number of girls and women who were arrested explained that their cross-dressing was a result of influence from a parent. For men left alone to bring up a daughter and with a business to run, it was sometimes easier to dress the child as a boy, which is what happened to Lillie Brown, a New York shoeblack. In 1882, she was arrested for theft and in court, she explained that her mother had died when she was very young and her father put her in boy's clothes to assist him in his tailoring business. His fellow-workmen would have allowed a girl to sew but not to cut – and a cutter earned three times more money than a seamstress. When the father died, she was left alone and worked selling newspapers and blacking shoes. The newspaper had sympathy for her plight and concluded if, but for the watch incident, whether 'Lillie Brown would not have done much better as a boy than as a girl.'[16]

For those women who grew up in boy's clothes, the better wages, greater respect and freedom were difficult to surrender. John Bradley at Dublin's Kilmainham Gaol told authorities that her mother had always dressed her as a boy and after her death, she did not want to alter her clothing.[17] Similarly, Frank Williams was admitted to a Cincinnati hospital in 1905, but having a terminal illness, confessed he was Frances Lamonche and that her mother had encouraged her to become a boy, as she believed that boys succeeded in life better than girls. Four years earlier, her mother had died and Frances became homeless, sleeping in barns and porches.[18]

It is possible that other parents who had wanted a boy forced their daughters to switch genders. It was claimed the President of the French Republic, Jules Grévy, was so disappointed in having a girl that he raised her as a boy.[19] Other parents believed in the equality of upbringing, such as John Harvey Kellogg of breakfast cereal fame, who brought up his daughter Clara Louise Kellogg as a boy.[20]

Sometimes, during family troubles, women had no recourse but to cross-dress in order to help out. In 1685 in Scotland, Sir John Cochrane had been taken prisoner as part of the rebellion against James II, and was condemned to be hanged. In a much-written-about story, his 18-year-old daughter, Grizel Cochrane, undertook an 'almost unexampled instance of female heroism and filial affection.' When Sir John's death-warrant was expected from London,

Grizel dressed herself in her brother's clothes, took her father's pistol and horses, and twice attacked and robbed the mails. Having found the warrant, she took it home and burnt it. This allowed enough time for Sir Cochrane's father to appeal to King James's confessor (not to mention to make a payment of £5,000) to allow for leniency,[21] and he was pardoned.

Even short outings could be pleasurable for women when they were taken as a man. Another trek across country was undertaken by Madame de Genlis. From a noble family, she found fame as a harpist and writer, and in her memoirs she recalled how her brother-in-law had been taken ill and, unable to gain any information, she decided to visit him. She and her servant cross-dressed in clothes lent by a male servant and she recalled that at each post 'I was delighted at being taken always for a man.' Playing on their disguise, the servant 'chucked one of the maids under the chin, who bluntly rejected her saying, "You are too ugly".'[22]

In a century when mortality was high, a number of stories mention that girls and women were living with other family members or were adopted. In 1854, 14-year-old Eliza Ann Peacock suddenly disappeared from the home of the family who had adopted her. They desperately looked for her, placed ads in papers and offered a reward until she was finally traced to New York where she was working under the name of Edward Murray. Her father hurried from Philadelphia and Eliza rushed into his arms in 'the greatest delight.' He had adopted the illegitimate child seven years earlier from Britain but she had secretly harboured a desire to return to search for her mother.[23]

Throughout history, some women have been forced into marrying men chosen by their family but in some cases, however, they rebelled. In Yale, USA in 1883, two men were working on the railways: the older was about 60, the younger about 16. Ten days or so after they arrived, the older man was taken ill. At the hospital, it was discovered the younger man was in fact the wife of the older man and they had eloped from San Francisco because her father and stepmother had wanted her to marry a man of their choosing. Once recovered, the husband returned to San Francisco and sent for her and she sailed to meet him – this time in women's clothing.[24]

In 1862, a piece entitled 'a Sussex romance' appeared in the *Pembrokeshire Herald*. It began by reminding readers how common it was for women to cross-dress:

The story of running after a lover in masculine attire has very often been told but in one of the principal towns in Sussex, the same course from exactly the opposite motive, has it is said, been very lately adopted. As the story runs, a young lady not out of her teens, pretty, and in well-to-do-circumstances had pressed upon her by her friends a matrimonial engagement to which she had the greatest aversion. To escape the persecution which this brought upon her, she did as many a heroine of romance has done before – ran away from home.

To make her escape, the unnamed woman procured male attire, 'doffed her pretty locks of raven hair' and made her way to another town, getting a job with a fruiterer where she 'worked hard and with satisfaction to her employer.' When she was laid off, she then secured employment as a plumber's assistant and in this capacity 'toiled up and down long ladders, over scaffolding, and in many other inappropriate positions, often bearing heavy burdens.'

In the meantime, her family and friends were using every possible means to find her. Handbills and advertisements were published and searchers combed the area; detectives were even sent to try and find the missing girl, all to no avail.

Back at her place of work, some lead went missing and suspicion, for reasons which were not made clear, fell upon her. A policeman took her to the station and charged her with theft. Despite an investigation showing the accusation was unfounded, her sex had been discovered. When her details were entered into the *Police Gazette* (a police newspaper that shared details between forces), she was recognised. The Superintendent of police, a 'man of kind heart as well as of tact and judgment', saw to it that the young lady was 'decently apparelled', took her to his own home and communicated with her family. She was returned and the Superintendent of police received a modest reward from the family who agreed to drop the unwanted marriage plans.[25]

It would, of course, have been easy for a woman to say she was escaping an arranged marriage. In 1844, a young boy was seeking lodgings in South Queensferry, Scotland but the landlady became suspicious and sent for the local vicar to assist her. The young lady, who appeared about 20, told them she was from Greece and that friends had insisted on her marrying an 80-year-old man in a ceremony that had taken place that morning. She was so disgusted that she disguised herself and went on the run. However, when pressed for more details, such as the names of her friends, she refused to answer. She spoke fluent Greek and French, her English was very good and by her manner, the landlady and vicar deduced that she was from a 'superior condition in life' but that was all they could find out. They didn't believe her story but had no means to find out who she truly was. As with many of these stories, the fate of the woman is unknown.[26]

In a patriarchal society where women were dependent on men, it is not surprising to find a number who wanted to be with their sweethearts. Some of their efforts backfired, such as the woman in 1830 who was caught stealing a pair of breeches so she could follow her beloved, a felon who had been sent to Australia. It is not known if she too was transported for her theft.[27]

Being with your loved one could be very difficult in the past. Class structures and social mores were rigid and for centuries, women were little more than possessions of men who could marry them off for political or monetary gain. So, finding ways to be together with the person you really loved could require ingenuity.

Only rarely are women of colour mentioned. One Australian aboriginal woman, Harriet Paroo, angered the authorities at the Aborigines' Mission station at Warangesda, when she resolutely refused to be confined to their boundaries and was reported several times for 'masquerading in the garb of a man.' She had several sweethearts but as they were on the opposite side of the river, her practice was to rig herself up in male clothes and swim across to them. For this and other more serious little peccadillos, she was ordered to quit the station but the authorities did not find it so easy to get rid of her. In open defiance of the manager, Paroo continued to visit but nothing more was recorded in the newspapers.[28]

A number of women would leave a false trail to make their escape. A bundle of female clothes was found in Baltimore that were found to be the property of Caltha Eads, a society belle of Springfield. During the hue and cry over her disappearance, she was arrested for masquerading in male attire in the company of a Nathaniel Henderson. Once notified, the family sent a telegram asking for the couple to be held until Caltha's mother arrived, however, she had already been released and had left the city. It emerged that Nathaniel had decided to go to South Africa for his health and asked Caltha to accompany him but her family refused consent. In the face of her determination, the family finally relented and the lovers were married.[29]

Even prison could not stop a determined woman. According to the *Hull Packet and Humber Mercury* 'a prisoner confined for debt had been accustomed, for some time, to receive the visits of a fair friend, who was supposed to be his lawful spouse. It having been discovered, however, that the lady had no claim to that honourable title, she was excluded from the prison.' So, she dressed as a man, but 'the lynx-eyed attendants of the Gaol, who are notorious for penetrating disguises and unveiling deception, again unmasked the deceiver, and she was once more expelled, and refused admittance for the future.' Undeterred by this further setback, the 'fair swain dreamt up the idea that his debt was due to the fact that she owed him the money'. She was arrested and sent to the same prison, together at last.[30]

Not all stories had a happy ending. In 1892 in Hidalgo, Texas, two State rangers and a guide were searching the area for some horse thieves when they came across two Mexicans riding the same horse. Ordering them to stop, the man in front cried out, 'I'll die before you shall take me,' and drawing his gun, fired at the rangers. They fired back and the man fell from his horse, dying instantly. The other leapt from the horse, cradled the dead man, sobbing and begging him not to die. It emerged that the couple had eloped as, being 18, her parents had refused to let them marry. They were looking for a priest when they were stopped and thinking the rangers were sent by her parents, she had begged her lover to protect her, which he did with his life.[31]

Others cross-dressed to conceal affairs. In 1884, George Strickler, a wealthy Pittsburgh farmer, became obsessed with Rosa Snyder, a very pretty girl of about 19. He dressed her in male attire, took her into his house and introduced her to his wife as an insurance agent. Rosa would deliberately visit at a time when it was common to invite people to stay if it was late at night. Strickler would also visit Rosa at her place in town. When Rosa asked him to do the fair thing and support her, he agreed to pay her $500; the following day, he and his wife set out for a six-month visit to Kansas and Colorado.[32]

Concealing affairs may not have been always about heterosexual couples. Homosexuality would definitely have to be concealed and a number of stories exist about men employing 'young' women in male attire. These women may have appeared as pseudo men as a means of avoiding the legal ban on men being with men, or it may have been a way to deal with the mental stress of being homosexual.

Occasionally, rather than the daughter or wife dressing in male attire, it was the parent. Women would work as men in order to bring in higher wages and many stories mention their children. A tale which appeared in numerous papers is that of Harry Lloyd, who lived for twenty-five years in

London with Elizabeth, his daughter, who was 26 years old when the story broke in 1910. It appeared that Frenchwoman Marie Le Roy had developed a deep 'sisterly affection', as many newspapers described her relationship, with another woman who was pregnant. To save the woman's reputation, Marie became Harry and they married, bringing up Elizabeth together, which, the *New York Tribune* commented, 'a great many women would like to do.'[33] After Harry's death, Elizabeth was amazed to find her 'father' was an unrelated woman. The media portrayed Harry as a noble woman who came to the aid of her friend, but the reality is that it was highly likely a lesbian relationship or Harry was transmasculine.

Any 'sexual deviance' could have dire consequences. Women could be locked up in asylums for reasons given by male members of the family, and many women we would today regard as lesbian or trans were incarcerated despite having no mental illness at all.

Whatever the reason, escaping the family could be fraught with difficulties and some women became destitute. Among the sick and infirm beggars waiting outside the police station at the Paris Palais de Justice for the daily distribution of soup, a young girl clad in male attire was discovered because she had fainted. When recovered, she said she had put on men's clothes to escape from being molested during her wanderings in the street in search of employment. Bystanders had a quick whip-round for her and no more was heard from her.[34]

For some, it was too much and there are numerous stories of suicides, such as Nina Baker from Colusa County who had run away from home for reasons unknown. Becoming despondent, she tried to drown herself in the sea but could not sink and had given up the attempt. Having been arrested for attempted suicide, in court she was offered 'suitable raiment' but refused to 'don dresses', saying she preferred male attire. Her father was communicated with but nothing more is known.[35]

Why some women who cross-dressed committed or attempted suicide may never be known. Quite a number took place after the woman had been caught, either in prison or when threatened with imprisonment. Perhaps the thought of having to give up their freedoms and revert back to the constraining life of a woman was too much – some stories leave more questions than answers.

A young woman dressed in men's clothes, wearing an 18-carat gold gentleman's ring and gold studs, jumped into the Thames in 1880. A witness said the last words of the twenty-ish, fresh-complexioned, good-looking girl were 'I die for him' but when the body was recovered at Dartford some ten miles away, in her pocket were two photographs of herself, one in male attire, the other in women's clothes.[36] Her identity was never discovered.[37] Was the 'him' herself or a male lover?

At the Ashton-under-Lyne Guardians meeting in 1910, a report was presented concerning a visit to the Macclesfield Asylum, which included details of a female inmate who was labouring under the delusion that she was a man. The explanation given was that she had worked for years as a man; had resided in common lodging-houses for men; and had become so 'practiced being a man until she came to the conclusion that she was one.'[38] In 1859 at Poitiers, 17-year-old Augustus Baudoin cross-dressed because men earned more than women but she had been found guilty of theft. In court, she refused to give details of her family, so was removed to the female ward but her repugnance of showing herself in women's attire among her fellow prisoners was so great, she committed suicide by hanging herself from an iron bar.[39]

Some tried to escape by convincing their families they had committed suicide. Elisa Copiato, aged 16, disappeared from her house in Porto San Giorgio, Italy and when her clothes were found on the beach, it was thought that she had killed herself. In the meantime, a young man was engaged as a coachman and later became engaged to one of the household servants. One day, a man glanced at the coachman, quickly walked up to him and called out 'Elisa.' The coachman tried to escape but was caught and was found to be the missing girl. She claimed that her 'strange behaviour' was due to being in love with a young man of whom her parents did not approve.[40]

A variety of family situations could inspire a woman to don male attire and run away – a harsh parent, or love, or escaping an arranged marriage. Some mothers were forced to leave for the upkeep of their family. Whatever their reasons, many were taking their lives into their own hands and only a handful of these courageous women can be presented here.

Chapter 5

For Love, or Hate

For the majority of cross-dressing women who appeared in the press, any relationship mentioned was inevitably heterosexual. However, for women we would now consider gay, societal pressures meant most of them were forced to marry so while heterosexual relationships are mentioned, without supporting evidence we cannot assume all the relationships were heterosexual. Nor can we assume the relationship existed at all – women knew that citing love meant they could often get out of trouble. What is clear is that most of the women who cited a man as their reason for cross-dressing were trying to get away from him, to prove his infidelity, or to punish him. Clearly, most of these women were not happy, something which could start at the engagement stage.

Sarah Blaymires of Leeds, described as 'of interesting appearance', was charged in 1861 with assuming male attire. She had been walking down the road when a policeman suspected her sex, particularly as she was wearing women's shoes. In court, Sarah explained that for nearly seven years, she had been seeing a butcher and a month earlier, he had promised marriage but not trusting him, she decided to get away for a while. She had visited a number of towns and was everywhere received and treated as a man. She was on her way back to see what the butcher had been up to in her absence and whether he had missed her, when she was arrested. The magistrate warned the 'fair adventurer of the risks she ran by indulging in a course … so dangerous' and discharged her.[1]

Married woman also wanted to get away, and in 1857 in Philadelphia, two young men were arrested as suspected pickpockets. When it was found they were women, they explained that they were on a ten-day 'spree' when one woman took advantage of her husband's absence to travel a little, and preferred the male attire for that purpose. They too were discharged with a warning.[2]

Whether someone was discharged or punished varied on the personal opinions of magistrates and their views on cross-dressing. Jane Medlen, described as a married woman of Stepney, was charged with loitering dressed in male attire, supposedly for the purpose of committing a felony. She explained that her husband had been acting strangely and was determined to watch him. The magistrate said it was a very 'silly trick' but discharged her.[3] Jemima Flemming from London took advantage of her husband being laid up in hospital and put on his clothes 'for a lark' in 1871. The magistrate described her as an outrage against public decency and she was left to find six months' bail money.[4]

Most of the stories in newspapers of woman cross-dressing offer only snippets, usually listed along with hundreds of other crimes treated with equal brevity. However, a number do include more detail which allows a small glimpse into the motivation of the women, and into how courts treated them. A good example is the story of Etty Kilduff in 1882, from Melbourne, Australia, as it contains classic elements of these types of cases.

This story was repeated in numerous newspapers, most simply listed under the police reports with no dedicated heading, and most simply replicating the story exactly as it appeared elsewhere. Copyright rules were limited at this time and articles could be copied multiple times. Most referred to the Kilduff case as a 'peculiar' one, but the *Mount Alexander Mail* enlarged the story under the heading 'Extraordinary freak of a married woman.' In all the reports, Kilduff's appearance was commented on, some describing her as a 'fine-looking woman' or as 'well-preserved, stalwart'. Her appearance was so masculine that it 'was difficult at first to realise that she was a woman masquerading in male attire,' and 'until she spoke it was impossible to say by her appearance to which sex she belonged.' The *Mail* adding admiringly that she 'presented rather a dashing appearance.'

Etty was the wife of an omnibus driver and had taken 'masculine costume' for the purpose of watching her husband, as she feared he was not entirely true to her. She pleaded that in her anxiety, she did not have time to wait and think if what she was doing was wrong and seemed 'keenly sensitive of the delicate position in which her foolish conduct had placed her.' She expressed her sorrow for the silly manner in which she had acted and as she stood at the bar, in front of the dock, she shaded her face 'out of very shame with her hand.'

The magistrate told her that she should be ashamed of herself for going about the streets in a man's dress and warned her that if she repeated such a 'freak', she would be severely dealt with.

What is common in stories such as this and other accounts is the liberal use of words and phrases such as 'foolish conduct' and 'silly' to reduce the 'freak' to something minor, which worked in Kilduff's case as the bench took a lenient view of the escapade. In addition, Mr Hill, a court attendant, stated that he had inquired into Kilduff's account and found it to be perfectly correct so she was allowed to go home.[5]

Even when women were easily identified, there was always the problem of how to describe her – or him. Witnesses tripped themselves up trying to navigate the gender pronouns, often generating a great deal of laughter in court, as can be seen in a story from 1863 of Ellen Doughty of London, a 'young woman, of considerable personal attractions.' Samuel Bridges had seen a man hiding in the shadows and called the police, who arrested Ellen. In court, as Samuel gave his testimony he began to trip up, 'I gave him – her I mean – into custody. She hardly spoke a word, and he – I beg pardon, the young woman I mean – hardly said a word.' Ellen explained that she was watching her errant spouse who was apparently carrying on an affair with a woman who had two children. An inspector of Thames Police confirmed her story, saying that his investigation had found she was a very respectable married woman and that her husband was indeed faithless. She too was discharged.[6]

In 1864, Mary Ann Withnell was charged with being riotous in Shoreditch. A constable said he saw the defendant lying on the pavement dressed in male attire and thought she was a man until he saw a quantity of hair hanging about her shoulders. She was lying there because, having drunkenly insulted a man, he, thinking she was also a man, had sent her flying. Mary said that friends had persuaded her to assume the disguise to search for her husband who they assured her 'was more attentive out of doors to her sex than was quite correct; and, once having adopted the step, she became excited under the influence of a little liquor.' The magistrate fined her 5 shillings and she was required to re-dress before walking away.[7]

For the most part, women who claimed the excuse of love, or lack of it, were taken at face value and not seen as liars or tricksters, even though the reason they were in court was because they were 'masquerading'. In some cases, as with Kilduff's and Doughty's, checks were made to see if there really was a man involved, something that was relatively easy to do if the woman was local. For those from out of town, checks could often take several weeks of sending letters back and forth and in the meantime, the woman was either let out on bail or imprisoned. For these women, it is rare that their story is followed up.

Some magistrates were satisfied that shame alone was sufficient punishment. Lottie Jackson, in 1886, described on the charge sheet as an actress of Albany-street, Portland-road, was charged with assaulting Amy Dumas at Victoria Station. She was further charged with being dressed in male attire for a supposed unlawful purpose. It seems that Lottie had attacked two women as she suspected the fidelity of the gentleman to whom she was engaged. With the intention of following him without detection, she assumed the garb of a man. She discovered her suspicions were well-founded when she found her fiancé paying attention to the two young ladies and, having followed them to the railway-carriage, the fracas occurred. As there was no real damage done, Jackson was discharged on the grounds that she had suffered enough shame, embarrassment and ignominy.[8]

Often the women were only dismissed by the court if they promised they would never don male clothes again. The 'natural' order of things was restored by these women's promises and for the most part, they seem to have kept them as most of the thousands of names which appear in the press never appear again. Of course, they could have changed their names, and many did use aliases – not just to avoid bringing shame on themselves and their families, but to buy time when out on bail while officials were trying to trace their origins.

When women did not keep to their promise of returning to their feminine garb, authorities and the public expressed surprise and struggled to understand why they would jeopardise their, and their families', good name by persisting in such 'folly'. There was little a court could do, however, unless they could be charged with indecency or creating a public disturbance, as there was no law in the UK to charge women who cross-dressed. This left the magistrate little option but to admonish the women as 'silly' or 'foolish' in the hope that a good telling-off would mend their ways.

For many, women did indeed look 'silly' in their attempts to be men. Those who remained within a family home and so experienced men only in a domestic setting had little concept of how a man interacted with the outside world, particularly in male-only environments. Men's behaviour, body language and speech would change in non-domestic settings and women, attempting to imitate them, may have had a cruel awakening when they ventured out into the world. This could explain why a lot of disguises failed on the woman's first outing. One case to illustrate this is from 1880, when an Officer Sullivan in Cincinnati was at the train station waiting to investigate a man suspected of being a woman. On board, he searched the compartment and quickly found a figure clothed in a black suit, straw hat and new box-toed shoes, reclining on a seat. Some people struggling with the 'she/he' pronoun would often resort to using 'it' as Sullivan does when he says, 'it wore a mass of curly hair at the back of the head, and a small black moustache.' Having been taken to Central Station, Kate Bench confessed that she lived in Grand Island, Nebraska with her husband Fred, and explained, 'We lived happily the first two or three years. I had two children, but they are both dead.' Through tears, Kate explained that they had been married for nine years but 'he is so close-fisted, stingy, and cruel, that I have left him twice in my own clothes, and he has caught me each time. Finally, about four months ago, I went to work for some neighbours, who advised me to buy a man's suit, and leave disguised in that way; so I got money enough to buy these clothes at the house of a friend.' Kate was on her way to Chicago when she thought she saw Fred, so leapt off the train and started walking. It was when she had got back on the train that she was discovered because, falling asleep through exhaustion, her moustache fell off and she woke to find several men staring at her. Kate was trying to get to Buffalo to see a sister and be protected as, 'I know my brothers would whip my husband if he comes for me. I hope they will let me go east, for I can never live with him again.' The police decided there was nothing to charge Kate with and let her go.[9]

Escaping cruel husbands often feature in stories of cross-dressing. In 1870 in Horncastle, William Wilson, described as a common sailor, was charged with vagrancy and sentenced to fourteen days in prison. On admittance, William refused a bath before confessing, 'I am a female.' She said she had been married for ten years but owing to the ill-treatment of her husband, she left him and had ever since been obtaining her living in male attire. Once dressed in 'the garments proper to her sex', there was a great deal of sympathy for her and she assured the court she now wanted to get into a respectable way of living.[10] No checks were made on her story and she disappears from view, so whether she did return to 'a respectable way of living' is not known.

The cruel husband excuse was a good way to gain sympathy and with many cases, we cannot be sure of the veracity of the story as they are taken at face value. In 1895, a passenger called Nystrom arrived in New York from Southampton. Nystrom, who had travelled as a man, was found to be a woman when she refused vaccination by the port doctor. She then confessed that she had adopted the disguise in order to escape from her husband who she claimed had treated her with cruelty. The story soon spread among the passengers and a subscription was raised of £20:[11] all on the word of the woman.

Occasionally, there are stories of men forcing women to dress in male attire: the police of Boston arrested a young and good-looking woman, apparently from a respectable family in New York State who had been married for about three months. However, her husband had treated her very badly, pawned nearly all her clothing and had 'upon some pretext, and partly by threats, prevailed upon her to don male attire.' Having been spotted, she was arrested and her husband followed her to the station house. She expressed much gratification at her detention by the police, as she hoped it would relieve her from her husband's cruelty.[12]

It was not just married or engaged women who followed their man but also lovers and mistresses. Edmund Kean, a well-known Shakespearian actor, had an affair with Charlotte Cox, the wife of a London businessman. In 1849, a letter was sold at auction revealing that during their affair, he had told his tailor that two ladies, a Mrs Cox and her sister, would call 'to be dressed in male attire.' Kean's intention was to abscond to America with them both, but the affair was discovered and in 1825, Mr Cox successfully sued for adultery. Kean was ruined by the adverse publicity.[13]

In 1858 in Lewiston, Maine, a young man boarding at a hotel was discovered to be a woman. She was occupying a room with a Mr Ward and the landlord, having found out their secret, promised not to report them if they separated. However, they moved to the town of Greene where they were arrested. It turned out that Ward was a married man with children.[14] And in 1841, a 'suspicious looking chap' and his mistress, dressed in male attire, were discovered. She turned out to be the wife of a New Orleans resident, and her romantic enterprise 'to have sprung from the love of her new lord being so strong as to induce her to break her marriage ties, and fly with her lover to his wild and rocky retreat.'[15]

Very occasionally, there are stories of a ménage à trois and a rather convoluted example took place in London in 1852. A police officer called at John Rose's beer house on the complaint of a tailor whose bill had not been paid. A suit had been made for Mrs Roses' brother – 'Young Alfred', who then turned out to be her sister, Sophia Cecilia Pierson who, according to Mrs Rose, had been married days before to a young man named Moody. Mr Rose, said his wife, would ensure the tailor was paid. However, when the police officer called on the tailor to update him, he was told a different story. He was, said the tailor, pretty sure that Moody was actually John Rose having frequently seen him and 'Alfred Browne' riding and walking together.[16] What the background was to this convoluted story we can only speculate.

On occasions, women felt driven to try and kill or maim their lovers: in 1910, a girl in Rome dressed as a boy and murdered Felice Nardiello by shooting him through the heart. She then threw herself on the body 'sobbing passionately.' It seems that Felice had broken off their engagement a few months earlier and when she heard he was about to marry someone else, she plotted her revenge. She dressed herself as a boy to ensure that she should not be recognised.[17] In 1893, a wife was sentenced to 18 months' imprisonment for disguising herself in male attire and throwing vitriol into the face of her husband, blinding him in one eye.[18]

In 1857, a woman applied for lodgings in Troy, Ohio clad in a 'miserable suit' of grey jacket and pants, oil cloth coat and straw hat and without shoes'. Officers became convinced he was a female and when challenged, she readily admitted it. Georgiana Gendler was 'an intelligent, good-looking woman of nineteen' from Springfield, Massachusetts who had assumed male attire a year before to follow and wreak revenge on her seducer. She had been employed as a rafter and had just come from New York City from where she walked to Philadelphia but broke down with fatigue. The police, rather than prosecute her, promised to either return her to her family or to find her 'employment suitable for her sex'.[19]

When female same-sex couples were mentioned, it was often played down either by the newspaper or by the woman herself and was invariably presented as a 'close friendship.'

In 1865, Sarah Geals, a 'masculine-looking person', was charged with shooting at James Giles, a London boot and shoe manufacturer. Sarah had been employed by James for nine years under the name of William Smith and was married to a woman called Caroline. When James's wife became ill, he engaged Caroline to look after her. After his wife died, Caroline remained as housekeeper and ultimately married him. It was she who told him that William was a woman, nevertheless, he made William the shop manager. But it was not successful and James shut the shop, although he continued to pay William a wage. All remained on friendly terms and William visited them often – but things were not working out. While the British press presented the story as one of female friendship, the Australian press were more direct and referred to Sarah, as she was now called, 'as jealous as if she had been a real man.'[20] Sarah had written to James:

> Sir, I have been thinking of our quarrel, but you give me the cause, and not Caroline. I know she would come and see me often, but you keep her away. She is very submissive, and you do not care how hard she slaves, like some poor drudge of a servant. If you loved her you would not allow it in her declining state of health. Since you have had her you have broke her spirit. If the dinner is not ready to a minute, look at the agitated state that she is in, frightened almost to death. As I told you last Sunday, I am the woman for spirit, and you held my arms and they are black and blue this day. I am still inclined to come to terms to save any more bother or further trouble, as you know what I mean – the affair between you and me that has taken place at Bow. The best thing you can do is to supply me with a few pounds, and I will go to New Zealand, and then you will be rid of those you have acted as wrong to. I must have an answer to this. Tell Caroline to send me a few shillings, and I will pay her again. This is not her fault, but yours. I wait the answer.

James decided to send the letter to his solicitor, so Sarah went to see him. 'Well,' said James, 'what is your pleasure with me?' She didn't reply but put a pistol to his cheek, pulled the trigger and ran away. Luckily for James, the pistol had not been properly loaded and failed to fire. At her trial, Sarah claimed she never intended to shoot him but just to scare him in order that he took better care of Caroline. The jury cleared her of attempted murder but did find her guilty of intent to do grievous bodily harm, for which she received five years' imprisonment.[21]

There are no examples of women in my research leaving or abandoning their children, either to the husband or other family members. Women would usually cross-dress when they had lost everything, particularly their children. When Hannah Snell was abandoned by her husband and then lost her 7-month-old daughter, she took to wearing male attire for the first time, enlisted on a ship and went off in search of him – she later became a very famous female sailor. In 1897, a tramp was found riding the rails in Pennsylvania and when he refused to leave, the police were called. Laura Corey, of Cumberland, Maryland, told police:

> My husband was a worthless man, who took me all the way to Binghamton, N. Y. to get rid of me. We had a child, which died in Binghamton, and after the little one was buried I got tired of standing the abuse of a drunken man, so I made up my mind to go back to my people. I had not the money to pay my fare, so I jumped a freight train. The conductor of this train was kind to me, but said that while he would cheerfully carry male tramps, he drew the line at tramps in skirts. I then decided to adopt male attire. The clothing I wore when arrested I begged from a railroad employee near Albany, N.Y. and continued my journey thus attired unmolested.

She was sent home on a passenger train.[22]

Women often adopted male attire in order to earn a living, particularly if they had been abandoned and left to raise their children by themselves. Some did pursue the father, such as Alice Lindsay who went into a London pub in 1889 dressed in male clothing, specifically to accuse a man of being the father of her child.[23]

Love, or the pursuit of it, plays a big part in the history of female cross-dressing. Even where it was untrue, a story of lost love was often invoked to generate sympathy and a dismissal of charges. Alongside women making up stories, the newspapers would regularly do the same, making it difficult in some cases to determine the truth. After reading through thousands of stories, one develops a 'feel' for fictional stories such as this one about 'a very intelligent woman indulged by her father in literary pursuits and was left in the lurch and disguising herself as a man went to work for a professor and helped him complete a book. After it had finished, he was set to travel but couldn't take his young assistant as the only way he could take another person was a wife. She instantly confesses, they married and lived happily ever after.'[24] Despite being offered to readers as a news article, it is entirely possible the piece is complete fiction.

If such fictional stories were being created, it only proves how popular stories of love-struck cross-dressing women were with the reading public. But in reality, stories did not need to be invented for there are thousands of genuine and tragic examples to pull at the heartstrings.

Chapter 6

A Nymph of the Pave

A great deal has been written about female prostitution but one aspect rarely covered is those who cross-dressed. Like other women who wore male attire, they did so for a variety of reasons: to avoid the police; to surreptitiously approach a possible client; as an erotic lure in a time when men rarely saw a woman's outline; or to attract homosexual men and women.

Whatever the reason, the prostitute is only one of three types of women who cross-dressed with the aim of being seen publicly as women, not men: the actress, whose cross-dressing was largely designed to bring an audience into the theatre; the sports player, for ease of playing but arguably to also bring in an audience; and the prostitute. Other women cross-dressed for the purpose of being removed from the public gaze.

Prostitutes' accounts contain similar elements to other stories: the recognition of her as a woman; a crowd forming (there is the possibility that cross-dressing was deliberately used to attracted a crowd as cover for other prostitutes); the reliance of the 'lark' argument; and leaving the man, whose clothes she had taken, lying in bed. One story from 1830 incorporates all these elements. Eliza, 'a very pretty woman in male attire' had been arrested in London when a crowd formed around her. It was one appearance in a long line of criminal convictions. She and her two sisters had been found guilty of a range of offences – indeed, their father, according to *The Morning Chronicle*, had been 'living by their prostitution.'[1]

When asked how she came to appear in such a 'garb', Eliza replied, 'why for a lark, to be sure,' but to suggestions she might have stolen the clothes, Eliza scornfully tossed her head and denied it. When pressed, she admitted, 'The fact is, that the clothes I have got on belong to my last night's bed-fellow, named Scrivener, a baker, from Watford, whom I have been on terms of intimacy with for some considerable time past.'

'And pray where,' asked the magistrate, 'is he?'

'At home, in bed,' she replied, 'where else could he be, when I have his clothes on my back? No doubt he is by this time rather anxious for my return.'

The magistrate asked the arresting officer if Eliza was a 'nymph of the pave' or 'pavement,' (a prostitute) and the officer admitted he had seen her walking the 'flags' and had no hesitation in saying she was a 'gay' woman.[2]

Some prostitutes cross-dressed not as an erotic lure but simply to avoid being recognised by the police. This is reflected in a piece from 1848 when Paris police tried to make the *bourse* (metro) 'less immoral' as 'many facts of a strange character have come to light, that ladies of a peculiar class have been found dressed in male attire, carrying on affairs in love and money upon a large scale.'[3] Similarly in Cardiff, Ann Amos was arrested in sailor's clothes in 1856. The journalist noted that 'since the Mayor's caution to these unfortunate characters to keep out of the public streets has appeared, many of them have adopted the male costume, for the purpose of continuing in their abandoned and wretched course.'[4] Eighteen years later, the problem had not gone away. When Phoebe Edwards was charged with causing an obstruction, the magistrate complained she was one of a number who were in the habit of getting drunk, disguising themselves in men's clothes and 'generally conducting themselves in such a way as to be a great nuisance in the locality.'[5]

For the most part, prostitutes cross-dressed as an erotic appeal to men. There was not a great deal of opportunity, outside of marriage, to view the female outline and with so many prostitutes, some needed an 'edge' to make them stand out. In fact, it was so common that King James I instructed London preachers to harshly condemn the practice, which clergyman William Harrison did in his 1577 book, *The Description of England*:

> What should I say of their doublets with pendant codpieces on the breast full of jags and cuts, and sleeves of sundry colours? Their galligascons to bear out their bums and make their attire to fit plum round (as they term it) about them. Their fardingals, and diversely coloured nether stocks of silk, jersey, and such like, whereby their bodies are rather deformed than commended? I have met with some of these trulls in London so disguised that it hath passed my skill to discern whether they were men or women.

'Trull' meant prostitute and Harrison is deliberately linking cross-dressing woman with prostitution.

In the same period, a number of women appear in the Bridewell and Alderman's Court Records of London, 1565–1605. Colby College lecturer, R. Mark Benbow, examined the records and found a number of cross-dressing women accused of prostitution, including a spinster, Dorothy Clayton, who in 1575:

> contrary to all honesty and womanhood commonly goes about the City apparelled in man's attire. She has abused her body with sundry persons and lived an incontinent life. On Friday she is to stand on the pillory for two hours in men's apparel and then be sent to Bridewell until further order.[6]

Margaret Wakeley had 'a bastard child and went in man's apparel' in 1601 and other records show women had been apprehended for wearing men's clothes and living a loose life.

What drove many prostitutes to cross-dress was male desire (women rarely had the financial means to employ prostitutes) and while today, the terms prostitute and prostitution refer to those who sell sex, this has not always been the case. In previous centuries, such terms had been used as a more general description and could often mean a woman of sexual laxity (a woman who lived with a man without being married); a woman who had illegitimate children; or those who were sexually active without receiving money.

Most of the stories of cross-dressing prostitutes featured here come from court cases reported in nineteenth-century newspapers. However, despite implications, it can be difficult to definitively identify some of the women as prostitutes because newspapers could be reticent about describing them as such. There is usually little accompanying detail or commentary by the police, courts and journalists about why women were cross-dressing but what is clear is that most cross-dressing prostitutes did not seek to live as men, or remain cross-dressed for any length of time – which made them easy to recognise as women. And rarely did prostitutes bother with male names, other than the occasional attempt to fool the police.

A distinctive feature of cross-dressing female prostitutes is the location in which they chose to ply their trade. Many worked in large cities and where there were crowds, there were usually prostitutes, such as at the notorious Vauxhall Gardens. When the Gardens' licence was due for renewal in 1853, the court worried about 'disgraceful scenes':

> nearly the whole of the women present were prostitutes, and the greater part of them were dressed as men; and at six or seven o'clock in the morning they were turned out of the gardens in a half-drunken state, and the scenes that took place in the neighbourhood were of the most

disgusting character, so much so, that no respectable female residing in the neighbourhood could look out of the window of her house.[7]

It is unlikely that 'nearly the whole of the women' were prostitutes but they would take advantage of masque balls or other travesti parties. An editorial for the *Leicester Chronicle* in 1869 complained about both sexes cross-dressing:

> A disgusting nuisance has been growing for some time past in our parks and other places of public resort. It is that of the appearance of men dressed as women, in company as to the character of which there can be no doubt. One of these masqueraders has lately made Rotten-row his favourite haunt, whilst another frequents several theatres. As if this were not enough, it has become anything but an uncommon occurrence to meet in places of public entertainment, women disguised as men.[8]

A second distinctive feature of cross-dressing prostitutes is that they were predominantly disguised as sailors or soldiers, serving the area around naval docks or barracks. An example was Elizabeth Harrison, a 'nymphe du pave' in Cardiff, who was taken into custody in 1864 for being involved in a drunken squabble near the docks. The constable suspected from her 'shrill voice, effeminate manner, ladies' boots, and superabundance of hair, though she was dressed as a seaman, that she was concealing her sex.' Apparently, she had on other occasions appeared in the 'toggery' of a seaman.[9]

A similar case in Greenock, Scotland concerned a woman known only by her surname, McCann, who was tried in 1886 for appearing in male attire on the public streets. According to the *Birmingham Post*, 'One of the blue-jackets of *H.M.S. Ajax* had fallen asleep in a house in Dalrymple Street.' This was a street close to the docks where the battleship was stationed and McCann had taken his clothes and 'paraded Dalrymple Street for some time.'[10]

Both women were recognised due to their appearance or activity, for example, McCann was 'parading' in the street. Often what gave them away was the voice, hair, or in some cases, small hands or feet. In London a 'handsome young woman,' Ann Smith, described as an actress, was charged in 1872 with being in male attire supposed for an unlawful purpose. The prisoner who was 'the beau ideal of a sailor' was placed in the dock in 'the uniform of a sailor, with a good conduct ring, and her cap bore the name *H.M.S. Immortalité.*' It was the size of her feet which had betrayed her. Ann said she was sorry if she had done anything wrong and she had merely put the clothes on for a joke; the clothes belonged to John Smith, a seaman on board the *Immortalité*.

However, John, if indeed that was his name, was so drunk that he was sent out of court and Ann was remanded, still in her male attire.[11]

There is no evidence of prostitutes stealing men's clothes, rather they 'borrowed' them for short periods leaving the man in some location in a semi-naked state. Occasionally, the man dared them, as Fanny Caffray in Melbourne in 1880, was. She had, it was claimed, 'for some time past led a dishonourable life' before being found by a constable in Victoria Street in men's clothes, the owner of which had apparently dared her to go out in them. The Bench ordered her to be imprisoned for three hours in order that she might have an opportunity of altering her costume to suit her sex, before being discharged.[12]

Despite the number of cases listed, few women persistently cross-dressed – although this only means others were not caught, or gave aliases. There are exceptions. Lucy Nicholson, along with Mary Ann Davies and two other Cardiff prostitutes, was charged for soliciting in Bute-road in 1870. The prisoners, said *The Cardiff Times*, 'belong to the swarm of loose girls which infest Bute-road.' Lucy had been in the habit of walking about in men's clothing and had once been brought before the Bench on that charge. The magistrate told her, 'I feel inclined to give you one more chance, what do you say? Will you never dress in male attire again?' but when she refused, he tried another tack by suggesting she leave town. When Lucy agreed to go, and to the women's astonishment, he dismissed them.[13]

Only a handful of prostitutes can be traced historically – most appear briefly and then disappear again. However, some have extended histories, such as Ann Youngs. In 1870 she, Elizabeth Daris and Elizabeth Sparrow, described as 'girls of loose character', lived together in Military Road, close to Colchester Garrison, a major military base. Although little on Elizabeth Daris can be found, Elizabeth Sparrow has been described elsewhere as a 'loose character', indicating she was a prostitute. Ann Youngs was described as a 'dissipated looking woman' and had a history of prostitution, particularly with soldiers. She received twenty-one days' hard labour in 1872 when found guilty of trespassing in a field with a soldier,[14] and later that year, she was accused of stealing 15 shillings from a private, John Smith. However, 'John' decided not to press charges as he would not like to 'disgrace himself in the Court House' – although it is more likely he did not want to give his real name – so Ann was discharged.[15] It was not until 1875 that the press openly labelled Ann as a 'prostitute' when she was accused of stealing from her landlady. She tried to claim the theft was committed by a soldier who was staying with her but she did not want to name him. Her story was rejected, she was found guilty and sentenced to two months' hard labour.[16] In the 1870s case, Ann and the two Elizabeths were charged with 'being riotous' in Military Road. Two (Youngs and Sparrow) were in men's clothes, 'one of them in the dress of a private of the 2nd Dragoon Guards, with boots and spits' who was sleeping at the house. They were each sentenced to seven days' hard labour[17] but despite Ann Youngs' various arrests for prostitution, this was her, and Sparrow's, only mention of cross-dressing.

Colchester Garrison appears again some four years later in 1874 when Lydia Grores, described as 'a girl of loose character', was apprehended dressed in soldier's clothes.[18]

In a time when working-class people owned few clothes, and men often had one suit of clothing, most of the women obtained uniforms from men who had fallen asleep – which partially explains why prostitutes wore male clothing on an intermittent basis. It seems they wanted to chance their luck in the short time before returning the uniform to the slumbering male, and three of the cases listed above mention that the man had supposedly fallen asleep. Sometimes the men were helped into sleep by plying them with alcohol. A case from 1876 caused considerable amusement at the Western Police Court in Glasgow by the appearance of a young woman dressed in 'fantastic male attire'. The woman, Mary M'Gregor, was charged with causing obstruction on the foot-pavement in Broomielaw. It was alleged that Mary, who was 'an unfortunate,' had enticed a Chinese man into a house and while there, the man had taken so much drink that he fell asleep. During the time he was unconscious, Mary took off his upper garments, dressed herself in them, and left the house to go 'swaggering' about the pavement. As her sex was quite apparent, and the appearance she presented somewhat ludicrous, a large crowd soon collected. She was fined 5 shillings, or in default, she was to remain in the cells six hours longer. During all this time, the unfortunate man was in a sorry plight; with no clothes, he could not leave the house and had to patiently wait in bed until his garments were returned.[19]

Less frequent were occasions when the man actually lent his clothes to the woman. A 'Sailor Girl' at Sunderland police court was charged with being drunk and riotous. Early one morning, she had been rollicking about in a 'very shameless manner' and was arrested. It transpired that a sailor had been 'larking' with the prisoner and had lent her his clothes but when she went off, she left him in the lurch without a rag to his back and his ship ready to sail. Considerable amusement was created in court by the 'ridiculous appearance of the prisoner.'[20]

Even when women were known (or suspected) to be prostitutes, there could sometimes be difficulty in deciding what to charge them with. In 1854, Ellen Dixon appeared in the dock in the clothes of a sailor, charged with being disorderly. The magistrate asked, 'But how was she disorderly?' To which the arresting constable replied, 'She was dressed in sailor's clothes, as she now is,' but the magistrate was unconvinced, 'I don't know that is any proof of disorder. What did she do?' The constable explained that Ellen and several other women were creating a disturbance by 'shouting and singing and everything in that way'.

'Was she drunk?' asked the magistrate.

'She had been drinking,' said Bullen, 'and she had some sailor companions with her.'

When asked for an explanation, Ellen said she had been to Charlton Fair but the magistrate was not convinced, 'Did going to Charlton Fair make you assume a man's dress? You know that in itself is very disgraceful.'

'But it was a masquerade affair,' Ellen retorted to laughter from the court.

The magistrate replied wearily, 'Men do not dress as women, although it appears that women dress as men. Is this woman known to the police?'

The constable replied, 'I know her very well; she is on the town.'

Reluctantly, the magistrate admitted he could not find anything to charge Ellen with and said, 'although she acted in a disorderly and disgraceful manner by assuming a dress that did not belong to her, still she has committed no offence. I hope this will be a sufficient warning to her, for if ever she comes here again she will be punished.'

Ellen made a speedy exit from the court amidst much laughter.[21]

Then there were magistrates who were simply confused. Eliza Fordham was charged with being a disorderly person and being in the street in male attire. In the dock, she was dressed in trousers, a nautical jacket and cap and presented 'a very respectable appearance.' Initially, the court took her to be a man until a police Superintendent informed them that Eliza was female. When an examination discovered her hair, which had been artfully pinned up, a roar of laughter arose at the girl's expense. When arrested, Eliza claimed she had put the clothes on for a lark but the magistrate struggled to understand. 'Did you feel very cold in your own clothes?' he asked, which amused the court enormously.

He seemed confused about the exact nature of her clothes and asked, 'Why is she only charged with having a top-coat on?' The Superintendent replied, 'She is charged with wearing male attire' but the magistrate wearily replied, 'Don't most of the women wear the breeches?' to more roars of laughter from the court. Turning to the girl, he asked what had induced her to wear such clothes but she would not answer. 'Take her away home,' said Dodds wearily, 'and get those clothes off her, and mind you don't do it again'.[22]

Similarly, a Cardiff woman named Ellen Thomas, who appeared in military uniform in 1861, was charged with being drunk and causing an obstruction. The magistrate asked if 'the soldier' had been examined and when told she had not, he ordered her removed, amidst the laughter of those in court and the jeers of the crowd outside, in order that her gender might be tested by a female searcher. When she returned properly attired, Ellen admitted to drinking freely and as a result had, for a lark, put on a young man's clothes who lived in the house. However, the magistrate insisted on ascertaining who the uniform belonged to and asked the prosecution to write to the soldier's commanding officer but a young man stepped forward and admitted to being in the 21st Foot and that he was on furlough. He had no hand in the lark, he claimed, for his clothes were taken while he was asleep in bed.[23] Ellen Thomas had a long criminal record as a prostitute and can be traced through newspapers and archives.

Once women had attracted a client, there was always the question of where to take them. Ann Youngs had been found in a field but there is little evidence of other outside activity. Many of the women would have tempted the men back to brothels. In 1867, Margaret Douglas was arrested in Belfast and during her court appearance, she was told by the magistrate, 'It is most improper for a woman to appear in the streets dressed in men's clothes. Is she married?' The arresting officer said he knew her well, and she resided in May's Lane, the mistress of an improper house.[24]

In Newport Police Court, John Hodgkinson, a labourer, and his wife, Elizabeth Hodgkinson, were charged with knowingly permitting their house to be used for immoral purposes. A few months prior, they had bought a cottage at the fashionable village of Malpas and to the surprise and indignation of the locals, the house soon became the scene of disorder and the 'resort of soldiers' and other men, brought there principally by a lodger named Ellen Hardman. On one occasion, said the arresting officer, he had seen Ellen walking around Malpas in a suit of mason's working clothes.[25]

The magistrate asked, 'Did she appear to manage the clothes pretty well?'

'She did not appear to be able to keep up the trousers very well,' replied the officer, which greatly amused the spectators.[26]

In another case concerning a brothel, a girl of the town, Jane Gillett, was brought into court dressed in the uniform of a private of the 2nd Regiment. She was charged with conducting herself in a riotous and indecent manner at Colewort Barracks. Jane was 'one of the unfortunate girls residing at the Fortune of War, a beer-shop in Portsmouth.' One night, she took the 'regimentals of a soldier who was then in bed in the house, attired herself in the same, and perambulated the barrack-yard, with "a yard of clay," from which she puffed the Indian weed.' The unfortunate soldier was left in 'durance vile' at the house in question for want of his clothes. The magistrate inquired where Jane's own clothes were and another girl called out that she had brought them into court. He asked the girl if she lived in the same house and she admitted that she did, along with fourteen other women. 'It is a disgrace to the town,' said the Major, 'and I hope the house will be indicted.'[27]

Examples from other countries include the story of Mary Wild from Tasmania. In 1853, described as 'a dissolute character' and well-known to the police, she was charged with 'misconduct in being in a common brothel in Brisbane-street.' The magistrate 'reminded her of certain pranks she had played, by dressing in male attire and blacking her face' – using soot as a beard or moustache. She was sentenced to three months' imprisonment.[28]

In 1885, a charge of keeping a disorderly house at Adelaide, Australia was heard against Louisa Clarke Wells. The police had been watching the house – one of the prostitutes was only 15 – and Louisa was notorious for frequently appearing in the streets in male attire. The charge was not sustained and she was discharged.[29]

Intensive studies of location can reveal patterns of prostitutes crossdressing. Anthony Rhys has studied areas in Cardiff and his findings include Ann Williams, who ran a brothel with her 'husband', Ned Llewellyn. She was arrested in 1855 for 'promenading Bute-street' 'habited in the garb of a sailor'. In 1856, Caroline Williams of Whitmore Lane was 'dressed in male attire' in Bute Street – she worked for Mary the Cripple's brothel in Whitmore Lane. Amy Amos, who was just 17, was arrested in Bute Street in sailor's clothes and in 1861, she was living in a brothel in Peel Street. Elizabeth Ford had been a prostitute on Whitmore Lane since she was 17 and was still recorded as such when she was 32. She was arrested in 1860 for 'standing at the doorway of the brothel at 25 Whitmore Lane making a great noise and dressed in men's clothes.'[30]

A rare example involving a woman of colour was the case of Ellen O'Neil, a known prostitute who was charged several times with helping to run a 'disorderly house' – a euphemism for a brothel. In 1896, Ellen appeared at Penarth Police Court, charged with obstructing the thoroughfare by looking 'very coy in "breeks",' which was 'the source of illimitable delight to a crowd of about one hundred persons on account of her novel make-up.' Not able to find her guilty of anything specific, the magistrate dismissed the case.[31]

Another reason that prostitutes cross-dressed was to attract homosexual men and while there is not a great deal of writing on this subject, such behaviour can be traced back to the fifteenth century.

In 1403 in Italy, Florence's local authorities founded an 'Officio di Onestà' (Officers of Honesty), a scheme designed to increase the region's population and to combat homosexuality – so they built a brothel. Workers in brothels were forbidden any practices which might subvert the fight against homosexuality, for example, women in men's garb and 'unnatural' ways of intercourse.[32] A number of prostitutes in Florence had preferred to dress as men (and were punished for doing so), and in late medieval Venice, some adopted men's hairstyles.[33] In response, the Venetian authorities in 1480 decreed that women were not to cut their hair cut short in 'mushroom' style, as they did so only to 'conceal their sex and strive to please men by pretending to be men, which is a form of sodomy.'[34]

It seems to have had little effect for, by the late medieval period, prostitutes in Venice, Florence and Rome often appeared in local courts wearing men's clothes. Indeed, 'cross-dressing so signalled a woman's sexual availability in Venice that, when books depicting fashions became common in the later sixteenth century, the typical Venetian courtesan was shown wearing men's breeches beneath her womanly skirts.'[35]

In Britain, cross-dressing prostitution cases have been recorded from the late seventeenth century at a time when women were first appearing on stage. Prior to that, young male actors represented women and 'the page's body size and his clothes were so sexually appealing to men that some female prostitutes dressed as pages in the street.'[36] There is little writing on using girls for pederasty but a rare example is from Australia in 1882. The writer drew attention to cattle drivers, one of whom was in a Port Darwin camp with a young girl dressed as a boy. While he made no accusations about that particular man, he continued, 'but in most cases these feminine "boys" are the victims of their masters' basest passions. That is the fact, and I do not see why the matter should be minced. There has been too much mincing of it already.'[37]

Until 1861, men found guilty of a homosexual act in Britain could face the death penalty and even when that sentence was abolished, they were often sentenced to many years in prison and social exclusion. However, being caught with a prostitute, even if she was in male attire, would only generate the usual fine. A pseudo-homosexual story appeared in 1833 at Cambridge when author and magistrate, Robert Mackenzie Beverley, wrote a pamphlet on the state of life at the university. He included a reference to undergraduates throwing drinking parties at which 'a Thais, in male attire, occasionally adds a zest to the entertainment.' 'Thais' was a famous Greek prostitute from around 300 BC. In his pamphlet, Beverley states that he was invited to three parties 'of which the principal amusement was understood to be the presence of public women, dressed as Undergraduates.' He did not, he assured his readers, accept the invitations but that twelve or fourteen young men were present at these 'harlot-festivals.'[38] Five years later, according to the *Hull Packet,* another Cambridge undergraduate who took a female in male attire into his lodgings was dismissed from the university.[39]

During the research for this book, only one woman was found who used female prostitutes. The reference comes from a 1903 article entitled 'Sexual Perversion' in the Australian newspaper *Truth*. The piece includes a description of a woman from Lonsdale, Melbourne who had been arrested for prostitution as she was 'always about the brothels'. However, a medical examination found her to still be a virgin, which puzzled the police until it became clear that she was there:

> not to meet men, but women. She has been thus gratifying her abnormal passions under the eyes of the police for the last 10 or 15 years. A remarkable characteristic of this sexual pervert is her great physical strength. She is a woman in sexual organism, yet with the muscular strength of a man. She is always ready to fight men with her fists, and can punish those who ill-treat female prostitutes. She is to be seen almost every night in Melbourne in the vicinity of Lonsdale-street.[40]

Iwan Bloch in *The Sexual Life of our Time* wrote of female same-sex brothels:

> They have their parties, and even their balls, at which the virile tribades appear in men's clothing, and (as also when at home) use male

nicknames. There also exist female prostitutes who devote their services entirely to urnindes. This tribadistic prostitution is especially widespread in Paris. Such prostitutes are called *gouines*, or *gourgnollies*, or *chevalières du clair du lune*. Theatrical agents are said to be especially occupied with tribadistic procurement. There also exist tribadistic brothels in Paris.[41]

It was not just women who cross-dressed: male prostitutes did the same and could be mistaken for cross-dressing women. John Travers (or Scavers) dressed as a female and was charged with loitering in public streets, apparently for some unlawful purpose. It was known that John frequented a 'low public-house in Whitechapel' and a police constable said he had frequently seen the prisoner dressed as a female and had supposed that she was a woman of the town. Despite John's claim that he had done it for a frolic, the magistrate said he suspected it was 'a crime of the foulest character' and 'in order to put a check upon persons detected in such abominable practices', he would put a bail of £50 with two sureties of 25 shillings each and that 'he be of good behaviour for the next six months.' The prisoner put on his bonnet and was hissed at by the bystanders as he left court.[42]

The extraordinary Charlotte Charke, a cross-dressing actor and labourer made famous in the eighteenth century by writing her memoirs and describing her life as a man, also wrote a novel, *The History of Henry Dumont*, which described a 'male-madam'.

The presence of the cross-dressing female prostitute in literature is not extensive but it is worth mentioning *Memoirs of a Woman of Pleasure* (popularly known as *Fanny Hill*) by John Cleland, written in 1748. It was the first openly pornographic work published in the English language and is one of the most banned and prosecuted books in history. In it, the fictional Fanny describes going to a masquerade ball with fellow prostitutes, Louisa and Emily, who were dressed as a shepherdess and shepherd. Emily meets a man who flirts with her, and she believes he is playing along with the disguise but when he leads her away for sex and discovers she is a woman, 'the mixture of pique, confusion and disappointment, that appeared in his countenance, joined to the mournful exclamation: "By heavens, a woman!"'[43]

Despite Cleland's coverage of various sexual acts in the book, he, in keeping with the times, condemns homosexuality and the extract is couched in such terms as to take away the responsibility from Emily. It is made clear that Emily is under the impression that the man has seen through the disguise, that she is only joking and is portrayed as being under the influence of drink.

The number of women identified as cross-dressing prostitutes is probably much higher than discovered in this research and further work is required to explain those stories where an implication exists but no further evidence is included in newspaper reports. Certainly, it is a persistent theme from the earliest of times to the twentieth century. Emily Wilkinson was arrested in London in 1918 in a captain's Army Service Corps uniform and charged with 'insulting behaviour' – short-hand for soliciting. She claimed, 'I could get off better with the boys when in uniform.'[44]

When considering why prostitutes cross-dressed, we have to question the theory that it was predominantly an erotic lure for heterosexual men. If this was true it would be expected that cases would appear across the country equally but they do not – almost all the instances recorded in this study are in the vicinity of London (including outside theatres); naval ports; or areas with significant military barracks such as York, Pontefract, Newcastle, Birmingham and Colchester. No examples have been found at mercantile ports or significant non-military or non-naval cities and towns. It raises the question: were cross-dressing prostitutes deliberately targeting homosexual men? More work on this subject is definitely needed.

Chapter 7

Usurping His Occupation

When society permits one half of its population to earn more than the other, for no other reason than their gender, it should come as no surprise that some individuals will cross that boundary to earn themselves a better life.

Throughout history, women's employment was often limited to that of helpmate for males and few could act independently – and those who did have control were still constrained by restrictive societal attitudes. Well into the late nineteenth/early twentieth centuries, women's jobs were more difficult to find than men's – and pay was always a great deal less (in 2020, the gender pay gap in the UK is still on average 9–15 per cent).

For those women with sturdy frames and appearance, cross-dressing could offer an opportunity to earn higher wages or to have a life with more freedoms. Even for those born without a masculine appearance, prolonged working in a job could alter the physical body so it became more androgynous and less likely to be identified as biologically female. Indeed, there were so many ways for women to pass undetected that thousands were doing so. The examples found of women doing jobs usually reserved for men filled nearly two hundred pages, so it has been necessary to highlight only a few of their stories here.

Until relatively recently, divorce was difficult to attain for those not blessed with wealth and it was often socially unacceptable. It was therefore quite common for a man to simply leave and get married elsewhere; bigamy was rife but the wife, left to hold the family together, would often struggle on women's wages. One option was to cross-work but this in itself was fraught with difficulties. If the woman remained in her original location, she ran the risk of being recognised by neighbours and, as cross-dressing was a disgraceful thing to do in society's eyes, she risked exposure and possibly arrest. Those who did remain locally showed either a great confidence in their ability to completely change their appearance or a certain naivety.

Relocating brought additional problems as it often became necessary to pretend family members were other people. Mothers became fathers, or children become nephews and nieces, which must have put enormous pressure on them to remember all the lies.

Despite many women citing better wages as their reason for cross-working, only a few examples provide a pay comparison. A young woman in Minnesota told the local newspaper in 1853 that she earned about $4 a month while men were getting from 20 to 40. So, when she heard of a logging expedition up river, she cut her hair, donned male clothes and went to work as a cook for one of the gangs at $30 a month. Despite close quarters, none of the men took off their clothes to sleep in their shared bed and seldom changed their coarse flannel garments, so as she remained in camp during the day while the men were out in the woods, her disguise went unnoticed. That was until one day, as she chopped firewood, one of the men said, 'That's a woman.' Rumours spread through the camp until she felt forced to cash in her wages and leave – but she still earned more in one month than she would have done in a year on women's wages.[1]

Another American woman petitioned President Wilson for a permit to dress as a man, on the grounds that in male attire she could earn more than twice as much as when hampered by skirts. The *Flintshire Observer* quoted the difference in earnings in sterling – £3 a week. Using online historic exchange rates for 1913, this equates to around $4 a week, or just over $100 a week extra in today's money.[2] It is not known if the petition was granted.

Most women who successfully cross-worked were either quite young and could appear androgynous, or had worked for many years in a male role so had become more like men physically.

The Chevalier D'Éon was a man who self-identified as a woman but did not want to wear dresses. When forced to do so in 1774, she complained bitterly that she was 'a prisoner of war in skirts' (a sentiment many women would have recognised). Mary Johnson told immigration officers at Ellis Island in 1888 that she had been handicapped 'by nature' and so for the last fifteen years had 'masqueraded as a man.' She admitted she had 'learned to walk, talk and work like a man and ever since then life has been so much more easy and pleasant.'[3]

It wasn't always a simple case of 'learned to walk, talk and work like a man' – there were practical considerations to be taken care of. Hair had to be cut and most women simply used shears or scissors. Others went to a barber where they could also sell their hair – the longer the better as wig-makers paid more for lengthy locks and the money could then be spent on male clothes. A young girl, 'masquerading in male attire' in Petone, New Zealand went to a barber but he, guessing something was wrong, refused to serve her. She found another shop where they did cut it, before taking the 8:40 train to Wellington – after which nothing more was heard of her.[4]

For some women, there were other practical considerations such as large breasts. A well-dressed young man, James Murray, drove into Guelph, West Canada, and tried to sell some horses for suspiciously low prices. The chief of police thought he 'presented a rather robust appearance about the chest' and asked why he had so much clothing bound around there. James replied that the doctor had ordered it as a remedy for a severe cold – but he turned out to be Mary Bell from Toronto. This is a rare example of chest binding.[5] Alison Oram, in her book *Her Husband was a Woman*, describes how William Holton used chest wrappings in 1929 and notes that in her study of 200 cases, this is the only one when binding is mentioned.[6]

A smooth chin and upper lip would not have generated comments in younger women as they would have looked like young beardless men. For older women, the lack of a five o'clock shadow could be a problem and some tried to blacken their faces with soot or wore a false moustache. Some would have realised that by deliberately shaving, they could cultivate a beard but while a number of bearded women did cross-dress, none have been found who admitted to deliberate shaving. When Mary Field was arrested and charged with breaking into two houses at Brenchley, Kent, she had false beards and curls, and a number of other things used for disguise in her possession.[7]

Continuous physical labour can cause women to develop musculature similar to males, losing their characteristic feminine 'curves'. Harsh conditions and limited food can also create a slender body shape so that often the only way to make a quick decision about someone's gender is by their clothing. As American drag queen RuPaul put it, 'We're all born naked and the rest is drag.'

In the past, clothing convention was often set by society for both women and men. Women wore dresses and skirts, and men wore trousers. But as soon as that formula was interfered with, it became difficult to determine who was which sex, and that mattered at the time. Women who wished to cross-dress would cultivate visual indicators that gave an initial impression of maleness, such as hats, smoking, or being seen with a woman on their arm – further emphasised by walking and talking like a man if they could.

Before women could even apply for a job, they needed male clothes and they were not always easy to come by. There were no unisex clothes and for most of history, the moral and sometimes legal codes around clothes were very strict and the one sex did not wear the clothes of the other. Due to numerous stories about French women applying for permission to wear male attire, some thought this was applicable in their own country. While French women were sometimes given permission, it did come at a cost – they were charged a yearly fee.

Lack of money could present a problem in the beginning of a cross-working life and theft of clothes is a common theme. In 1860, Maria Cummings from Durham was arrested on suspicion of stealing a pair of shoes and stated in court that she had come from Ireland as a working woman at the harvest. But she was 'obliged to submit to a much lower scale of wages than the men' so she changed her attire, got a new job and received men's wages.[8]

Some women fashioned trousers out of other clothes, such as an unnamed girl in 1836, who was one of those rare individuals who remained in their local area. The girl had suddenly disappeared from her father's house and her parents had looked for her without success, worried that some calamity had befallen her. A neighbour recognised her and she was arrested. When the magistrate asked why she had done it, she replied that she had frequent disagreements with her mother and so resolved to leave but thought it would be easier to obtain a situation as a boy. She turned her cloak into 'a pair of trowsers', purchased a jacket and hat for a few shillings and, in this new character, 'obtained a situation'.[9]

Women could sell their own clothes to buy male attire, as the selling of clothes was very common in the nineteenth century. Almost everyone wore baggy garments as tight-fitting clothes were not practical to work in and small women could get away with buying boys' clothes to bolster their androgynous look. Catherine Coombes, who appeared regularly in the press, thought buying boys' clothes 'strange at first' and practised by walking 'about the streets for a long time, to make myself look as manly as possible,' because 'you can't make yourself a man at once, you know.'[10]

Occasionally, women cross-worked not from choice but because they were instructed to do so – such as the 'ludicrous circumstances' in Suffolk in 1805 related to 'amuse some of our numerous readers'. A gentleman with a small independent fortune was facing a fine for keeping a liveried servant and not declaring it on his taxes. In court, he brought in the supposed livery servant

– a female in men's attire. As the judges knew of no law to prevent a man putting his maid into livery, the charges were dropped.[11] Nobody asked the woman what she thought of it all and although at first glance it may be a story of penny-pinching, the fact that the woman is presented as a pseudo-man could also be seen as a possible indication of homosexuality on the part of the employer.

The types of employment where women worked as men were wide-ranging; some, like the female barman, have received a great deal of coverage both then and now, mainly because their stories are often quite detailed and provide longer narratives. However, as they have been covered extensively elsewhere, they are not included here. Numerous women also worked as doctors, surgeons and even policemen. For thirty years, Fernando Wisson was a policeman in Seville until badly injured. Fernando told hospital staff that she was a Frenchwoman, born in Paris in 1836, and had assumed male disguise when she was a girl, serving in the French army before emigrating to Seville. The article ended on the wistful note that 'the police have lost a valuable servant by the discovery of her identity.'[12]

Other employments were more unusual. Tom Kellett, a hangman in Ireland married a 16-year-old girl in circa 1826 and when faced with more work than he could cope with, dressed his wife in men's apparel and she covered for him. She is only one of a handful of female executioners – two are known from Ireland[13]; and in 1749, a French executioner at Lyon, responsible for more than sixty executions, got drunk, accidentally revealing he was a woman.[14]

Other unusual jobs included steeplejacks, those individuals who make perilous climbs up buildings, church spires, and chimneys to build, maintain and repair them. In 1781, shortly before it was rebuilt, the spire of St Mary's Church, Leicester, was ascended by a steeplejack named Wright, accompanied by his wife, who was as expert a climber as her husband. The woman, dressed for the occasion in male attire, helped her husband in the repairs and her courage was so admired that a number of the townsmen entertained her to a supper and presented her with five guineas. Two years later, this same woman ascended the spire of Trinity Church, Coventry, to carry out repairs alone.[15]

One way to avoid detection was to have a job that included travel, such as the courier role held by a well-known European, Louis Herman. Having fallen sick and discovered to be a woman, she confessed she had worn male clothes for forty years and had never been suspected.[16] In 1905, a deserted wife's struggle for a livelihood resulted in her assuming masculine clothes and working as a sailor; then a waiter in Sweden and Norway; and a builder's labourer in Berlin. During the last job, she would climb the highest scaffolding and 'performed exhausting physical labour at giddy height without a tremor' – 'the best hand in his gang,' said the foreman. Chance led to her discovery and she was ordered to abandon masculine clothes or a more severe punishment would follow. She said she intended to go to America and restart life there in male attire.[17]

A famous character in California was Charley Pankhurst, a stage-coach driver, better known as 'one-eyed Charley', who lost an eye in a desperate fight with a robber. On death, it was discovered that Charley was Charlotte Pankhurst, who many years before had eloped from her father's house with a postmaster.[18]

Working with a husband was beneficial in a number of ways; not only could he protect her disguise but the dual male income would have made them better off. A Manchester couple were charged in 1871 with being drunk and disorderly and in court, the wife explained that sixteen years earlier, her husband made her cut off her hair and sell it, dressed her as a man, and together they went about the country as house painters. When discovered, she had been separated from her husband for some years and the man she was arrested with was her nephew, with her pretending to be his uncle. They were fined 5 shillings and costs – but she left still dressed in male attire.[19]

How long women worked as men varies greatly, from a few weeks to whole life-times. Often, we only have the woman's word, but sometimes supporting evidence comes from those who worked with them. Catherine Coombes had been married for sixteen years in 1871 and cross-dressed the entire time with the knowledge of her husband, who 'would not work'. When she lost her job as a school tutor, Catherine's brother taught her how to be a painter. Her husband cut off her hair and she worked in male attire for forty years.[20] For twenty of those, she appeared in and out of the newspapers; in 1901, the *Rhyl Record* added some rare, but cautious, understanding for those women who decided to live as men:

> it is not to be wondered at that enterprising and energetic girls who have their own way to make should sometimes, as in this case, seek to enjoy the advantage of man's higher industrial caste. The striking superiority of pay which men receive as compared with women – even when the work is the same – must look very unjust as viewed by the eyes of the feminine competitors; and while the disparity continues there will doubtless be

occasional attempts on the part of women to right themselves by hook or by crook. It may be doubtful, however, whether the ingenuity and perseverance displayed by women such as this one would not be as productive if applied in one of the acknowledged feminine callings.[21]

Cross-working women enjoyed the freedom and privileges which came from passing as men, so much so that when discovered, many refused to give up their jobs or their male attire. Some claimed they simply wouldn't know how to wear women's clothes. Jane Anderson, arrested in 1859 in Cincinnati, said she had worn male attire for three years, in which time she had travelled considerably, including being a cook on an Erie Canal boat. If forced to throw away her male attire, she told them, they must furnish her with a female wardrobe but she wouldn't have hoops, as she 'wouldn't know how to navigate in them.'[22]

Losing a job could make life very difficult, especially if no references were given by the employer, so out of desperation some women turned to wearing male attire. Alice Evans had been in service but lost her situation in 1865 when her mistress complained she was always reading instead of working. For two nights, Alice slept under the arches of London Bridge until a young man told her she could get work on the docks if she dressed in men's clothes. She went to a second-hand clothes shop and changed her outfits but still could not get work. Having become desperate, she was about to drown herself when a policeman saved her life. However, as attempting suicide was a criminal offence, she was arrested and brought before Southwark Police Court. The magistrates gave her up to her friends with a caution.[23]

It is possible to trace some women through several years of arrests. In 1858, a young woman 'in the costume of a railway labourer,' was charged with trying to attempt to obtain money under false pretences. Elizabeth Ann Holman was described as a short and very boyish-looking girl, her hair cropped and parted on the side 'like that of a boy'. She was so well disguised that it was almost difficult to believe that she belonged to the 'softer sex.' About five years before, she had become acquainted with a man named Pearce, a shoemaker. She moved in with him and they had two children, one of whom died; the other lived with her sister in Cornwall. Only during her confinements had she 'left off her male attire' and she was so attached to male clothing and her 'unfeminine but laborious vocation,' that she declared she would never 'leave it off, if the gentlemen were to transport her for it.'[24] Elizabeth had a number of previous court appearances, all in male attire, and was described variously as a road- and field labourer in Devonshire and Cornwall and a miner – all, so she explained, to earn higher wages.[25] In one case, when cleared of theft, she stated she would never wear anything other than men's clothes or work as anything other than a labourer.[26]

For women who were discovered disguised as men, there was, generally speaking, a great deal of sympathy and they were often praised for being responsible members of society – poverty was generally seen as laziness and the fault of the individual, not of the state or society. That sympathy increased when employers also praised the individual. A noted theme throughout the stories of employment is that the women were often highly spoken of in terms of reliability, hard work and politeness.

In 1857 in New York, Edward Craw was employed as a street vendor selling apples. His manager described him as the 'best boy' he ever had. Earlier, Edward had worked as a cabin boy and cook, the Captain stating he was 'exceedingly modest and well behaved.' At times when other sailors indulged in obscene conversation, the Captain noticed that Edward would blush and walk away to some other part of the vessel and often told off sailors for their vulgar jests. Nonetheless he was a great favourite with the other sailors. On being discovered while selling apples, she was made to wear 'proper attire' but the other boys refused to work with her and 'to protect her from annoyance' she was taken into custody by the police. She had dressed in male costume to obtain better wages, she said, and had been successful, even managing to save some money. She carried a large dirk-knife, and when asked its use, declared it was to take the life of any man who attempted to trifle with her honour.[27] Tom Smith was a labourer at a Lancashire paper works in 1878, described as 'a capital worker, a favourite with everybody'. He slept alongside some of the other men in cottages near the works but owing to unexplained circumstances, was eventually discovered to be female. Managers offered to 'buy her clothing more suited to her sex' and retain her services but Tom declined and left, still in male attire. The police were notified but then lost all track of him.[28]

Most women went out of their way to avoid attention but there were those who were far more daring. An unnamed 16-year-old shop assistant in Glasgow gave the 'greatest satisfaction to his employer' in 1861 and in his spare time would speak at revival meetings where he 'held forth most eloquently.' Having impressed some of the Glasgow ministers and the wealthy patrons, he was invited to dine with them but pressed his luck too far and was discovered. The escapade was written off as a 'romantic freak'; she was returned to the parental roof and no more was heard of her.[29]

Even when women had been admired in a work environment, it did not mean that admiration continued after they were discovered; in fact, they were rarely permitted to carry on in their job. When a woman from England at the time of the First World War chose to live apart from her husband, she dressed in male clothes to hide from him. She eventually obtained the position of foreman in a printing office where she was highly respected by the other workers. As a man she had been called up for military service but having confessed to being a woman, she offered to take the responsibilities of a comparable position as a foreman. But the military authorities, while commending her 'pluck', refused to keep her on in the role so she discarded male attire, gave up her foreman position and started life again as a woman.[30]

Johanna Johnson was arrested in Australia in 1873. She explained to the court that men's clothes suited her better because when she wore women's clothes, she was called a man and 'bad names.' She went on to say that she was accustomed to wearing men's clothes and had even fought in the army, where her face was disfigured by an injury. She told the court doctor that she could earn more money as a man and wanted to save to return to her native Germany. She was told she could not be permitted to wear male attire and if annoyed by boys when in her proper costume, she could bring them before the court. The case was dismissed but she was remanded until the police could procure female costume. However, as she had given her clothes away to a poor woman, she was released, still in male attire.[31]

It is rare to find stories about women of colour cross-working. In one example, Eliza Randall was in charge of the engines and machinery in two mills in Elbert County, Georgia, and was a first-class mechanic. The owner of the mills had a number of female prisoners working for him, including Eliza, who was serving a life sentence for murder. He said she was the best hand on the place and her efficiency as an engineer had made her famous throughout the region. He approved of the male attire, as it was safer for Eliza around the machinery and he 'wouldn't have her hurt for the world.'[32]

'A decided step towards the equalisation of the sexes has been taken by the director of Kew Gardens' began an 1896 article in the magazine *London*. The director had, as an experiment, engaged two young ladies as gardeners on condition that they wear trousers. 'Mrs Grundy will, no doubt, raise her hands in horror at the idea,' wrote the journalist, but added, 'after all, lady-gardeners in trousers are much better equipped for the work.' As soon as the article appeared, the director was inundated with applications from girls, but he wanted to wait until he saw how the experiment worked. 'Up to now,' the article continued:

> the florally-disposed novitiates have every satisfaction. They are ready to tackle all kinds of rough work, just like the men. No distinction is made. The director could not engage them as regular gardeners, although they had previous training but as "boys." This involved the wearing of the articles of clothing mentioned, a condition with which the fair ones cheerfully complied … thus is another door for the employment of women thrown open, and, as the trousers are only worn when at work, the question of New Womanity does not rise.[33]

The *Cambrian News* in their coverage of the story added the rather contradictory note, 'the other day a woman was driving a horse in Aberystwyth. She was so attired that nobody could have told she was a woman,' adding, 'most women in these days wear hats and ties and coats very like those articles worn by men.[34] The *North Wales Express* noted, 'professional lady gardeners are, of course, nothing new, but they have hitherto created so much remark that they have sometimes actually dressed as men to escape observation.'[35]

By the turn of the century, it was becoming apparent a change was needed in many areas of employment where women worked, not least in the police. In Chicago, there was a fear that female police would be handicapped by their dress whenever it was necessary to give chase to a runaway but rather than allow trousers, a 'model skirt' was designed. At first glance it appeared to be 'just like any other ultra-tight garment until the necessity arises for chasing a wrong-doer trying to escape. Then the policewoman pulls a string and immediately the skirt becomes a pair of Zouave's trousers, in which she can run with freedom and ease. The skirt is of blue serge, and has a pocket large enough to carry a magazine pistol.'[36] They never caught on.

The main objection (after simply wearing male attire) was a concern that women were taking men's jobs. In 1892, in a piece about a female butcher, *The Morning Call* wrote:

> the gentler sex is gradually pushing man aside and usurping many of his occupations is beginning to assume a serious phase and the question has been pertinently asked if women will not in time compete with men for every point of vantage in the financial and industrial world. It seems

that they are capable of doing almost any kind of work that is done by man. Their choice, of course, lies along the line of light employments, but they do not scorn to do blacksmithing and light machinists' bench work in the factory, harness making, etc.'[37]

After the First World War, women's employment began to change and trousers became more convenient clothing for many jobs. However, attitudes towards women wearing trousers did not shift significantly until the 1960s, when unisex jeans and trousers became popular. It was not until the mid to late twentieth century that women could freely wear trousers in whatever job they were doing.

Chapter 8

Hard Labour

Women have always done laborious jobs, often working as assistants to fathers, brothers and husbands. In 1871, the *Pall Mall Gazette* wrote, 'anybody who has travelled much will have found many places in which women take the hardest part of agriculture and other labour.'[1] 'Other labour' covers numerous types of jobs that women have undertaken for many centuries. For example, in 1282, thirty-six hodwomen (those who carried bricks) worked on the construction of Builth Castle.[2]

In historic periods when the death rate was high, many women were widowed; others were deserted by their husbands or became unmarried mothers. All had to earn a wage with no man to support them. However, women's pay was rarely sufficient to support a family and they began to take jobs usually reserved for men. In Wales, the *Cardiff Times* noted in 1893 there were 'six women classed as builders, seventeen carpenters and joiners, two bricklayers, seven masons, twenty paper hangers, plasterers and whitewashers, four plumbers, ten painters and glaziers, but no slaters or tilers.' 'Which,' they added, 'is the only branch of the building industry strictly confined to the male sex. The same is true of England, where there is no female slaters or tilers. On the railways 12,615 men were employed and 36 females, of the latter 29 were porters and servants, and 7 officials and clerks.'[3]

Stories of women taking laborious jobs appeared in the newspapers precisely because of the work they were doing; we would never have known about them otherwise. They elicited few comments and no real surprise. In 1846, the *Bradfield and Wakefield Observer* simply noted that a 'female navvy' from Newcastle was breaking stones on the railway at Bingley and 'right lustily does she lay on.' For twelve years, she had been working for most of the railways in the North of England, and 'so efficient in her vocation, that she earns 2s 6d a week more than men employed in the same description of labour.'[4]

Even when jobs for women were available, there was very little curiosity about why some women would choose to cross-dress instead. When individuals related their stories, the courts showed little interest in particulars, perhaps due to a lack of time given the number of cases they had to deal with but the media rarely gave much detail either or followed up on the stories. An example of this is the 'unfinished' story of 16-year-old Eliza Evans, who explained to a court how she had escaped detection in 1840. Eliza had been attached to a young man, who left their village in Hampshire to obtain work on the railroad. Eliza, finding it impossible to live without him, had gone in pursuit but failed to find him. Without money, food or the means of reaching her home, Eliza had been reduced to a state of great distress. She decided her only recourse was to get work as a man on the railroad. With the assistance of another woman, she obtained a pair of trousers and converted her flannel petticoat into a shirt, resembling those usually worn by navigators. She got a job in a brickyard and was set to work wheeling barrows of clay but after one day, she found this work too difficult. She spoke to the manager, who gave her a job which suited her better as it was 'a lighter sort of work, and younger people, and even females, were employed at it.' There are many questions left unanswered, such as why Eliza persisted in her disguise if other women were employed? Also, if she was in such dire distress, how did she acquire the trousers and why did the woman collude in her plans to pass as a man? More often than not with these stories, we cannot get to the root of why women cross-dressed due to this lack of curiosity by the courts and press.

Eliza had spent only a couple of days passing as a man, which may have been the reason she worried about sleeping alongside men in the rude cabins provided for the labourers. Some were only constructed of stray pieces of wood, plastered over with mud and other bits of rough timber, with crude benches covered with straw for sleeping. Workmen paid 1s. or 1s. 6d. a week for their lodging, with two or three sharing one of these 'boists' (boxes). On the first night that Eliza assumed men's apparel, she slept in one of these boists with two men; and on another night, the weather being severe, she joined three others. Fearing her sex would be discovered, she decided to sleep where the bricks were heated, rather than go through the stresses of sleeping in the boists with the men. However, many homeless people also took refuge in the warm kiln at night and some had done considerable damage by clamouring over the bricks, so a policeman patrolled the area – and discovered Eliza. In court, the young woman's story excited a great deal of interest, although the nature of this interest was not discussed and the magistrate dismissed the charges. Furthermore, a subscription of 40 shillings was raised among the workmen and others, which paid for a coach-hire home, to where Eliza returned and was never heard of again.[5]

Eliza's story is typical, containing the classic hallmarks of women treated kindly by men in authority despite the general aversion for women in male attire. Various motifs are common: 'following a man'; a hard-working ethic; a modest desire not to be found out; and the agreement to either assume 'proper' attire or to return home. These 'plucky women' stories rarely contain the language used to describe other women, such as 'creature' or 'freak', and rarely are offending words put into italics.

Few journalists provided explanations of how women avoided detection when living in such close proximity to men, perhaps due to a sense of propriety. There are, however, the occasional explanations: 16-year-old Sylvia (Sidney) Hammon ran away from her Ohio home in 1885 and after taking various jobs, she was discovered working on the railways in Chicago. A young roommate explained that Sidney was always the last to retire and always extinguished the light before preparing for bed. They occupied separate couches and in all that time 'he never once woke up in the morning without finding Sidney up and dressed and ready to leave the room.'[6]

Marie Campbell had been working in the shipbuilding yard for about five years and at her lodgings, she slept in the same bed with a male lodger for about four months 'without any one having a suspicion that she belonged to the softer sex.' Marie, who had been left an orphan, wore male attire to better maintain herself and had previously worked as a surfaceman on the railways. But when asked if any of the men knew she was a woman, she replied, 'Do you think I would have let these blackguards ken?'[7]

The surprise of men who shared beds with cross-dressing women is a common feature in reports. At a quarry at Montmartre in 1860, a man was arrested on suspicion of stealing a bottle of liquor. In court, the prisoner on being asked his name, said 'I am Catherine B -!'

'Catherine!' exclaimed the Commissary, 'Why that is a woman's name!'

'And I am a woman,' she replied, 'though for a long time past I have been working as a quarryman, and was previously *garçon* to a public-house keeper.'

A colleague begged for him to be released as it was all a joke. 'The man!' exclaimed Commissary again, 'Why the prisoner is a woman!'

The colleague appeared confused, 'That can't be,' he replied, 'inasmuch, as for more than a year he has slept in the same bed with me, and in a room in which there were several other men; and if he had not been a man, we should certainly have known it!'

Meanwhile, the prisoner had been examined and Catherine was definitely a woman. The court showed no sympathy and she was sent for trial, not only for stealing the bottle of liquor, but also on a charge of 'wearing without authorisation a costume not of her sex' in keeping with French laws which prohibited women wearing men's clothes.[8]

A similar harsh punishment was passed in 1853 when a woman named Duhamel was sent to the Tribunal of Correctional Police in France, on a charge of vagabondage. When the President asked her occupation, she said she was a chimney sweep. 'What!' he exclaimed, 'A woman!'

'Yes,' she replied, 'And why not? Besides, you see I wear man's clothes.'

The woman claimed to have a home in Bondy, just outside Paris, but the President informed her that, 'Inquiries have been made about you there, but nobody knows you.'

'Ah,' replied the woman, 'No doubt you asked for me as a woman, though I am only known as a man. And I am not a lazy fellow, either, I can tell you. During the summer, when there were no chimneys to sweep, I occupied myself in harvest work, and did more work than the men.'

Despite her claims, she was found guilty of being a vagabond and sentenced to a month's imprisonment.[9]

There are a few other female chimney sweeps in the record: in Wales in 1891, there were 112 male chimney sweeps listed in the census, with two women from Swansea and Monmouthshire.[10] In 1829 in Somers Town, a district of north-west London, a man had his chimney cleaned by a poor girl, about 11 years old, in 'a most ragged and pitiable state'. She ascended the chimney dressed as a boy and on being questioned why, she said her father had dressed her as a boy for the last five years and sent her out to sweep chimneys. She slept with the other boys at night on sacks in the cellar. The man severely reprimanded the 'unnatural parents,' ordered them to clean the poor girl and clothe her in the dress belonging to her sex.[11]

The word masculine appears frequently in stories of cross-dressing women but the meaning varies. Intelligent women were often described as having 'a masculine mind' or attitude and many robust-looking women, or those deemed unattractive, were described as masculine-looking. During the nineteenth century, there was a fascination with ultra-masculine women and several became notable for this alone. Examples from earlier centuries were often discussed with perhaps Marged ferch Ifan (1696–1793) the most well-known. However, the fascination with them was precisely because they were women. When women cross-dressed, it was noted on a number of occasions that their build aided their disguise. A girl in the East End of London, finding it difficult to earn a livelihood, assumed a youth's clothing and sought employment at the docks. According to the report, 'having a masculine physique, she experienced little difficulty in practising the deception.'[12] Sarah Madge's death in 1899, aged 67, appeared under the headline 'A Masculine Lady'. Sal, as she was popularly known, had worked at the Whitehaven Collieries, regularly wore a man's peaked cap, a jacket and waistcoat; enjoyed a short clay pipe; and sat astride her wagon horse.[13]

For others, the use of the word masculine was intended as an insult – one used frequently about the women who worked in coal mining. Women had been working in the coal industry from the earliest times but when production rose rapidly in the eighteenth and nineteenth centuries, their numbers increased. Children of both sexes, often half-naked, would drag tubs of coal through narrow, low shafts with chains running between their legs:

> Girls, from five to eighteen, perform all the work of boys. There is no distinction whatever ... in wages or dress. They are to be found alike vulgar in manner and obscene in language; but who can feel surprised at their debased condition, when they are known to be constantly associated, and associated only, with men and boys, living and labouring in a state of disgusting nakedness and brutality, while they have themselves no other garment than a ragged shift, or, in the absence of that, a pair of broken trowsers [sic], to cover their persons.'[14]

In 1842, a law was enacted that banned women and girls from working underground but it was not always successful. Many women felt compelled to take men's clothes and jobs, often aided by unscrupulous employers wanting to keep paying lower wages. Four years after the law was enacted, at an inquest into an explosion in a mine at Chorley, it emerged that women were still working underground. The coroner remarked on the illegality of the practice but some of the jury said it was impossible to prevent, one juror noting, 'The women are fonder of working in the pits than anywhere else, and you cannot keep them out, because there they get good wages ... When disguised, they are very hard to detect. A young woman used to pass our door from a pit at Blackrod, and I said one day to my wife, "That's a clever young fellow"; but my daughter said, "Nay, she's a wench".'[15]

For those women accustomed to working underground, switching roles could bring new difficulties. A woman who lost her job pulling carts down the mine found new work as a brick setter's labourer. She was said to have the strength of a man, easily able to carry up a 'burn' of bricks or mortar on her head to the top of the building. However, she was barracked by women living nearby who, 'expressed their indignation of the step by hooting but she says she must do it or starve.'[16]

Most women changed from underground jobs to working on the pit brow, the area above the mine shafts. It was easier to do that work in trousers but this created fascination and much commentary. The women (and some male supporters) argued that dresses were impractical and even dangerous if caught in engines.

A naïve, or perhaps deliberately malicious, piece of writing appeared in 1856 entitled 'Female Labourers' which began, 'how unnatural the word sounds in this English land of ours, where women are treated with more respect, and more deference is shown them, than in any country in the world.' The writer, oblivious of the true nature of female labour, went on to comment that this 'masculine species of employment' was 'degrading to the female character' and that the:

> kind of attire rendered necessary by the masculine nature of the employment, and the blackness and dirt with which these females cannot avoid being covered, can scarcely fail to undermine their modesty and self respect, while it is notorious that their association with the course [sic] description of men employed in that branch of labour, exposes them to every deteriorating influence of language, manners, and habits.[17]

His opinion was not unique; there was a tendency to see women covered in dirt as somehow more immoral than others. The rest of his article heaped criticism on them and showed no understanding of the difficulty working-class women faced in finding work.

During the 1860s and 1870s, the fascination with coal women in trousers grew as more and more females started wearing them. When R. H. Isaac, the stationmaster at Kidwelly, wrote his memoirs, he recalled, 'in those days (1860s-70s) I have seen gangs of women, dressed as men, working on coal and iron stone tips, and loading and unloading iron-stones and coal to and from railway trucks.'[18]

In addition to the word 'masculine', others frequently used were 'unsexed', epicene, androgynous, Amazon, or unfeminine. A journalist visiting Merthyr Tydfil in 1854 considered the young girls he saw breaking up masses of coke and limestone with large and heavy hammers as 'unfeminine' and 'masculine in form as well as habit'.[19]

Another wrote:

> at Wigan, in Lancashire, for instance, we have met with numbers of these females clad in male attire, and working with the spade amongst ordinary male labourers. There is nothing in their dress or demeanour to distinguish them from those of the other sex. They drink and fight like their male companions, give utterance to fearful oaths, and exhibit a degree of masculine vigour unusual in their sex. The evils arising from the existence of this state of things are easily apparent.[20]

Yet another journalist provided an unpleasant description of the 'unwonted spectacle' of one of the female colliers returning home:

> It was difficult to believe that the unwomanly looking being who passed before me was actually a female, yet such was the case. Clad in coarse, greasy, and patched fustian unmentionables and jacket, thick canvass shirt, great heavy hob-nailed boots, her features completely begrimed with coal dust, her hard and horny hands carrying the spade, drinking, tin, sieve, and other paraphernalia of her occupation, her not irregular features wearing a bold defiant expression, and with nothing womanly about her except two or three latent evidences of feminine weakness, in the shape of a coral necklace, a pair of glittering ear-rings, and a bonnet which as regard shape, size, and colour, strongly resembled the fantail hat of a London coal-heaver; she proceeded unabashed through the crowded street, no one appearing to regard the degrading spectacle as being anything unusual.[21]

There were those who defended the women:

> In the works the women, chiefly young females, are engaged in manual labour from morning to night, hearing all the common language and observing all the usual habits of the unrestrained and half-civilized men. The dress of these wretched females can scarcely be distinguished from that of the men. In voice, manner, appearance, and actions they have become unsexed ... if their habits are somewhat masculine owing to their ultimate association with the other sex, they are by no means worse in that respect than the thousands of their fellow women in Manchester and the other innumerable manufacturing districts of England ...

When the position of these females is compared with that of the various classes we have enumerated, and many others that we can name, the "unsexed" persons referred to are, in fact, more objects for envy than for commiseration.'[22]

Some even attempted to understand the lack of work available to women:

wages reduced to such a point in many descriptions of female labour that the workers barely exist in such abject poverty that their lives are passed with almost no pleasures. Added to them are numbers of women forced into employments unsuited to their sex, of such rough and coarse nature that it destroys in men that respect for women which it is essential for human happiness to preserve. Of this description is the work done on the coal banks of Wigan, where thousands of women and girls, clad in men's clothes, work at the pit's mouth; also the female nail and chain makers of Staffordshire, where their coarse work has almost unsexed the women.'[23]

However, it is clear that it is the loss of men's respect for women, 'essential for human happiness', that the writer truly mourns.

In the 1870s, the government tried to ban women's work on the pit brows – causing many of the women to send a delegation to the House of Commons. No legislation was put in place but complaints about women 'taking men's jobs' continued.

As with many situations when women cross-dressed, it provided an opportunity for women we would now regard as lesbians or trans to be able to live their lives openly. In Durham, an unnamed individual worked in the colliery for fifty years as a man, both in the pits and on the farm. When he died in 1895, he had been married for thirty years.[24]

Other hard labour jobs did not receive similar mass publicity as the Pit Brow Lasses and the Welsh Tip Girls but there was a wide range of such work undertaken. A piece from 1896 states that California had been famous for women who had followed the occupations of men including 'female stage drivers and women stage robbers.' Nannie Hutchinson of Yuba County was forced to earn a living when her father died, leaving her and her mother alone. She applied for a job as 'Pete' in the lumber mills of A. M. Leach and Co. and 'laboured industriously throughout the entire period of its construction, boarding in camp, taking rough fare with the men, and mingling with them in the evenings as unconcernedly as though he had been accustomed to it all his life.' For three months, Pete walked along the narrow plank beside the flume with a heavy pike pole, keeping the logs moving but one day, he had a fainting fit and fell into the flume. When it was discovered Pete was a woman, she was treated kindly and eventually married one of the loggers.[25]

Women cross-worked not simply to earn more but to take control over their finances. The history of women's employment and wages is complex but women were often dependent on men and some needed, or wanted, to break that dependency. 'Plucky' Emma West of Quinnimont, Virginia apparently left home because her parents were trying to force her to marry. She donned male attire and took a job on a farm; however, when she was arrested and charged with being a female in disguise, she admitted she dressed as a man to command better wages and had saved nearly $400 – over which she had complete control.[26]

Catherine Clancy, a native of County Waterford, was discovered in the workhouse. She explained that she had spent fifty years as a man among the farmers in the counties of Waterford and Tipperary, ever since she was 18 years old.[27] Marie Herve, who was admitted to a hospital at Dinan, France for partial blindness, was well-known in the local district for taking employment on local farms and was considered an excellent workman. Marie had first adopted a masculine costume when her parents died some sixty years earlier, leaving her destitute. A peculiarity of the case, it was noted, is that the barber at Dinan Hospital had to shave her twice.[28]

As with Marie's story, a consistent feature was the women's hard work and reliability. In Wellington, New Zealand, a young Italian woman was found masquerading in boys' clothes and working as a common labourer in a local brickyard. Although she had only been there about a week, the manager said he would not wish for a better or more exemplary worker. She was discovered when recognised by a friend. According to the reports, she had married but found that her husband already had a wife and family, so she left him. She was unable to find a job as a woman, so adopted male attire and worked at Wanganui as a driver and at Pulmerston North as a carrier of parcels.[29]

Even if people disapproved of the disguise, if the woman's story was seen as honourable and worthy, she was often rewarded for her 'plucky little woman' attitude. In 1854, it was discovered that a Prussian woman named Hubschen had worked in male attire for five years as a railway navvy in the Drôme, an area in the south-east of France. She had an infirm husband, four starving children and had been struggling to find work until she disguised herself and

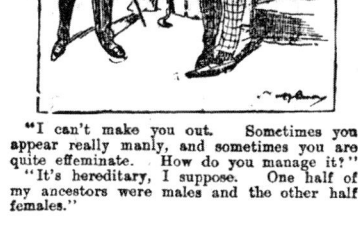

'Half and Half': a cartoon from the *Abergavenny Chronicle*, 17 September 1909. (*Welsh Newspapers Online*)

Jane Dieulafoy (1851–1916), the French archaeologist. (*Wikimedia Commons*)

Writer Ménie Muriel Dowie (1867–1945). (*Wikimedia Commons*)

Ellen Penrose who 'shocked the good people of Coney Island, USA by parading about the streets in male attire', *New York Journal*, 4 May 1897. (*Library of Congress*)

A romanticised image of Grizel Cochrane who reputedly saved her father's life. From *True Stories of Girl Heroines* by Evelyn Everett-Green (1901). (*Internet Archive*)

British sailor Hannah Snell (1723–1792), who claimed she was abandoned by her husband and lost her child, so she dressed in male attire. (*Wikimedia Commons*)

'Girl-Boy': a cartoon accompanying a story of a woman in male attire, *Cardiff Times*, 21 January 1888. (*Welsh Newspapers Online*)

Postcard of a pit brow lass, circa late nineteenth century. Women working in coal mining caused controversy by wearing trousers under their skirts. (*Author's collection*)

Rhani of Jhansi (1828–1858), an Indian queen who fought in the Indian Rebellion of 1857. (*Wikimedia Commons*)

A cantinière in Algeria in 1845. (*Wikimedia Commons*)

Marie-Angélique Duchemin (1772–1859), also known as Angélique Brûlon, a French soldier and the first woman to receive the Légion d'honneur. (*Wikimedia Commons*)

Amelia Vella, the 'girl sailor', pictured in the *Evening Express*, 11 November 1898. Images like this showing individuals in both male and 'proper' attire were always popular. (*Welsh Newspapers Online*)

A female lieutenant from *The Woman in Battle* by Loreta Janeta Velázquez (1842–1923), who supposedly served as a soldier in the American Civil War. (*Internet Archive*)

Mary Anne Talbot (1778–1808), a British sailor and soldier who served in the French Revolutionary Wars (1792–1802). (*Wikimedia Commons*)

Emilia Plater (1806–1831), a Polish-Lithuanian noblewoman, revolutionary and soldier. Images of female soldiers were often femininised. (*Wikimedia Commons*)

An extract from a report about sailor Mary Anne Arnold (1825–?) with the familiar heading of 'another female sailor', *The Cambrian*, 4 January 1840. (*Welsh Newspapers Online*)

Audiences flocked to see the legs of British actor, Lucia Elizabeth Vestris (1797–1856). (*Wikimedia Commons*)

Famous image of French actor, Sarah Bernhardt (1844–1923) playing Hamlet. (*Wikimedia Commons*)

American actor, Charlotte Cushman (1816–1876) playing Romeo. Audiences saw nothing odd in a woman dressed as a man playing a romantic role with another woman. (*Wikimedia Commons*)

Portrait of Catherine the Great (1729–1796) riding astride a horse, long before it became fashionable to do so. (*Wikimedia Commons*)

One of the most famous male impersonators, Vesta Tilley (1864–1952). (*Wikimedia Commons*)

A HIGH KICK.

A HEADER.

Lady footballers pictured in the *Evening Express*,
2 November 1895. (*Welsh Newspapers Online*)

The bicycle allowed a great advance in women wearing trousers. (*Wikimedia Commons*)

'A "Rational" Bride': image of a New Zealand wedding with the bride in 'rational dress', *South Wales Echo*, 13 October 1894. (*Welsh Newspapers Online*)

Dorothy Curtis who, during the Second World War, went to work in a Birmingham munitions factory. She sent a photo home captioned 'trousers'. (*By kind permission of Glamorgan Archives Ref: DXFX/19*)

Postcard from around the late nineteenth century highlighting concerns about gender confusion when women wore trousers. (*Author's collection*)

Portrait of James Allen who gained notoriety as a 'female husband' and was married to a woman for twenty-one years. (*New York Public Library Digital Collection*)

A postcard dating to 1911 showing the horror caused by women wearing 'pants'. (*Author's collection*)

Australian Edward De Lacy Evans (circa 1830–1901) married and had relationships with women, and would today be regarded as transmasculine. (*Wikimedia Commons*)

Pharaoh Hatshepsut (1507–145. Writers would often designate h a queen, not a pharaoh, as in this image, but not all 'male attire' ca defined by Western dress. From *Temple of Deir el Bahri* by Edoua Naville & Somers Clarke (1894) (*Internet Archive*)

quickly gained employment. She worked hard and her wages enabled her to support her husband (whom she claimed was her 'father' and her children as her brothers and sisters). When her identity was discovered, her fellow workmen and neighbours gave gifts – and she was offered a job 'more suited to her sex.'[30]

A few days later, Empress Eugenie, the wife of Napoleon III, heard about Hubschen's case. The Empress was a strong advocate for women's rights and had previously arranged for the Ministry of National Education to give the first baccalaureate to a woman. She also attempted to get the Académie Française to elect George Sand, the cross-dressing author reputed to be bisexual, as its first female member, but the request was denied. The Empress became a patron for two of Hubschen's children and she sent them where they could get a good education – on the condition they did not get ideas above their station.[31]

As was always the case, women had to take care not to be found out. In 1863, John Bell was employed at Dundyvan Ironworks in Scotland as a labourer, working with a number of brick-layers and soon became expert in carrying a hod. This, however, was not to his liking so he got a job moving iron from the shears to the mill furnaces, reportedly doing his duty remarkably well. He paid double price for his lodgings, so as to get a bed to himself, and on no account would he allow anyone to sleep with him. Unfortunately, one Saturday evening, John got tipsy and, on reaching his lodgings, was unable to take off his clothes. The landlady, taking pity on her lodger's helpless state, began to assist in the operation when another lodger was startled by her calling to him, 'Bob, I say, Bob be gorra he's a woman.' John (aka Maria Cummings) tried to bluff it out and continued to walk around in male attire but did not return to work. When asked, John stoutly denied having admitted to being a woman and left to get employment elsewhere.[32]

In another place, a girl who had taken a job on the docks because of her 'masculine physique' was washing at home when one of her colleagues walked in on her. She lost the job.

Often, discovery only happened when the woman was injured, or died. Margaret Neilson, who had worked on the London wharves for six months loading steel plates, was severely injured. But before she died, she told the doctor that her husband had ill-treated her, forcing her to leave and adopt male attire to support herself and her children.[33]

By the late nineteenth century, moves were being made to prevent women taking labour-intensive roles and increasing examples were appearing in the media. However, the driving force behind the call for change was often less concern about the women and more about the loss of men's jobs. On the docks, women were working 'like men' and trade unionist Harry Orbell, while denouncing the degradation to which women were subjected, campaigned for their jobs to be given to men. The corn shippers followed, instructing that no more women were allowed on board their ships.[34]

Today, a number of women work in construction, on the docks, railways or elsewhere in heavy manual jobs but it should not be forgotten that historic women also took such employment out of necessity – for higher wages, to support families or simply to get away from the restrictions put on their lives.

Chapter 9

For Nefarious Purposes

When women cross-dressed, it was generally assumed by authorities that it was for nefarious or criminal purposes, despite the fact that for most women it was not. Even in those cases where criminality was involved, particularly with swindling and blackmail, the woman had often been cross-dressing for some time and did not specifically do so to commit the crime. When they did opt to change clothes, it was often linked to relationship troubles, especially jealousy. In 1904, Lavinia Coulson disguised herself as a man to commit a vicious acid attack on Hannah Maria Kenefick, whom she thought was too close to her husband. Maria lost an eye and the judge at Leeds Assizes sentenced Coulson to three years in prison.[1] Occasionally, the intention was as a disguise in order to escape. The first arrest in history using a telegraph was that of Hawley Harvey Crippen, famous in the annals of history for murdering his wife. Crippen, and his lover, Ethel 'Le Neve' Neave, were on board a ship heading for America but he had been recognised by the ship's captain who sent a telegram to the authorities describing Ethel as 'Accomplice dressed as boy. Manner and build undoubtedly a girl.'[2] At the trial, she was charged with being an accessory after the fact but was acquitted.

Beggars and pickpockets cross-dressed to blend into the crowd but in reports, they are often only mentioned in passing, perhaps to avoid inspiring others. Similarly, items about people pawning items are usually brief, including one from 1849 when a woman offered a stolen watch to a pawnbroker in Edinburgh. When caught, she said she had been too ashamed 'to offer the watch for sale in the garb of the fair sex.'[3] Rachael George was apprehended at Newcastle-Emlyn fair in 1829 for stealing a mare and when describing her, the journalist put the offending words *dressed in male attire* in italics. He added, 'this is the third offence for which the above *lady* will make her appearance.' Again, for emphasis the word *lady* is put into italics, as if to question her sex.[4]

A few reports have more extensive narratives, including an extraordinary story dating to the seventeenth century when fear of witches was at its peak.

A method of discovering witches – 'pricking' – had been developed based on the belief that a blemish on their skin could be the mark of Satan. A needle was pushed deep into the mark and if it caused no pain or bleeding, then the person was a witch. Thousands of people, mainly women, were maimed or even killed by this practice, while the men employed as 'prickers' received huge wages. It may have been this that tempted Scotsman John Dickson to apply for a job in 1662 but when it was discovered that John was a woman called Christian Caddell, the public was shocked. The *Inverness Chronicle* was astonished at the horrors done by a woman, with no comparison of the horrors carried out by 'pricking' men. Christian was put on trial and subsequently transported to Barbados for life, after which nothing more was heard of her.[5]

The public reaction to the news that a woman had committed a crime in male attire was often horror. When Lizzie Leonard was arrested in Brooklyn in 1884 charged with stealing a gold watch, she said, 'People run around me and look at me as though I had committed murder,' looking at the crowd that had followed her from the court-room. She said defiantly, 'I think I have a perfect right to wear such clothing if I want to.'[6]

Most crimes associated with women in male attire are secondary to the cross-dressing. Some stole the clothes necessary to achieve the disguise, or stole money to buy them. In 1910, Emily Gordon was sent by her stepfather to collect a debt of 30 shillings but having obtained the money, she used it to have her hair cropped and buy boys' clothing. She was three weeks into a boy's job when she was discovered. Unfortunately, she had not moved far enough away, her stepfather recognized her and had her arrested.[7]

Jessie Leeson, described as a 'somewhat masculine looking woman' stole clothes belonging to her landlady in 1867 before going to the Gunmakers' Arms, in Nottingham, where she remained for two or three days. Taking the name 'Sir Harry Clifton' and saying that he was waiting to meet an uncle before going sailing may have been a step too far. The 'young gentleman's' anecdotes were so entertaining he became very popular, courting attention that made discovery inevitable. It turned out that Jessie was actually 'a ballet dancer at one of the singing rooms' and the magistrate did not take a lenient view of her escapade – it is not known what happened to her.[8]

Many things were stolen by women in male attire – for example, in Cardiff, Lilian Matthews stole a child in 1893. William Johnson, actually Elizabeth Johnson who had been in male attire for nine years, and William Blake were charged with stealing two geese, because they were starving.[9]

Some of those convicted of a crime made it all the way to the prison before being detected. In 1875, in a case the media called an 'extraordinary instance of concealment of sex,' William Seymour, a cab-driver in Liverpool, was convicted of a felony. Once discovered, she explained that she had left her husband because of his ill-treatment of her and had been a cab-driver for nine years, during which she had been successful in concealing her real sex. In court, the indictment had to be altered (as it did for all cross-dressing individuals in order to prevent appeals) and she was found guilty and sentenced to three months' imprisonment.[10]

When caught committing a crime, women could often be released with a simple caution if their story was full of the requisite necessities to engender sympathy and, in 1886, one unnamed woman fitted those criteria. She had stolen a few articles from her employer where she had been working as a porter, disguised as a boy, for four months. Her mother, appearing as a character witness, said her daughter had only donned male attire when she tired of failing to find female employment and had bravely taken a boy's job to support her starving brothers and sisters. Hearts warmed to the 'noble girl' and something approaching pity was expressed for the unfortunate magistrate who had dared to commit her for trial. However, a local vicar pointed out that she had long been in the habit of masquerading in men's clothes; it was no sudden onset of distress and the story was untrue in other details. All sympathy disappeared.[11]

Other women tried pure bravado. In 1896, Police Constable Gibbs stopped a man in Cricklewood at 1.15 am and asked what he was carrying. The man replied, 'What is that to do with you?' and cheekily handed the officer some keys saying, 'Take them home and tell the servants I shall not go riding this morning.' The officer was not so easily duped and arrested him. Mary Ann Hester was described in court as 'a woman of superior education' who worked as a laundress but had no home. She claimed she had left her skirt in the stables as she wished to go for a ride so was 'borrowing' the clothes – but it seemed she had a long criminal record and so was given a month's hard labour.[12]

Trying to bluff a way out of trouble was common for many women, particularly when in court. Raymond O'Dowd explained, to a rather confused magistrate, that he was wearing earrings because he was Irish and it was a custom in his country – but a female searcher was brought in and Rose Fertray's mother was sent for to take her home.[13]

For some, creating a fiction was the only way they could live their lives but such fictions brought additional problems as the disguise itself could be seen as 'nefarious'. Sarah Baker, a laundress from Edmonton, was charged alongside a man with felony but when the man was asked his name in court, he said, 'I had rather not give a name.' When asked for his reasons, the inspector replied that both prisoners were women. When the man was forced to provide a name, he said he was Edward Baker, the 'husband' of the other prisoner. Edward, who had 'quite a masculine appearance', refused to give a female name and throughout the article, pronouns used to describe Edward were put in inverted commas. It was reported that the couple had gone into a shop and were seen 'nudging' one another, before getting into conversation with a female shopper. They offered to buy her a drink and went to a public-house where the 'young man' bought her some gin. Almost immediately, she became insensible and later believed she had been drugged. When she recovered, she missed her muff and umbrella and suspected the couple of stealing them. Seeing the 'young man' – 'for the sake of distinctiveness,' the journalist wrote, the woman was called 'young man' – the woman accused him of theft. Her case was sent for trial on the charge of 'being in male attire for the purpose of a felony'. But in court, Edward explained that she was employed by Sarah as an ironer and, in a spirit of fun, put on the men's clothes and went into town. During the trial, it was proven that Sarah had left the muff with the barmaid – and furthermore, as she had an income of £120 a year, she did not need to steal. Edward was her servant and they decided to go out for a lark. The jury found them not guilty and believed the assumption of male attire was nothing more than a drunken freak.[14]

Stealing livestock is a common element in cross-dressing stories – a dangerous endeavour as the penalties could be severe. In 1806, Helen Jeans stole two horses and was caught in the act of selling them at a fair. Had she not been arrested then, it was said, 'it would have been impossible afterwards to have identified her person.' She was sentenced to transportation for fourteen years.[15] Sisters Elizabeth and Mary Loosemore stole two heifers at Mariansleigh, Devon in 1830. As two women driving cattle would have excited suspicion, Elizabeth dressed as a man and called herself John Hill. They managed the 26 miles to market with no difficulty and returned home 'passing, unrecognised, persons who had known them for years.'[16] However, they were caught and sentenced to death but it is not known if that was carried out.

Robbing a house could be risky, particularly if the owner was present. William and Sarah Webb were indicted in 1826 for robbery and for 'putting in bodily fear the person of Catherine Cotterel' in Australia. Sarah, in male attire, had threatened Catherine with a musket and they had stolen mostly clothes. Police pursued them through the bush and when arrested, Sarah claimed she was coerced by her husband, who denied it. Had the jury believed her, she would have received a lesser sentence. However, they did not and both were sentenced to death.[17] William was executed but Sarah's sentence was commuted to three years' hard labour in a factory – and to have her head shaved. She was an old offender and had 'occasionally committed depredations in male attire.'

As with many sensational stories, they received more newspaper coverage than those considered more mundane. In many, the word 'romantic' is used; indeed, a great number of the women's stories are described as romantic – although the meaning of the word has changed and prior to the twentieth century, it meant something 'remote from everyday life'. One robbery in 1861 was described as 'committed under peculiar and romantic circumstances.' An inspector had been called to a house at Bessborough-gardens, London where he found a broken poker in the hall with human hair and blood sticking on it; more human hair was strewn about and a pail apparently containing blood sat on the floor. There was plenty of evidence of a break-in and various items were wrapped in bundles, ready to be taken. A young man had been seen leaving, carrying some boxes and a bag, but where was the 25-year-old servant, Mary Anne Newall? Had she interrupted a burglary gone wrong and paid with her life? Where was her body?

Detectives discovered that the man had boarded a train to Brentwood and from there, they tracked him to Yarmouth. At a lodging house, the detective asked if a young man had recently arrived and was told that a Mr Barker was staying and was due back shortly. The landlady (described as a 'buxom spinster') told the detective that the young man chatted, smoked and was very agreeable, noting that he ordered his dinner 'at quality hours'. She also explained how he 'arrayed himself in a handsome suit of gentleman's clothes' to take her to the theatre. On Sunday morning, he had advanced himself so far in her opinion that she arrayed herself in her best and went to church with him. In fact, Barker had chatted up local girls with the 'air of an accomplished lothario; smoked cigars, sported a fancy tobacco pipe, and played his assumed character to such perfection that the good people of

Yarmouth never doubted for a moment that they were honoured with the society of a tip-top metropolitan swell.' When Barker returned, the detective arrested him but as he was not allowed to search a woman, he demanded to see the contents of his pockets. The box was also searched and items from the house taken into evidence.

In court, the defence played on Mary's eccentricity, such as courting women and suggested she was of unsound mind as her journey had been easily traced and she did not hide while in Yarmouth. Unfortunately for them, she had a long history of being associated with missing items in various employments. On this occasion, to make her escape, she had staged the scene including gluing the hair on the poker – and the blood was found to be non-human. One journalist wrote, 'she had indulged in the comical extravagance of putting on male attire, of smoking cigars, making love to her landlady' and spoke in a voice 'peculiarly unfeminine.' She had a portrait of an actress in male attire in her pocket, and her defence argued she had been influenced by a monomania for romantic fiction and had thought herself a heroine in a melodrama. She had spent time as a patient in Cambridge Hospital and her father and grandfather had both died insane. She was, he said, of a weak mind. The judge said it was one of the strangest cases that had ever come into his court but, as the property was all recovered, he suggested that she should be dismissed. The jury disagreed and found her guilty – she was sentenced to eighteen months' hard labour.[18]

Another romantic and sensational story occurred in 1893, this time involving blackmail. An unnamed couple had been involved in a scandal involving the murder of two women and a child that had rocked Paris, even bringing down members of the government. The unnamed woman and her male partner escaped to London and started a new scheme: she would entice men to a house, or correspondence would be secured from him, and the man would then be blackmailed. The case was further complicated by what the *Western Mail* called, 'the most astounding part of this astounding story':

> incredible as it may appear, it is nevertheless a fact that within the last few weeks the pair were living in London as man and wife. The lady herself took the part of the husband, and the disguise is described as being the most artful and complete one that could possibly be imagined.

However, the pair overplayed their hand. When they blackmailed a prince for £7,000, they were not sent to trial, as it would have 'been of the most sensational character', but they were forced to repay all their victims (although they still managed to flee the country with a great deal of money). A bemused journalist wondered how the men had been fooled, considering that 'on the whole few would accuse her of being beautiful.'[19] As both of them were cross-dressing and a trial was avoided, it is likely their victims were high-profile homosexuals.

The number of women in male attire appearing as highway robbers or bandits is considerable. Some like Mary Frith, better known as Moll Cutpurse, who continually dressed in male attire, have gained fame; and Grizel Cochrane entered Scottish lore when in the seventeenth century, she robbed her father's death warrant from a mail coach, giving time for a successful pardon to be argued.

Most stories of highway women and bandits in male attire are relatively brief and often appear in columns containing 'interesting snippets' of news. For example, in the 'North of Siam, many women are now forming bands of robbers, they go about the country dressed in male attire. They mark their bodies with certain characters, or 'charms' to make them invulnerable to attack.'[20] In other cases, a cross-dressing female bandit in Romania was credited with eighty-six murders and hundreds of crimes of violence and theft;[21] and when an unnamed couple was arrested in 1866, the man admitted to dressing the young woman in male attire in order to assist him in robbing people.[22]

A rather strange story appeared in 1832 regarding a young man sent to the workhouse to get the weekly allowance for his own and some other families. On his return, he was attacked by a man demanding the money but when the young man called out, 'Murder! Thieves!', people came running and captured the highwayman – who turned out to be the lad's own mother. The affair, noted the *Kentish Gazette*, had been suppressed but the editor of the *Leicester Chronicle* added his own note to the story: 'the matter ought not to be so hushed up – the parish authorities should investigate it.' Presumably, the mother had thought if the money was stolen, the workhouse would replace it.[23]

A great sensation was caused throughout the State of Montana by the arrest of a female highway robber who, with others, had been a terror to villagers and farmers for many months. The police laid several traps but failed to capture them until they saw a boy in the vicinity of an attack on a Chinese man. The boy was stopped and searched, and a watch was found from an earlier robbery. The boy turned out to be a woman called Bertha Helen Forslund, also going by the names of Charlie or Bertie Miller. After being locked up, Helen sent a note to a 'Henry Miller' asking for his help but the detective who delivered it arrested the recipient – who turned out to be Henry Clark, the leader of the gang. Helen had met Clark on her father's ranch in Oregon when he induced her to elope with him and join him in robberies. At first, she did not like the work but when she saw how easy it was to make a big, strong man give up all his property, she became fascinated with the life and began to work alone, taking one section of the town for herself and Clark, another. Helen cheerfully related to police some of the robberies she and Clark had committed, including one when she was walking down a street and saw a woman lying asleep in bed. She entered the house, grabbed the sleeper by the throat and made her give up $30. Helen was said to be, 'perfectly composed in manner despite her attire' and when asked if she did not desire a dress to wear, she replied that she had worn male dress so long that she did not care for woman's apparel. The case caused such interest that shops in town displayed pictures of her in both female and male attire.

In a chatty letter to one of her victims, she added, 'The officers here treat me very well; they allow me to wear men's or women's clothes, just as I wish; they call me the highwaylady and say I'm a dandy ... I don't know whether to appear in court in dress or in pants. Weimy says I look better in pants; I think my name will be pants before they get thought with me ... Yours in haste and in jail.'[24]

Very rarely do stories of cross-dressing women include violence, however, there were those who broke that pattern. In 1905, a reporter interviewed Tilly Woods, the American highwaywoman 'Tilly-the-Hold-Up in the prison where she was being held'. He spent most of the interview dodging her fist as she described how she hit men from behind with a 'blankjack'. At other times, she lured them into conversation before banging their heads against brick walls. She also kicked out their teeth, battered their heads with stones, and broke noses. The police sergeant added, 'it never takes less than half a dozen policemen to bring her in when she's drunk, and when she's sober it takes the whole reserve squad.'[25] Josepha Perez, the 'She Wolf' of Gallicia, also committed multiple robberies, tortures and murders, including 'the most revolting acts of ferocity on her victims'.[26]

Marie Semit, a Russian, dressed in male attire and led a band of highway robbers in the Province of Smolensk in 1910. Originally a school teacher, she had 'pronounced radical tendencies' and with her gang attacked a monastery near Pfkow, killing several monks. She was sentenced to twenty years' imprisonment.[27]

Physical descriptions of many of the women often use unflattering terms but it would seem that many did have quite masculine appearances, either naturally or from exercise or shaving used to enhance the disguise. Occasionally, there were beautiful women – such as the dashing highwaywoman, Barbara Danelia, who captivated Russia with her exploits. She was noted for being very polite and gentle while relieving many men of their possessions. Several times she was caught and managed to escape – often by the gaoler releasing her, even when dressed in male attire. Danelia was described as an excellent rider who could jump anything; an excellent shot; and a beauty. She was very popular among her own people, whom she seldom attacked, and poor travellers apparently never had anything to fear.[28]

Some stories, which appear true on the surface, have the feeling of fiction. One such tale from 1827 involved Donna Maria de la Concepcion Dauvedra from Jaen, who was the beautiful and only child of wealthy parents. Her father had been killed by partisans and sometime later, during a fete, a band of armed men broke in, causing her mother to have a heart attack on the spot. Instead of being terrified, Donna 'conceived a violent passion for Hongueta, the chief of the brigands, and accompanied him into the mountains.' Consequently, all her houses and lands were confiscated; nevertheless, she often returned in male attire and was received by the farmers, who refused her nothing. On one such visit, they were invited to sit and eat at a table served by an old servant of Donna's family. The servant drew a knife and was about to stab Hongueta when Donna suddenly rose and 'blew the servant's brains out.' A price was put on Hongueta's head and a peasant determined to gain the reward joined his troop. Serving him breakfast, he took a gun and shot Hongueta, threatening Donna if she moved. After cutting off his victim's head, he delivered it to the magistrates and received his reward. Donna, despite her protests of innocence, was sentenced to death, later reduced to life imprisonment.[29]

Another somewhat fictional-sounding story concerned a female brigand in Persia. She was described in a book by Baron de Bode entitled *Travels in Luristan* (1845) as 'when yet a spinster, she used to dress in men's clothes, saddle her horse, and, armed with a lance, would sally forth into the desert, there to waylay travellers.' One man who was attacked received several wounds but inflicted several more on his assailant. He then sought refuge at an Iliyat (a Persian tribe) encampment where the chief of the tribe washed and dressed his wounds, the chief complaining that his daughter was not there to help as she had been wounded that same day. The man asked to see her – and immediately recognised his assailant.[30]

For women convicted of crimes, punishments varied widely and many were simply released with a caution. Others could receive more severe, even bizarre penalties. In 1849, Wilson Ramsay of Australia was the Superintendent Surgeon of the prison ship *Inchinnan*. He devised his own punishments, making Mary Stephens wear his trousers, much to the horror of witnesses. 'Surely,' wrote the *Sydney Morning Herald*, 'if it had been necessary to punish the disorderly and disobedient, some punishment might have been contrived not so offensive and disgusting as encasing the delinquent in Mr Ramsay's trousers.' When the superintendent admitted in court that he had used this punishment, the disgust 'depicted on the countenances of almost every spectator in Court could not have escaped the observation of Mr Ramsay.' Ordered not to do anything like it again, an unrepentant Ramsay wrote a letter stating, 'I have no hesitation in re-asserting that under similar circumstances I would resort to a similar punishment. And in case the emigrants had been males, I would very likely have put petticoats on them.' In addition, Ramsay had further punished women by exhibiting them on the poop deck. 'The punishment,' wrote the *Herald*, 'of placing the women in trousers is indecent and indelicate enough, the placing the women on the poop when so clothed, to be subjected to derision, scorn, and filthy language, was unpardonable and offensive.'[31]

Some women realised they could use their understanding of themselves to attract other women. In Berne, Switzerland in 1906, Salome Lejeune was tried for fraud. 29-year-old Salome and 18-year old Lina Pauly had become friends but when Lina expressed a desire to be married, Salome posed as a Dr Krause of Strassburg and courted her friend via correspondence for four years. The girl's brother, managing to acquire most of Lina's fortune, called the police and Salome was found guilty and sentenced to a month's imprisonment, the costs of the trial, and expulsion.[32]

From the mass of evidence collected on cross-dressing women and their crimes, most did not receive extreme punishments and were either dismissed, were fined or given a short spell in prison. Only occasionally was transportation or the death penalty used. Ann Hereford (known as 'Nan') was a prolific thief and often in and out of prison: 'her pugilistic prowess would never lead to the question of her sex had she not been betrayed.' In 1690, she was in Newgate Prison and set it on fire in an attempt to escape, but was caught and executed for arson.[33]

It should be remembered that this study only covers those women who appeared in newspapers – many others did not make the news and can only be found in archives, such as those at Glamorgan Archives. For example, Martha Alice Hodson, was charged with committing offences 'while masquerading as a man.' She was fingerprinted and her photograph appears in the Fingerprint Register.[34]

Irrespective of whether they appeared in the newspapers or the archives, details about women's lives are often limited and they frequently disappear into obscurity. This makes it difficult to draw conclusions about their emotional and mental state and, in most cases, why many committed their crimes.

Chapter 10

Soldiers

Women who disguised themselves to go to war have fascinated people for centuries, from those who led armies to those who served alongside ordinary servicemen. Women like Calamity Jane, who dressed in men's clothes, or Joan of Arc, whose statue in Paris is perhaps the only public sculpture of a cross-dressing female soldier. And not just individuals, but whole armies of women: from the legendary Amazons, after whom most women warriors are named, to the Dahomey of Benin, who featured in a 2019 documentary by Lupita Nyong'o (whose character in the film *Black Panther* was based on the Dahomey). However, these women did not disguise themselves and they achieved their reputation because they were women.

A few of those who cross-dressed gained fame such as *Lakshmibai*, Rhani of Jhansi, who was killed leading rebels against British rule in 1857. She has been featured in numerous novels and films and was the inspiration for the Rani of Jhansi Regiment, a 1942 women's army fighting for Indian independence. Courtesan Azizan Bai fought in the same war in male attire but was captured by the British. Other women who have gained fame include Mary Anne Talbot, Emilia Plater, Lola Montez, Hannah Snell, Phoebe Hassell, Dr Barry and Dr Mary Walker, and many others have become familiar. However, this chapter is designed to highlight a few of the thousands of women whose fame exists only in a line or two in a newspaper – and many of their real identities will never be known.

Arguably the first female cross-dressing soldier was Epipole of Carystus of Greek mythology, who fought against Troy. When discovered, she was stoned to death. This extreme judgement is rare, as men throughout history have been fairly indulgent of female soldiers and tended towards benevolence.

From ancient times onwards, there was a small stream of stories until the eighteenth century when ballads and broadsheets featuring female soldiers and sailors became extremely popular. 'Mother Drum' claimed she was inspired by the ballad of Mary Ambree, a female soldier who was at the siege of Ghent.[1] Another name from the eighteenth century is Aal de Dragonder (Aal the Dragoon), who was stabbed to death during an altercation over a game of cards sometime in 1710. When discovered to be a woman, her body was donated to Rotterdam Medical School. The skeleton and stuffed skin were put on display holding a sword and sitting on the stuffed carcase of a horse. As only criminals were denied burial, this has been seen as some sort of 'posthumous punishment.'[2]

The earliest consistent records of cross-dressing female soldiers come from the French Revolution, and because so many women were disguising themselves, a new law was enacted: 'Ruling Number 22 of Chief of Police Dubois of the 16th Brumaire of year nine,' (7 November 1800) that banned any woman from wearing men's clothes. However, for those women whose jobs required more modest clothing, women could apply for a police permit.

The new law was not particularly effective and the subsequent Napoleonic Wars (1803–1815) saw the number of women fighting as men soar. This rise may have been related to the growing number of newspapers; as more stories appeared about female soldiers, other women possibly followed them, although few admitted this. Difficulties in extracting accurate figures are compounded by fictional accounts – so popular was the 'gallant little woman' that it was worth inventing a story or two, and many women used one or more aliases so it can be difficult to trace them in the historical record.

Nevertheless, a whole book could be written just on Napoleonic women and it is difficult to extract just a few examples. Some gain much fame, such as Theresa Figneur or 'Sans Gene' ('without embarrassment'), 'whose name figures honourably in the military annals of France'. Her autobiography details life as a dragoon from 1798 to 1812 but although dressed as a man, she did not disguise her sex – or at least did not intend to. When she married, in uniform, the official asked dryly, 'Which of you two is the bride and which the bridegroom?' to which Theresa took exception and stalked out.[3]

Another celebrated fighter was Angélique Brûlon, who became the first woman to receive the Légion d'honneur in 1851. Virginie Ghesquiere reached the rank of Sergeant (her nickname was 'pretty sergeant') and she too was apparently awarded the Légion d'honneur, as was Theresa Figneur. Sadly, many of these awards have not been recognised and it was not until 2016, when British woman Marsie Taylor, a veteran of the Second World War, became the first 'official' woman to receive the medal.

One particular class of women who were highly lauded were not only permitted to be on a battlefield but also permitted to wear trousers. The cantinières, or vivandières, were French women who, from the end of the eighteenth century, were attached to regiments, received rations and accommodation, and were licenced to sell alcohol (to prevent adulterated and possibly dangerous liquors sold by charlatans). The cantinières had a particular costume: a glazed hat; a blue petticoat with a tri-coloured border; red or *garance* military trousers; boots; a short cloak; and a keg slung round the shoulder with a small basket containing one or two glasses, and a few loaves. A *plaque* on the arm denoted their number and the corps to which they belonged.

Despite their role as sutlers (those who sell provisions to an army), they regularly rescued men from the battlefields, tended their wounds and performed deeds of heroism – many having their names inscribed on rolls of honour and awarded medals.

The high reputation of the cantinières saw their corps being copied in other countries including during the American Civil War and in France, they survived as a unit until the First World War.

The reasons women gave for enlisting were varied but often centred around following their man. A young woman of Norfolk, being 'strongly attached to a soldier in the 24th Foot', resolved to follow him and share his fortune. Unfortunately, she tried to enlist in the 54th Foot and was sent packing.[4] A similar mistake was made by a Welsh woman who tried to join the 43rd regiment when her lover was actually in the 63rd.[5]

Following their man was a good excuse to use when discovered: it smacked of true love, bravery and patriotism which the public loved. Claiming she wanted to fight, see the world and have the same experiences as men would not have been as well received. Rarely were the men's identities revealed, making it an easy and useful excuse to get the woman out of trouble.

Women may have thought they could find love in the army and some did, but others may have married simply because society expected them to. Individuals we would now consider gay women or trans men may well have married gay men or hidden their identities in heterosexual marriages. As the *National Advocate* observed in 1894, 'it is strikingly noticeable that many of these Amazons were fatally attractive to their own sex.'[6]

Some couples did manage to stay together. A Napoleonic War journalist, observing the movement of prisoners, saw two officers, the younger of whom was wounded and an unhurt middle-aged man, comforting the younger. It turned out that they were husband and wife.[7]

Occasionally, a woman enlisted to escape a man. A 'lady of quality in Russia', having been pressed into a matrimonial engagement, abandoned her home and entered a Polish regiment, in which she served at the Battle of Austerlitz (1805).[8]

Some joined for retribution, such as Henrietta Spencer who enlisted during the American Civil War to avenge her dead father and brother.[9] Others went originally as nurses but when their service was over, rather than go home, they enlisted. At the beginning of the First World War, nurse Flora Sendes enlisted in a Serbian regiment when her hospital closed.[10]

Young women could appear as androgynous. When in their uniform, nobody suspected Charley Davis, or Jane Short, of the American Civil War 'to be a woman, she looks much more like an unsophisticated country lad of 20 years.' Her friend William (or Lou) Morris 'looks as little like a woman as her companion, and presents the appearance of a hardy boy of 18.'[11]

For other women, it was their voice which gave them away. Ellonora Prochaska was laughed at for speaking like a woman but claimed she was a tailor and, as it was 'only natural' that a tailor should have effeminate characteristics, she was left in peace.[12]

Hannah Snell was nicknamed Miss Molly Gray due to the smoothness of her face and chin. Conversely, others were noted for their masculinity. Jorgensen, who served extensively during the Franco-Prussian War, was a 'tall, angular woman, with a masculine voice and features, and gifted with great physical strength.'[13] Yet for most women who were depicted as soldiers or sailors, they were over-feminised in images with few looking masculine or like men. Only when photographs were available could it be seen what the individuals really looked like.

By the time of the American Civil War (1861–65), so many women were enlisting that newspapers were heading articles with the tired-sounding title of 'another female soldier'. A Cincinnati paper complained of the number of young ladies who 'excited by the numerous stories of women soldiers in the army, will persist in appearing in public in that city in male attire.'[14] And in 1879, the *Newcastle Courant* wrote, 'There are many stories on record of females who disguised in male attire have served as soldiers and sailors.'[15] In addition, numerous accounts, claiming to be true, were being produced and even today, the veracity of some are being questioned. Ever since Loreta Velasquez published her book *The Woman in Battle* (1876) detailing her life as Confederate Lieutenant Harry Buford, questions have been asked if she made it all up. The consensus is that she probably did, which is a shame as she included a rare explanation of how she disguised her body shape by inventing a wire support under her clothes to disguise her tell-tale waist.[16]

By the 1870s and 1880s, women soldiers had become so ubiquitous that long articles debating their place were beginning to appear. Many, supportive of the rising women's independence movements, were generally sympathetic, but most were not. Despite this, few women soldiers were ever censured; instead, they were often used as a stick to shame unpatriotic men. When Russian Harietena Korotkievitch was discovered, she was given permission to remain in the ranks because she had an excellent moral influence on the soldiers. When she was killed, her officers said she had 'shown all how to die nobly.'[17]

When a young girl asked the *Gendarmerie* for permission to wear trousers to fight, the chief commented, 'This is not the only case of the kind … and when there is such a spirit in the women it will go hard but the men do their duty.'[18]

In some cases, if women wanted to be treated like men, they had to face the consequences. During the French insurrections of 1871, a convoy of prisoners was being marched through Versailles and a gendarme was jabbing a male-attired woman with the point of his sabre until blood ran. 'Shame!' cried a spectator 'to treat a woman so.' 'Woman!' exclaimed the gendarme, 'that woman killed my captain and lieutenant and a sergeant with three shots from her revolver!'[19]

The mass of publicity about women in European armies gave the impression that it was a Western phenomenon. When a woman joined a Turkish army in 1839, the *Cornwall Royal Gazette* stated, 'Such a circumstance though it has been often witnessed in Western Europe, had never before been known in the East.'[20] While stories from the East and Orient (and stories of women of colour in general) are fewer in number than those of Europe and America, it does not mean they did not exist, only that they were not written about in Western papers with the same regularity. For those that are known, they follow the same pattern as Western women; some became famous because they were women but thousands more served in disguise.

In some countries, the mere idea of a warrior woman was viewed as incredible. When Fatimé Hanem, the leader of over 600 Turks, passed through the capital seated on horseback like a man, thousands flocked to view her. The 'Turkish females' were quite aghast, 'Mashallah! What a woman!'

they cried.[21] A young 'Indian woman' in Mexico was so respected and feared by her soldiers that they 'looked upon her as a supernatural being.'[22]

Oriental countries could be much more unforgiving of women dressing as men. In 1910, a piece entitled 'Barbarity in China' related the story of an ex-soldier who got into trouble and was sentenced to strangulation for dressing in men's clothes, 'thereby lowering the public morality.'[23]

Joining the army prior to the First World War was made easier as medical checks were either not carried out, or were quite cursory. Sometimes women did not even make it as far as the examination room and bolted before being asked to strip. Others tried to bluff it out, like New Zealander Harriet Muir in London in 1889. Having been charged with trying to enlist, the recruiting officer explained in court, 'he's a woman in man's attire', to gales of laughter from the spectators. Apparently, when the Sergeant had looked the recruit over, 'he' blushed so a doctor was called. The magistrate asked if there was a question about sex in the 'long string of questions which you put to would-be recruits?' and the bemused Sergeant admitted there were not, so Harriet was discharged.[24] Once stringent medical checks became mandatory, the number of cross-dressing female soldiers plummeted.

Occasionally, it was not the recruiting process which caught women out – sometimes it was the tailor. Margaret Macdonald had fallen desperately in love with Hugh Fraser so that when he was pressed for an American war in 1829, she too joined Hugh's regiment. When the regimental tailor measured up, he made certain discoveries, which he lost no time in communicating to the Colonel.[25]

Once they had enlisted, the most common reason women were discovered was through injury. Minor wounds could be treated safely and many reports of female soldiers state that they had been wounded numerous times without detection. However, more serious wounds, particularly if the woman was rendered unconscious, often proved the means of detection. Mary E. Wise, in the American Civil War, had been wounded three times but it was not until she was shot in the shoulder that she was discovered.[26] A woman who had served for six years and had risen to the rank of captain, was wounded in the breast.[27] Similarly, Leonora Prohaska fell in an engagement on the Gorde, in 1813, a bullet having pierced her breast. When she felt that she was dying, she revealed to her comrades that she was a woman.[28]

For some, their experience of serving was tragically short. After the Battle of Custoza (1848) during the First Italian War of Independence, a surgeon discovered among the wounded a young corporal with three injuries to the neck, left arm, and right leg. Herminia Manelli had cut her hair, dressed in her brother's uniform and joined his regiment but after a mere four hours had passed, she was wounded and died just a few days later.[29]

Some women knew only too well that treatment could lead to their discovery and took measures to avoid it. Mary Anne Talbot was wounded twice at the siege of Valenciennes (1793) and concealed her injuries, curing herself with the aid of lint, Basilicon and 'Dutch drops' (namely bandages, an ointment to 'draw' out items embedded in the flesh, and a diuretic often used to dress wounds). Hannah Snell secured the services – and the secrecy – of a black woman who helped her extract a musket ball and cure her wound.

Others resorted to more extreme methods, such as bribery. Johanna Stain, an Englishwoman (elsewhere described as German) with a 'stout masculine figure' had 'in a sort of freak' joined the army in 1788–9 and then served for ten years. She fought in eighteen battles and was wounded several times. On one occasion, her sex had been discovered by a doctor but she gave him $150 to keep quiet.[30]

Sometimes it was not a wound which led to discovery, but illness. When Sarah Taylor suffered from yellow fever in 1814, she swore the wife of a serjeant to secrecy[31]; and in 1898, Kieuase Ahmet (Beardless Ahmet) fell ill after three years' service and was discovered to be a woman.[32]

Some knew what being wounded or ill could mean and tried to prevent any medical intervention. Virginia Chesquieres had been wounded during the Peninsular War (1807–14) when she was recovering her colonel's body and her colleagues attempted to stem the wound in spite of her resistance. Nevertheless, she was discovered.[33]

Some were discovered for more obvious reasons, such as the sixteen enlisted women who served until a few pregnancies began to show.[34] And in 1839, a Turkish soldier was about to be promoted when it was discovered that 'he' was about to become a mother.[35]

One way to avoid detection from doctors was to become one yourself. One unnamed 'sinister-looking doctor' with a ferocious temper who served throughout the Peninsular War (and who also fought several duels) was, on death, found to be a woman.[36]

When it came to punishments or imprisonment, some women chose to out themselves. One private who had been in the ranks for about four months was about to be punished for a misdemeanour when she informed the commanding officer of 'her' sex.[37] A captured French woman, on revealing her sex, was released and immediately rejoined her regiment.[38] In fact, confessing and re-joining was a common strategy. Lizzie Compton had been in several regiments under several different names.[39]

After injuries, the most common cause of discovery was death. After the Battle of Waterloo (1815), a number of women's bodies dressed in male attire were recovered from the battlefield and in 1871, *The Graphic* wrote, 'It is now a frequent thing on the battle-fields round Pans to find the bodies of women, dressed in a semi-masculine attire.'[40] Ten years later in India, a journalist noted, 'at least four corpses are those of women ... dressed as men in the Mahdi's uniform, and had fought like men. The subject is not a pleasant one to any of us.'[41] A further ten years on in Manila, there was a similar sentiment: 'on going over the battlefield the startling discovery was made that many of the dead rebels were women in men's clothes'.[42]

There always seemed to be genuine concern at having killed a woman. In 1860, a British solider described how a woman 'fought against us with desperate valour. First, she fired at a soldier then cut at another with her tulwar [a curved sword]; and lastly, attempted to kill a Lancer, who ran her through the body, not knowing till afterwards that she was a woman.' She lay on the ground 'her long hair spreading out from her head, great firmness and energy expressed in her countenance, and the death-wound fresh and gaping.'[43]

For some, dead women on a battlefield were described in romantic terms:

> the ball of one of our riflemen had gone through her heart. From the small red wound the blood was still oozing in single drops, which I carefully caught in my handkerchief, to be preserved as a relic ... My hussars were visibly affected ... The corpse, in full uniform; the *kolpack*, [a helmet] with plume of glistening heron's feathers on the head; the light Turkish sabre by her side; was then carefully wrapped in a clean, large blanket, which we had with us, and so deposited in the grave, which we filled up again with earth. Then, regardless of caution, I had a full salute fired with pistols over the grave. I have preserved a small gold ring and a lock of her hair for a memorial.[44]

For those who survived, serving for long years and even being lauded for their actions did not necessarily count for much once the war was over. While a number were awarded pensions, many were not. At the end of wars, demand for government pensions was high and women were often refused on the grounds their enlistment had been illegal.

From newspaper reports, a high number of women supposedly received awards for their service. Catherine Lombaerts received the Order of the Iron Cross in 1830[45] and an unnamed woman convicted of theft in 1859 claimed to have won the Iron Cross.[46] However, there is very little research on, or official recognition of, such awards.

Recognition did come in other forms: an enormous number of ballads have been written about female soldiers such as Jeanne de Montfort, better known as Jeanne la flame. Emilia Plater appeared on Poland's banknotes, and there is the statue of Joan of Arc. Other monuments are rare but Ellonora Prochaska's life gave inspiration to various works of music and literature, including one by Beethoven, and in 1863, a commemorative marker was put over her grave at Dannenberg. In 1889, a monument was erected in her home town of Potsdam.

Others sought pensions and many newspaper articles detail women's petitions for consideration, indicating they did not mind being open about cross-dressing in a society where it was condemned elsewhere. Johanna Stain, who had bribed the doctor to conceal her sex, received pensions from both the Austrian and British governments.[47] Catalina de Eranso, known as the Ensign Nun, received 800 ducats annually, and permission to keep wearing her uniform. She 'had a declared abhorrence for the habiliments of her sex; nor was she ever known to possess the slightest feeling of affection toward the other' and indeed proposed to several women. She continued to be 'disguised as a man' until dying in 1650.[48]

Without a pension, life could be hard and the women had to find ways of coping. Both Hannah Snell and Mother Drum took on public-houses, both featuring fighting women on their signs. Mary Anne Talbot went on stage and others wrote up their exploits in books, articles, broadsheets and ballads. A number of women had served as spies, one of the most successful of which was actress Pauline Cushman in the American Civil War. When discovered, she was sentenced to death but was rescued and hailed a great hero – she later became one of the attractions at Barnum's Museum.[49]

For those who spent many years as men, giving up the clothes was hard. Lys Saint Mourel who died in 1747 continued in her uniform for the rest of her life;[50] and at Le Mans an old lady named Imbert, in recognition of her services, was given permission to wear male attire.[51]

The difficulties soldiers can have adjusting to life after serving in wars has long been recognised, but how much more so for those women who could not admit to their past? Post-traumatic stress disorder (PTSD) would have been hard for those women and occasionally, a notice of death raises that question, such as the young woman who had served as a Hungarian hussar and who committed suicide in 1853.[52]

By the First World War, the number of female soldiers dropped as medical examinations became more rigorous but these were not universal and many women still managed to enlist. In Italy, so common was the problem that the authorities were employing special detectives to 'scrutinise carefully all the soldiers, with a view to detecting by gait, manner, or behaviour, any women who may be masquerading among them.'[53] Flora Sandes was the only British woman to officially serve as a soldier in the First World War, although Dorothy Lawrence did so unofficially. When Dorothy tried to write about her experiences for a magazine, she was prohibited from doing so by the War Office who cited the 1914 Defence of the Realm Act, under which she could have been accused of treason. After the war, Dorothy did manage to publish her autobiography: *Sapper Dorothy Lawrence: the only English woman soldier* (1919) but it too was censored by the War Office. In later life, she was committed to an asylum and died in 1964. Her reputation has since been restored and Dorothy was featured in an exhibition at the Imperial War Museum entitled 'Women at War 1914–1918'.

In addition to British women, in the Austrian armies, 5,000 females were said to be in the front line dressed in male attire, many of whom were killed in battle.[54]

Conscription could also prove difficult for those women already cross-living as men. When American Harry Hoffman did not turn up for enlistment, the police went to arrest him. Lillian Myers then broke down and confessed that for the last ten years, she had been masquerading in male attire.[55]

So vast is the information on female soldiers that this chapter originally ran to over three hundred pages of mostly untold stories. Surely it is time, instead of lavishing attention on female superheroes, that we see these real hero women being celebrated in a film or two?

Chapter 11

Sailors

Women who went to sea have existed throughout history. While many worked and travelled in female attire, they lie outside the scope of this work, as do those who travelled as passengers on ships in male attire. This chapter focuses only on those women who attempted to live as professional sailors and while some, such as Anne Jane Thornton, Mary Anne Arnold and Hannah Snell, have gained fame, here only lesser-known examples from the extensive collection of stories found during my research will be covered.

Unlike female soldiers, where there is evidence from around the world, most of the female sailors and pirates so far uncovered come from the 'Western world'. This could, in part, be due to definitions, as not all clothes designated as 'male' includes trousers. The exception is China where, despite not being allowed on ships, many women did become sailors. However, the punishment could be severe and, in cases 'in which females have got on board disguised in male attire … they have invariably been thrown overboard.'[1]

Even in stories from the Western world, there are few women of colour. A rare example from 1815 was one William Brown, who served upwards of eleven years in the Royal Navy and was described as a 'smart, well-formed figure, about five feet four inches in height, possessed of considerable strength and great activity; her features are rather handsome for a *black*, and she appears to be about 26 years of age.' William was discovered while serving on the *Queen Charlotte* and it was said her share of prize-money was considerable – she declared her intention of re-joining another ship as soon as possible.[2]

Some of the earliest records of cross-dressing female sailors are linked to the press gangs that operated between 1664 and 1835, taking men into military or naval service by force. Being pressed could uncover those who were already cross-living – like Hannah Whitney who was seized in 1761 and sent to Plymouth Prison before being taken to a ship. Indignant at the harsh treatment, she let the authorities know her biological sex and then berated them for depriving the country of the services of a marine of five years' experience.[3]

Men could also be pressed from prison and a few stories include disguised women. In 1836, the *Daedalus* had been at New Brunswick, Canada when the captain had taken a robust and able-bodied seaman, Thomas Hanford, from the local jail. On the journey home, Thomas was ordered to reef the topsails in a gale, but nervous of ascending the masts, he confessed he was Sarah Busker. It seems it was not their only voyage as a man.[4]

Throughout the centuries, many tales were told of female sailors but it was the 1840s that saw a huge proliferation of stories. Many carried very detailed biographical details, more so than any other category of cross-dressing women. Newspapers were editorialising: in 1846, the *Welshman* wrote, 'two or three years ago there was a great run on female sailors. Every newspaper had its paragraph announcing the discovery of a female sailor. The result was a thorough conviction in the public mind that all sailors were female sailors – that there were no other sailors than female sailors in disguise; and now the curiosity would be the discovery of a male sailor, if such a phenomenon could be well authenticated.'[5] The *Belfast News-Letter* added, 'cases of this description are now so general that they cease to excite much interest.'[6] Indeed, many stories, like those of female soldiers, were headlined with the tired sounding, 'yet another female sailor'.

The arts also became saturated, with characterisations in theatre roles, ballads, novels and the like. Charles Dickens' *The Old Curiosity Shop* (1841) includes the unsavoury character of Sally Brass, who was rumoured to have been a female sailor in male attire.

By the end of the century, the phenomenon was stall causing comment. In a piece entitled 'Female Men-of-War's Men', the *Newcastle Weekly Courant* acknowledged:

> nearly every vessel that then ploughed the seas seems to have carried a number of women in her complement, and many of the lasses were quite equal to pulling an oar, serving a gun, or even hauling out the weather earring [sic] of a topsail if necessary. How they managed to conceal their disguise from their shipmates remains a marvel, but that they did so is indisputable, and even in our own times such deception has on more than one occasion proved successful.[7]

J. A. Scott of the Canadian Emigration Agency in Cardiff wrote to the *South Wales Echo* in 1898 recalling how twenty-five years previously when twenty deserters were caught, seven of them were females. He went to court to watch the trial and 'no one present could tell for certain which were the females in their sailor rig and white duck pants.[8]

Any sailor's story begins with the enlistment process and there are hundreds of women who attempted to fool recruiting officers; many were immediately caught and their efforts amounted to little more than a handful of humorous lines in a local paper. Some had more interesting stories, such as Margaret Grant who, in 1800, had been in the practice of continually enlisting for the money.[9] In 1811, an unnamed woman tried to enlist on board the *Valiant*, in Cawsand Bay, Cornwall but on being introduced to the officers, she dropped a curtsey instead of a bow.[10]

As the century progressed and medical examinations became more frequent, women could be caught earlier in the process. Harriet Palmer and Caroline Sarah Abbey offered themselves as apprentices on board a man-of-war in 1846. They had been employed at the Blue Bell Inn, Hull, one as cook and the other as barmaid, and had 'contracted a strong attachment for each other.' They claimed their sweethearts were sailors and having sent home 'glorious accounts from distant lands', the girls were inspired to follow them. After having their hair cut and purchasing male attire, they got the train to Manchester but running out of money, they walked to Liverpool where they attempted to enlist but were discovered by the doctor. This early story generated a great deal of press coverage and quite detailed stories of their lives appeared, allowing us to know more about them than most women with similar stories.[11] Like many other accounts, theirs included the common excuse of hunting a missing lover – but the probability is that they were running away together as a same-sex couple.

Alice Holmes from Massachusetts, who had hard and calloused hands showing 'how she has toiled from many years at sea', managed to get through the recruitment process because two male friends paid $25 each (about £600 today) to the doctor to pass her.[12] Johanna Stain also bribed the doctor[13] and there were probably many others who did the same.

When women were discovered, they provided a wide range of excuses for enlisting – some more imaginative than others. An unnamed woman was captured in 1813 having, she said, served for three years until being in a shipwreck, where all on board perished except herself. Finding the dead body of a seaman, she conceived the idea of dressing herself in men's clothing and later served on several ships. She continued, she said, because her share of the prize-money and wages amounted to about $200.[14]

In 1807, Rebecca Ann Johnston, a native of Whitby, Yorkshire, claimed she was forced by her stepfather to work on a coal ship, the *Mayflower* of Sunderland, threatening if anyone discovered her sex, he would murder her. He had also, Rebecca claimed, forced her mother to join a warship until she was mortally wounded at the Battle of Copenhagen (1801).[15]

James Wilson, a young sailor from the *Charlotte* moored in Belfast harbour, got so much 'grog aboard' as to be rendered insensible. Conveyed in a handcart to the police station, efforts were made to resuscitate the unfortunate sailor when it was discovered they 'belonged to the *fair* sex.'

An embarrassed Betsy Wilson of Whitehaven claimed she had adopted male attire because she was robbed of her own clothes in a lodging-house. In return, she stole the clothes of a sleeping lodger and decided to try a life at sea. She had been on two voyages before being discovered.[16]

The most common reasons cited for enlisting were either family or a man. Escaping cruel treatment by fathers, step-parents or husbands appears frequently. An unnamed girl in 1841 blamed 'an unamiable step-mother' for running away, aided by reading 'in the columns of the newspapers' a 'glowing account of an adventurous damsel who assumed the character of a mariner, and succeeded in preserving it for many years.' She claimed the 'ill delicacy' of being in male attire was preferable to prostitution.[17]

For others, it was their need to imitate family members that drove their actions, such as Glaswegian Annie Stuart (aka Thomas Stewart) who had been at sea for five years when she was discovered after a fall that broke her ribs. She said she had gone to sea because all her brothers had.[18]

However, most excuses involved men. As mentioned elsewhere, any story where a man took centre stage was well-received and women were treated with leniency so it became a convenient ploy when discovered.

When the *HMS Impertense* was in Plymouth Sound, a smart young sailor volunteered but when suspicions were aroused, the 'young spark confessed that *she was a woman*.' She had borne a child to a man who had been pressed and hoped to find him, which may have been an invented story because aged just 22, she claimed she had already served on a number of ships under the name of Tom Walker.[19]

In 1841, Eliza Carey from Ireland, supposedly in love with a lad, followed him to America. She worked as a cook but at one point was so seasick, she had to suffer the crew's traditional cure of being plunged overboard on the end of a rope, which she endured '*manfully*.' When docked in the Orkneys, she carried on a flirtation with a girl, who discovered her sex and as Eliza told the story, her 'countenance was thrown into an arch expression of playful humour' – a reminder to the reader that this interest in women was 'just a lark'.[20]

Nancy Clifford's sister had married a man called Anderson but when she died, Nancy fell in love with her brother-in-law. In British law of the time, a man could not marry his deceased wife's sister and so in 1897, they ran away together as sailors.[21]

A very detailed story appeared in 1827 when a policeman was informed that William Brown, a sailor on the *Laura* in Liverpool, was a female. Taken to court, Selina Augusta Hamilton refused to give any account of her family or why she had adopted 'such a novel line of conduct' and 'her resolution to retain her disguise appeared firm and unshaken.' She explained that she had adopted the disguise from choice; was determined to continue it; and that as she had done no-one any harm, she could not conceive what right anyone had to detain her. The magistrate agreed and dismissed her but the media kept digging. They found that the *Laura's* Captain Duffy told a different story. It seems that Selina was the daughter of a respectable merchant who owned several vessels. About three years earlier, when she was about 16, she left home to follow a young man, William Brown. She travelled to St. John's in Canada dressed in female apparel but he had already left. She went on to Quebec but arrived there only to learn that he had drowned in a river. From then on, she determined to follow his profession and taking his name, she worked first as a cook and then as a seaman on several vessels. She had, noted the newspaper, not only

> become quite familiar with the dress; but the *habits* of seafaring men. She could take her *jorum of grog* and her quid of tobacco, a box of which was found in her pocket. Her adventures with the *girls* have also been among her extraordinary feats; she had actually caused banns of marriage to be put up.

Returning to Liverpool, she was robbed by some girls and her sex was discovered. She subsequently married the same Captain Duffy and after her marriage, she could occasionally be seen pacing the deck of the *Laura*. He was heard to declare that 'she'll soon doff her woman's gear, if things don't go right, and take the command herself.'[22] Again, one is left questioning the William Brown love story and Duffy's sexual orientation.

The 'dying lover' is a familiar theme. In 1835, an unnamed woman fell in love with a captain who had to sail to America and when he failed to return, she donned male attire and went after him. However, he had died just a few days before her arrival. She too resolved to become a sailor and served on the *Belfast*, as cook and steward for £2 10s a month. One day, while she was 'washing in her berth with her jacket loose in the front, one of the crew caught an accidental glimpse of her bosom.' From then on, she was made to suffer – given the hardest jobs, such as going into the shrouds in foul weather; and subjected to gibes, jeers and curses. In port, she was dismissed, the captain keeping her wages for himself on the grounds that he had agreed to pay a man and not a woman.[23]

Other women claimed they were running from shame. In 1844, Sarah Bignell robbed her father of 7s. 6d. and, dressed as a sailor, went to join a naval midshipman who, she claimed, had seduced her 'from the paths of virtue.' In a letter to her father, she said she could not return home after the disgrace she had brought upon herself and her family. In court, Sarah claimed she had seen the midshipman just the night before but she would not then give his name as she believed to do so would result in his dismissal. 'He promised to take me as sailor on board his ship,' Sarah explained. 'He said that the vessel was under orders for the Mediterranean, and that when we arrived in that sunny clime, he would then have an opportunity of making me an honourable woman.' The magistrate was not convinced and believed the man's 'intentions towards her were not of an honourable nature, and that probably, when she arrived in a foreign country, he would desert her, and leave her to her fate in a state of wretchedness and poverty.' When the father added Sarah was 'in the habit of reading a good deal', the magistrate concluded, 'I am afraid she has been a reader of trashy novels, which have had the effect of tainting her morals, and have led to her present situation.' Attempts to persuade her to go home were met with refusal and Sarah declared she was determined to quit the country with the midshipman. The magistrate replied that if she would not see sense, he would send her to trial for stealing from her father and in the event of a conviction, she would probably 'cross the sea in a very different way from that which she intended', but nothing more is heard of her.[24]

Abigail Lindsey was seduced by the captain of the *Bradford*, who promised to marry her and by whom she had a child. When his ship sailed, he abandoned her and so she determined to find him and have her revenge. For five years, she served as John Browne, working as a cook but frequently having to perform the duties of a common seaman. She caught up with the captain in London and wanted to go ashore but just as her vessel was about to sail, she was denied permission to disembark. In court, she declared that she would have stabbed him if she had the opportunity. She was held in Bridewell and people came to gawk at her which she resented, declaring that if she were made an exhibition of any longer, she would 'destroy herself'. Orders were given that no person should be allowed to see her and a subscription was raised to send her home, but nothing more is known of her.[25]

For others, there were more practical reasons for becoming a sailor. Destitute Isabella 'Billy' Stewart worked on board the *Algonquin* in 1841 because she wanted a better life in America.[26] Similarly, an unnamed impoverished woman joined the *Fan* in 1842 and when discovered at Liverpool, she was followed 'by a crowd anxious to make themselves acquainted with her history. She had an extremely masculine appearance, and the hardness of her hands, caused by the labour on board the ship tended still further to conceal her sex.'[27]

Most of the women served on little-known ships but occasionally, famous vessels appear (although confirmation is problematic because women were not recorded in the official crew logs). According to a letter writer in 1836, three women served on the *Victory* at the Battle of the Saintes in the Caribbean in 1782, before it became Nelson's ship at the Battle of Trafalgar (1805). The women were apparently set ashore at Lisbon and money was collected to send them home. 'They had served at the guns most valiantly during the whole of the engagement, and had not received any injury.'[28]

Many women became captains but mostly wore female attire. The few cross-dressing individuals, for obvious reasons of maintaining their disguise, drew attention to themselves by taking such a prominent position. However, during the Galician Slaughter, or Peasant Uprising in Austrian Poland of 1846, a story emerged of a beautiful Galician girl who had an attachment to a young sergeant. He had been captured and was sentenced to transportation, so she dressed in male attire and managed to get herself on the same ship. Just as it approached Lisbon, she urged the crew to mutiny and arrested the captain, placing herself in charge. The men accepted her as their leader, believing her to be a young conscript of an unusually daring character. 'Thus,' concluded the article, 'the love of a young woman, who had not previously been out of her village, led to the escape of nearly 300 men.'[29]

Escaping detection was a continuous challenge and in a ship's cramped quarters, the women were forced to find unusual and often uncomfortable ways to keep their secret. 16-year-old Amelia Vella from Newport, Wales told a journalist how she shared sleeping quarters with five men and so would sit on the forecastle until the men were in their bunks, and then, 'I would turn in 'all standing,' as sailors say; that is, with all my clothes on, and when the foc's'le lamp was blown out I used to undress quietly in my bunk.'[30] John Wilkinson on the battleship *Vermont* in 1907 broke the rules by taking a bath after taps (a signal to note the end of the day at 9.00 pm) but the noise attracted attention.[31]

Some women's behaviour was too refined. In 1857, a sailor had 'retired manners, an unusual quietness of demeanour, an avoidance of intimacy with any of the crew, and a total abstinence from all intoxicating liquors' which soon attracted the attention of all on board. Despite that, there was little, wrote the journalist, 'of the really feminine in this strange creature's external ensemble.'[32]

The longer women served, the more easily they could pass as men – or more importantly, as sailors. Elizabeth Carter was described as walking with the 'gait peculiar to seamen' from her ten years at sea.[33]

Understandably, most of the known examples come from those women who were discovered and the reasons for discovery are myriad. Eliza Rice was arrested in Rye in 1857 for carrying a suspicious bundle, which ironically turned out to be her female attire;[34] American Bridget Dokay refused to stand a group of sailors a drink in 1861 and so one struck her in the breast and realised she was a woman;[35] and a suspicious sailor on the brig *Buswick* in Sunderland in 1838 grabbed a youth and pulling open their waistcoat, exposed a pair of breasts.[36] John Robinson, 'whose real name we forbear mentioning' wrote the journalist, sailed to follow a lover in 1864 but confessed due to excessive sea sickness;[37] and Charles Waddall, belonging to a man-of-war called the *Oxford*, moored at Chatham, was ordered to receive two dozen lashes for desertion in 1771.[38]

Some women were discovered despite receiving help from others. In 1902, Mrs Ratcliff worried that her husband, a cook on the *Lord Erne* leaving Barry, Cardiff might not come back from the USA so she persuaded him to smuggle her on board. Having bribed the cook's mate to keep quiet, she was not discovered for twenty-five days.[39]

Drink was a significant factor in the discovery of cross-living women. John Davidson, a sailor for twenty-three years was on *HMS Prince Edward* in Bristol in 1748 but having drunk freely, he became 'passionately fond' of his messmate.[40]

Probably the most common reason for discovery was through accident or death. Falling overboard was always a danger and William Macdonald, who had served for five years, did just that in 1814. He was recovered and stripped by his colleagues.[41] Billy Cridle, or Rebecca Young, had served for a year or more until on the way down from the masthead, he fell to the deck, about 20 feet, and was killed.[42] Hans Brandt on the barque *Ida*, of Pensacola in 1890, was killed by a fall into the hold.[43]

In 1873, the *Atlantic* was lost in Nova Scotia, and one of the bodies washed ashore was a sailor known as Bill who had served for three voyages. A survivor said, 'I don't know that Bill was a woman. He used to take his licker as reg'lar as any of us, and was always begging and stealing tobacco. He was a good fellow, though, and I am sorry he was a woman.'[44]

One particularly sad story occurred in 1877 when James Colton fell from the mast and was killed. William Bean had smuggled 'James', his wife, on board and when the stowaway was discovered, he was set to work without anyone realising she was a woman. As the funeral service was being read, a distraught William jumped from the mast and 'sank immediately'.[45]

When women were discovered, crowds would often gather to see them when they arrived back on land, especially in the 1840s and 1850s when female sailors were such a novelty. When Agnes Corbett was arrested, the front of the court was

> absolutely crammed by an anxious crowd, some of its members shouting, others laughing, and giving a description of the heroine to those who had not the good fortune to see the "female sailor" … others again were straining their necks over their fellows' heads, in order to get a peep at the window of the room in which it was alleged she was stowed away, and it was with the greatest difficulty that he (the magistrate) could make way through the dense mass of people into the barracks; but having, after much struggling, elbowing, and pushing, effected an entrance, he was introduced, puffing, panting, and blowing like a grampus, into the presence of the prize.

In the morning '*he*' was returned to court and the 'crowd in front of the office was very great, and it was as much as the constables on duty could do to prevent the mob from rushing up the stairs and into the board-room, in order to get a glimpse.' Agnes gave the familiar story of following her love only to find he had sailed elsewhere.[46]

Despite many women being attacked by crowds, rarely is impropriety recorded, however, one incident from 1857 occurred when Rachel Ramsden refused to acknowledge her sex so some men pulled down her trousers.[47]

Other difficulties of being discovered were that captains, or ship owners, would often refuse to pay the woman, despite having done the work. A few brave women did go to court to recover their wages, including Elizabeth Stevens in 1823. She had worked on the *Jane-Matilda* as a cook, steward and ship-keeper but the captain refused to pay her on the grounds that he thought he was employing a man. However, the magistrate disagreed and ordered him to pay 60 shillings in back pay.[48]

As with women who joined the army, female sailors who were discovered would often simply re-enlist. Martha Hudson had served for two years aboard a warship, where she suffered a gunshot wound, before being discovered in 1764. She simply declared her resolution to get aboard another ship, or join a regiment and 'there to serve her King and country to the last.'[49]

Frenchwoman Julienne Davy had served for many years as a soldier and when caught, declared her sex to avoid deportation. She then joined a ship but was captured by the British and held prisoner for eight years before her sex was discovered. Why she endured this and did not confess her sex again is curious, as prisoner conditions at the time were harsh.[50]

Susan Brunin of Newport had been at sea for fifteen months but when she enlisted on a new ship, the captain refused to keep the contract once it was found she was a woman. He told the police about her and they found her 'gallanting another lass about the town' and arrested her for being drunk. The *Pembrokeshire Herald* mused as to why she would 'expose herself to the hardships incidental to a mariner's life.' However, in court Susan explained that nothing whatever would induce her to leave off her 'fancy attire' – at which the bench gave her a harsh lecture on the impropriety of her conduct, and discharged her with some 'wholesome advice.'[51]

Life changed for many of the women after they were discovered: Jane Gallagher was a well-known Irish female sailor at the time and it was believed she had started cross-living when she followed a lover to America and beyond. When discovered, sometime between 1830 and 1837, her story fascinated William IV – he asked to meet her and they had wine and cake together. He granted her a pension of £10 a year, which she enjoyed up to her death.[52]

In 1802, a Mrs Cola became somewhat famous by serving on board a man-of-war. She resumed her 'proper attire' and opened a coffee-house for sailors.[53] Hannah Snell, and others, took to the stage and often earned good money. Several wrote up their memoirs and hundreds sold photographs of themselves dressed as sailors.

Even into the twentieth century, women were still managing to get on board. In 1904, a woman joined a ship at Swansea to follow her man.[54] In his book, *The Autobiography of a Super-Tramp* (1908), W. H. Davies wrote of a female sailor he had met; and another unnamed woman in Swansea tried to enlist in 1915.[55]

As elsewhere with cross-dressing women, many accounts of female sailors mention how hard-working and respected they were. Many wrote with awe that the female sailors often climbed the masts and repaired sails alongside the men, with apparently little fear. Most, however, seem to have been cooks although that was no easy task and they were often required to take on other hard physical duties.

From 1914, women could serve on ships in various categories without the need to cross-dress or cross-live, but it was not until the 1970s that they were officially allowed to join navies. And it was as late as the 1990s when women were at last allowed to wear trousers while serving their country aboard ship.

Chapter 12

A Pair of Pretty Legs

For centuries, the theatre was seen as a place of vice and the idea of putting women on stage was abhorrent to most in society – those women who did act were regarded as little more than prostitutes. Early women's roles had been played by young men but this created a dichotomy, because men who cross-dressed did so in defiance of Deuteronomy 22:5, the biblical ruling that men were not allowed to wear the clothes of a woman. In addition, there were concerns that a male body interacting with another male body could have a homosexual subtext.

In 1599, three leading men of the time – John Rainolds, an academic and churchman, and William Gager and Alberico Gentili, both experts in the law – debated in their book *The Overthrow of Stage Plays*[1] whether Deuteronomy applied to actors. Rainolds said it did, Gentili said it did not and Gager said it was wrong for men to wear women's clothing unless to save their life or for some public benefit. Nevertheless, women continued to be largely absent on the British stage until the 1660s, although they did appear in a variety of roles in other countries, such as the ancient Japanese tradition of *shirabyōshi* dancing, which included a female dancer and singer dressed as a man.

Not allowing women to represent women could have its difficulties; apparently, Charles II became impatient waiting until Juliet had shaved[2] so perhaps it is no coincidence that it was during his reign that women were first admitted to the stage. Almost immediately, women took to appearing in male attire and between 1660 and 1700, a quarter of the 375 plays in London included roles for women wearing male clothes.[3] Most of the plays had 'love plots' with the dependable motif of a woman in disguise seeking a missing lover or husband, although the shadow of homosexuality lingered. When Molière's play *Le Dépit amoureux* was first performed in 1659, Dorothée was disguised as a man and when she expressed her love for her husband, there were concerns about implied homosexuality. Despite women not acting in early productions of Shakespeare's plays, many of his works challenge the idea of gender by including cross-dressing and gender-ambiguous themes.

By the eighteenth century, what became known as *travesti* or 'breeches roles' were a popular fixture of the theatre and actresses such as Margaret 'Peg' Woffington and Charlotte Charke gained great fame in these roles. *Travesti* is taken from the Latin *transvestire* (*trans* – across and *vestire* – clothes) which led to the French words *travestir* and *travesti* to denote a disguise. In 1910, Magnus Hirschfeld coined the term *transvestite* using the same etymology.

As soon as women started appearing in male attire, there was criticism. A writer to *The Times* in 1787 expressed disgust over Sarah Siddons using her appearance in breeches as a means of attracting an audience to a benefit performance:

> However interesting the situation may be, our taste must ever censure the appearance of women in breeches ... playing the character of a man cannot bear an excuse; it is disgusting, and militates with every principle of female delicacy; and even, as in the situation before us, the assuming man's apparel as a means of disguise, though it may be sanction by *necessity* in real life, is contrary to decency as a public exhibition.[4]

The writer is acknowledging that there were occasions in real life when 'necessity' (stressed by the use of italics) made it acceptable for women to disguise themselves but this did not apply to the stage.

The nineteenth century saw travesti parts become lead roles in an era when the stage was to society as television is today. Plays generated the same passions as modern programmes – they produced celebrities; influenced fashions; and generated heated discussions – and there was a great deal of debate over travesti roles. From the mid-nineteenth century onwards, burlesque shows parodied all aspects of society and gender reversal for both sexes was a common feature – supposedly allowing the viewer to separate ideas of sexuality and morality.

In 1815, there were so many women in male attire that the *Morning Post* complained, 'if we go on at this rate, the original state of the Drama will be entirely reversed, and a sort of theatrical *annus mirabilis* will ensue, in which all the women will assume manhood.'[5] However, travesty roles were governed by a set formula that only included limited aspects of manhood. The plays (usually by men but women may have written some under male pseudonyms) were light-hearted comedies with the travesti portrayed as comic, farcical or pathetic, adding to themes of disorder and chaos. Many were set in foreign countries, emphasising that it 'couldn't happen here'. The role was almost always portraying a young man – fathers, husbands, men of importance or villains were rare – although an 1819 play called *Helpless Animals* included a 'malicious damsel' in male attire.[6] The women made no attempt to disguise their voices into a lower register and, for the most part, appeared clean-shaven although a moustache may occasionally have been used. No matter how brave the 'hero' might be while in male attire, she must always have those womanly qualities expected by society – often swooning in the face of danger resulting in the discovery of her sex. Once the disorder and chaos were over, the woman was not permitted to continue her disguised role but must always be relieved to be back in her 'proper' dress and surrendering herself back to male control.

Most of the actresses were young and pretty with attractive legs. Rarely did they look like men or unfeminine, and if they did try to appear like men, they were harshly criticised – such as the opera singer Benedetta Rosmunda Pisaroni, who was said to excel in male roles because of her ugly, unfeminine appearance, although contemporary images do not support the 'ugly' look. It may well have been that she deliberately used make-up to alter her appearance to further detract the audience from seeing her as a woman.[7]

Sometimes, there was confusion. In 1804, a new play was tried out at Drury Lane called *The Dash; or, Who But He?*:

> We understood him to be a young gentleman, but we were assured by several persons of discernment who sat near us, that he was in reality a female. He sometimes appeared in breeches, and sometimes in petticoats, and it was nearly impossible to say when he was in disguise and when in his proper attire.[8]

One of the intended purposes of the travesti was the erotic titillation of men and the theatre was one of the few places where scantily-dressed women could regularly and legally be seen. The costumes, although purporting to be male attire, were highly feminised, setting them apart from the costumes worn by men and reinforced with feminine glances and movements. They were designed to show off the female body and emphasised the bosom, legs, hips and buttocks, which were rarely seen in public spaces. A writer in *The Spectator* complained that appearance overshadowed talent, claiming women sought 'the loud plaudits of the unmarried gentlemen' adding, 'we are by no means sure that this taste ought to be encouraged in young women who go upon the stage.' The writer was worried that it made actresses trust more to a 'well-turned ankle' than talent and made them:

fonder of surtouts and tights than is entirely compatible with the good of their souls; it gives them notoriety, but it never secures for them respect … they aim at the sex of their auditors – it is as women they hope to please, and not as actresses.[9]

Lucia Elizabeth Vestris, popularly known as Madame Vestris, was extremely popular in travesti roles and audiences flocked to see her legs. When Violante Camporesi appeared in male attire, her appearance 'excited the admiration of the spectators the moment she appeared on the stage.'[10] Many of the well-known actresses had postcards of themselves in male attire which sold in their thousands.

Despite the popularity of the travesti role, it was surrounded by criticism. *The Examiner* in 1808 seemed to object to Dorothea Jordan's skin-tight stockings. 'I was completely disgusted at her appearance; and in this feeling I am sure I was accompanied by every rational person in the house,' but then the writer lavished detailed on her costume, 'She appeared in thin white breeches and stockings that fitted her like her own skin, and just over her waist hung a vest, still thinner, of most transparent black lace,' but then remembered himself:

> I shall not be exact in my description, lest I should appear to be writing upon anatomy, but if ever woman was ingenious enough to be effectively thought not actually naked, such a woman was Mrs Jordan on Tuesday. Every delicate female in the house must have felt wretched. The display was as absurd as it was immoral. *Viola*, though she put on male attire, was a most virtuous girl … *Viola* should have been really *disguised*, not undressed as a woman under *pretence* of being dressed as a man. Besides, Mrs Jordan has daughters, and I am told that these daughters sometimes witness her performances. For shame! For shame![11]

Despite the masses of criticism over travesti roles, there were those who defended the women. An unnamed writer in *The Examiner* wrote:

> That delicate animal who presides over the *Sunday Oracle, or Parson's Monitor*, which is no less emphatically than justly styled *The Smutty Gazette*, seems to be grievously offended with the appearance on the stage of women habited in male attire; and having exhausted all other epithets of disgust and vituperation, bursts forth every now and then with a declaration, that the practice is *nasty, filthy,* and *beastly!* Now

we will venture to affirm, that whatever objections might occur to the minds of persons of either sex against this practice, no man of *manly feelings* could ever have applied to it the epithets in question. The view of a beautiful woman, with her limbs and person dressed up as a man, could not in any but the most depraved of the most hyper-puritanical minds, have excited those *beastly* and degrading expressions.[12]

For almost two centuries, writers complained on religious, moral and political grounds against the travesti roles, mostly to no effect. Occasionally, there was even an attempt to stop a performance. In Rome, ballet dancer Guglielmina Salvioni was appearing in *The Countess of Egmont* in 1867 and her role required her to embrace her supposed lover. The police, who thought the public would be shocked by this amatory exhibition, ordered Guglielmina to discontinue but she refused, explaining the person she embraced, though dressed in breeches, was a woman like herself and the audience were aware of the fact. Four gendarmes were sent to arrest her on stage and she was placed under house arrest. However, there was a change of heart and the following night, Guglielmina was escorted by the gendarmes back to the stage where she was greeted with thunderous applause.[13]

Women rarely had the opportunity, despite the hundreds of plays that were produced every year, to stretch their performance abilities in good roles. Most plays were written by men, so male roles had more depth, with women required mostly to look pretty and behave on stage in ways that reflected their place in society. Generally speaking, it is only in the last fifty years that women have been seen in roles other than the subordinate, pretty side kick for men, so for those females wanting to take on more significant work, it is no surprise that they began to play roles such as Romeo or Hamlet. These cross-gendered breeches roles were different from travesti as there was no discarding of the disguise at the end of the play; the actress was the man.

Although there were many breeches roles, arguably the most famous were Hamlet and Romeo. Sarah Siddons was the first to play Hamlet in 1775 but she stuck to provincial theatres to avoid controversy. The most famous in the role was the great Sarah Bernhardt, who began playing him in 1899 and was the first to play Hamlet on film (in fact, it was the first Shakespearean performance on film). In the fencing scene, Bernhardt is quite convincing as a male but readers can make their own decision by watching the YouTube video.

Generally, she received great praise for her performances and when asked why she was so fond of male roles, Bernhardt argued that it was not the character but the 'male brain' she preferred. She was critical of female roles as 'mere play' – a matter of looking pretty and displaying emotions. Bernhardt's fame as a male lead attracted international attention and she travelled the globe, receiving reviews that ranged from vitriolic to rave. She became one of the most internationally watched breeches actresses of her day, and postcards were even produced of her in the male roles she portrayed.

Sarah Siddons designed her own costume that defied dress conventions for both male and female. She had done something similar when playing Shakespeare's cross-dressing Rosalind but had received negative reviews. Most critics thought she wore gender-neutral costumes because she was too fat – none considered she may have been trying for an ambiguity of appearance in order to concentrate on the role itself. Charlotte Charke, who became famous for her breeches roles, played Hamlet and even wore male clothes offstage.

Hamlet is one of the most popular male Shakespearean roles played by women and, like Romeo, is a young, possibly rather effeminate, man. In fact, claims have been made that Hamlet was not a man at all. Edward P. Vining, in his book *The Mystery of Hamlet* (1881), claimed he was a woman disguised as a man – and in 1921, Danish actor Asta Nielsen played Hamlet this way.

One reviewer offered Bernhardt a backhanded compliment, claiming that as a male impersonator, Bernhardt was a 'dire failure' and to say otherwise would be to 'cruelly insult her.' His argument was that she was too good-looking to play a man, that

> [it is] only the unsexed woman, the woman who, physically and physiologically, approaches nearly to the masculine – the monstrosity in short – who can deceive us as to her gender on the stage. Boys parts may be played by women, because in this case the demarcations of sex are not so distinct; and, as we all know, women's parts, in the old time, were successfully enacted by boys.[14]

Bernhardt herself believed young men's roles should only be played by women, as young men did not have the maturity (and older men could not get away with looking young).

After Bernhardt, Hamlet was not played by a woman until 1979 when Frances de la Tour undertook the role saying,

I didn't approach the part as a woman, I just studied the role as any actor would. I was dressed in trousers and jacket, so I could be seen as androgynous. My hair was long and curly and I wore no make-up, so I was just a young person. I think audiences readily believed this from the first soliloquy.[15]

Thirty-five years later in 2014, Maxine Peake's Hamlet was, according to the *Guardian,* 'almost pre-sexual.'[16]

After Hamlet, the most popular breeches role for women was Romeo. The American actress Charlotte Cushman became extremely famous for her portrayals but many argued her success was due to her masculinity. Unlike Bernhardt and Siddons who retained their feminine appearance, Cushman became the man.

Victorian audiences saw nothing odd in a woman dressed as a man playing a romantic role with another woman, as they believed it represented a purer, more spiritual way of expressing love without the taint of sexuality. However, unease about possible homosexual connotations did exist although they were rarely overtly voiced. The *Preston Guardian* referred to Charlotte Cushman as a 'laughable spectacle of a woman, dressed in breeches, making love to another woman in petticoats.'[17] One reviewer in *The Examiner* in 1828 wrote, 'to see a modest woman in male attire is revolting to delicacy … that one woman should make love to another, takes from the scenic interest.' And then the writer adds without a hint of irony, 'We are aware that the *Rosalind* and *Viola* of Shakespeare may be pleaded in excuse; but they are females disguised but temporarily; and moreover, in the days when Shakespeare wrote, all the characters were performed by males, which, though it might lessen the interest, certainly took away the whole indelicacy of the representation.'[18]

For some women we would today regard as gay, acting provided opportunities to be themselves. Charlotte Cushman had several wives throughout her life and French actress Cécile Sorel described in her autobiography an actress 'kissing her with such ardour that the audience was shocked'; another threw herself on Sorel 'with such erotic abandon that the authorities canceled [sic] the performance on the grounds of indecency.'[19] Anna Dickinson, the famous American lecturer on the Rights of Women and the abolition of slavery (and now considered a lesbian), sued relatives who tried to have her committed to an asylum citing as part of their evidence that she appeared on stage as Romeo in male attire.[20]

Female fans, none of whom would have been in the audience without a male escort, were not self-conscious about admiring cross-dressing women. This remained true in the twentieth century with actresses such as Marlene Dietrich and Katherine Hepburn.

Despite the popularity of women playing Hamlet, Romeo and other classic characters, it was the light-hearted plays that remained the mainstay for breeches roles throughout the nineteenth century – with critics paying particular attention to what the women were wearing. When Madame Vestris appeared as Captain Macheath in *The Beggar's Opera* in 1820, one critic wrote approvingly of her costume as, 'masculine enough as a dress, and yet feminine enough for her to wear them with ease.' Others, however, objected; ten years later when playing the same character, Madame Vestris sued two men for hissing and hooting at her with cries of, 'Off, off; no female in breeches!', so preventing her from performing. The men were fined.[21]

When women looked a little too like men, there could be disgust – as when a 'WB' wrote to *The Examiner:*

> in the name of decency, is all this to be tolerated, night after night, for months together in the very centre of British society? I cannot bring myself to dwell on the *outrageous impudence* of the girl ... Nothing more decidedly shocking to the public morals ever met my observation, and it was in witnessing the shameless scenes in which she figured, that I experienced the dreadful feeling of disgust to an extreme I never remember to have felt before; and what can be more abhorrently sickening than the disgust forced upon us at a Theatre, in spite of all the good nature we are supposed to carry thither?[22]

As with women who cross-dressed in real life, it was difficult to learn how to walk, hold their body, talk and sing like a man but there were those who were so good at impersonating men that some refused to believe they were women. In 1859, a Russian nobleman went to see Mrs Howard Paul imitating Sims Reeve and was so impressed, he asked to meet the tenor. It was not a tenor, he was told, but a lady.

'Impossible!' said the Russian; 'this is mere badinage. I am not so great a stranger in England that I am to be told that English ladies possess tenor voices.'

'But I assure you,' pursued the Englishman, 'it is no device, of man, but a singular truth – that was the voice of a lady, and a wonderful imitation of Mr Reeve, our first English tenor.'

'I have no doubt you believe it to be a lady, but there is some trick, some artifice here beyond your comprehension. No woman living could mimic the notes and intonations of a man so closely. Depend on it, you are the dupe.'

They took a bet of £100 and it was not until they went backstage and Mrs Paul sang again that the Russian believed it.[23]

There was also surprise that women were able to wield swords with effect. 'Mrs Nesbitt,' wrote the *Morning Post*, 'particularly in her masquerade of the Officer in the duelling scene, elicited the most rapturous applause. We have very seldom seen anything more effective on the stage at any period than the talents exhibited by this Lady last night.'[24] Some were determined to go where men would not. When the Great American Hippodrome arrived in Bradford in 1864, the advertisement carried the notice of Miss A. Hill who would

> appear in male attire, and go through the different changes of dress, fight her own combats, and gallop over the fearful precipices, lashed to the back of the Wild Horse of Tartary, a feat that has hitherto been avoided by actors, and who have had dummies to represent them in making the ascent, and will, lastly, lead her troops on to battle, appearing first and foremost in the struggle.[25]

By 1875, breeches roles were so ubiquitous that the *Daily News* commented that the '"Female Highwayman," the "Female Pirate," the "Female Soldier," the "Female Sailor," and nearly every variety of anomalous females, are familiar to popular romance.'[26] Uniformed roles were particularly popular in plays and songs, following the enormous publicity surrounding female soldiers and sailors.

Breeches plays were big money-earners and theatre managers wanted to capitalise by including clauses in the contracts that actresses must appear in male attire. The more well-known an actress, the more they tried to tempt her to cross-dress. However, even when bound by contract, it did not mean their appearance was a success. The *Morning Chronicle* noted, 'We know it sometimes happens that Managers, aware how many are attracted by the display of a pair of pretty legs (and there are no prettier than those of Madame Vestris), compel actresses to overcome their own natural repugnance.'[27] Some did refuse – a Miss Stephens was 'out of favour with the Managers, because she thus far insists upon maintaining the natural modesty of her sex.'[28]

Many actresses appeared nervous and ill at ease in men's clothing as it left them open to harsh criticism, and some demanded higher wages as a result.

In 1802, Madam Banti signed with the Opera House in London and was 'required to perform in male attire.' As she was expected to take the lead male role, she demanded the same pay as the lead female and was asking £2,500 to sing in breeches but had accepted £1,200 without breeches.[29]

Some avoided the problem by not dressing fully in male attire. Mary Anderson was reluctant to appear in 'boys' clothes' but did finally do so as Rosalind. The *Hampshire Telegraph* wrote, 'she had courage enough to wear a sensible costume in the forest scenes … not too much hose, but just hose enough.'[30]

If the woman was married, she would have almost certainly have required her husband's permission. A Mrs Topham's letter to her husband asked:

> They want me to play in breeches – the men all say they like me best without petticoats, and that I must *consent*: I have, it is true, often laid aside the modest appendages of our sex, but now that I'm married, Lovey, how will it look to be seen without even my under coat; but you shall guide – let me have your answer by return of post on that head.[31]

Some did not try at all. A piece appeared in the *Pall Mall Gazette* from 1890 entitled 'How I tried to become an actress' by 'One who shrank from the "Soldier Test".' An unnamed young teacher decided to become an actress and applied to Mr Irving at the Lyceum where she was accepted. She began as a soldier rigged out 'in tight-fitting trousers, high boots, and all the rest,' said Irving. However, she started to have nightmares about appearing on stage in male clothes and decided to give up all thoughts of acting.[32]

Occasionally, disapproval could be extreme. George Barnett had developed a passion for the actress Frances Maria Kelly in 1816 and had sent her letters but she had not replied to him. He wrote back saying,

> Had you not infringed the rights of your sex, I should not have thus addressed you … I love the sex, and once esteemed you as an ornament to it, till you roused my indignation by your impertinence and scandalous abuses … You are very partial to a disguised male dress; but let me not experience any more of your folly, for if you do, I'll secure you as an imposter, and punish you for your temerity.[33]

When she did not reply, Barnett went to the theatre armed with a pistol and shot at her. The bullet missed but he was arrested, found guilty on grounds of insanity and detained.

As the cult of celebrity grew during the nineteenth century, interviews with those women who undertook breeches roles stressed their 'normal' behaviour at home, but certain actresses continued to wear male attire outside the theatre. Cécile Sorel, after falling in love with an actor, donned male attire to spy on him and created an alter ego, giving him the name of Petit Paul and walking about the streets as him.[34] Hannah Webber, for some years a music-hall artiste and male impersonator in the United States, arrived at Liverpool in 1897 having worked her passage disguised as a cattleman. Her disguise was not discovered until she injured herself by lifting a 2-cwt bale of hay.[35]

Sarah Bernhardt wore male clothes at home but was sensitive to people knowing. She is also reputed to have had a relationship with Louise Abbema, herself a cross-dressing artist. In the latter part of the seventeenth century, the extraordinary 'wild' woman Julie d'Aubigny – better known as Mademoiselle Maupin and today regarded as bisexual – was involved in numerous scandals that including killing or wounding several men. As the law only covered men duelling (it was believed women could not fight), she escaped punishment. In a bizarre twist to her life story, she then began a relationship with a local merchant's daughter who was quickly sent to a convent to keep her safe. Just at that time, a nun happened to die so Julie broke in, put the nun's body in her lover's cell and set fire to the convent to cover their escape. She was caught, charged with kidnapping, body snatching and arson, and condemned to death by fire. However, she had moved to Paris and had begun an affair with a leading opera singer, and he managed to convince the authorities that her talent was so rare she should be pardoned. She was, and went on to become a famous opera singer – but could never stay out of trouble for long. It is believed she died in 1707 in a convent at the age of 33. Théophile Gautier's novel *Mademoiselle de Maupin* (1835) was loosely based on her.

It was not just women on stage who were cross-dressing but also members of the audience. A number of cross-dressing women mention attending the theatre, such as an unnamed woman in Brooklyn, New York who 'ran the town for a week, walking the streets, mashing all the pretty girls, attending the theatres, and on Sunday dropping in to hear Beecher in the morning and Talmage in the evening.'[36]

In 1869, the *Pall Mall Gazette* was complaining about the number of prostitutes in and around theatres: 'women in men's clothes had the audacity to appear in a private box, not hidden behind the curtains, but impudently defying the audience.'[37]

However, mistakes about the biological sex of individuals could be made. A man sat in a theatre in France with a handsome young lad at his side, when they were approached and told, 'The Commissary of Police desires to speak to you and the lady in his private room.' The Commissary advised the man it was illegal in France for women to wear male attire but the indignant father replied that the youth was his son. The Commissary looked the boy up and down before observing, 'Well, I see he has incipient mustachios – that is enough,' and they were dismissed without a word of apology.[38]

By the mid to late nineteenth century, the *travesti* and breeches roles had become so passé that it sufficed only to pass comment that the actress was appearing in male attire. Moral commentary had for the most part been abandoned, however, a new form of cross-dressing on stage was to take the place of these roles. By the 1870s, there was a rise in male impersonators and it seemed that no provincial theatre was complete without one. Unlike travesti and breeches roles, these were stand-up comedians, sketch artists and singers. Nevertheless, they were acts built upon years of familiarity with theatrical cross-dressing resulting in a carefully constructed image of what a woman, pretending to look like a man, was like. Audiences were accustomed to being 'in on the act', particularly when it came to double entendre; when something was read in a straightforward manner, it sounded very innocent but when told accompanied by winks and asides, it changed the meaning completely. When Marie Lloyd was challenged for being rude, she read out the song and it was deemed innocent – but when she then performed it again, complete with innuendoes, it was deemed immodest. The audience knew and willingly participated in this act and continue to do so with similar acts today.

As social changes crept in during the late nineteenth and early twentieth centuries, class resentment grew and the male impersonator gained great popularity by making fun of the foppish 'swell', the rich man who was effeminate in appearance from not doing manual work. Male impersonators became known for their satirical commentary on gender roles and making fun of men.

The earliest noted male impersonators were Bessie Bonehill, Hettie King and Vesta Tilley, although many others became internationally famous. Male impersonators had legions of female fans and many received erotic or romantic letters from them. Given that these women knew that the star was a woman raises questions as to their emotions.

With the advent of the First World War, male impersonators revived the traditional stories of women as soldiers or sailors, and presented the image of the perfect serving man. Indeed, Vesta Tilly was so successful, the army used her on recruitment posters and so many men enlisted, she was known as 'England's Greatest Recruiting Sergeant'.

Alongside male impersonators, the pantomime had grown in popularity, until in the twentieth century, it settled into being mainly a Christmas event, the most popular being *Cinderella*, *Aladdin*, *Dick Wittington* and *Puss in Boots*. In panto, the woman appears more androgynous than in male attire and the audience is left in no doubt the actor is a woman; in the same way, men take the roles of ugly dames. 'We employ girls for boy parts in pantomime,' said one manager in 1903, 'because the hero of a fairy tale is supposed to be a very beautiful man, and as the supply was not forthcoming, girls were taken on to supply the nearest approach to the ideal youthful hero.'[39]

The name, 'Principal Boy', conforms to the travesti tradition, reducing the women to a child-like state and therefore non-threatening. Similarly, Peter Pan is the boy who never grew up and therefore cannot take the role of the dominant male.

However, not everyone agreed with the tradition of Principal Boy:

> How refreshing it would be to see our dear old fairy tales presented at Christmas with the parts of the heroes enacted by members of the male sex. Slim Jack of Beanstalk fame, for instance, might be a real, slender, young man, not a corpulent or attenuated dame (often middle-aged) masquerading in male attire in which she looks supremely grotesque … An intelligent child must be confounded and sadly disappointed by seeing all the fairy princes and knights of his beloved story-books coming before him not as princes, not as knights, but only as "dressed up" women. Too well do I recollect one Christmastide a huge theatre poster, which depicted a stout lady, of very faulty anatomy, clinging to, and clambering up a frail-looking beanstalk.[40]

Throughout the nineteenth century, and despite the fact that many of the roles were comic or light-hearted, women on stage were usually represented as self-determining, independent and spirited, even if they did have to surrender it all at the end. For those women in the audience who longed for a similar escape, the cross-dressing roles must have been watched with interest, and perhaps longing. However, despite the popularity of cross-dressing roles, they did not add greatly to the fight for women's rights. None of the roles appear to challenge societal behaviour and no moves were made to reform dress because of breeches roles.

A similar situation exists today. 'Skirt roles' or men in female attire such as Les Dawson, Benny Hill, Danny La Rue, Dame Edna Everage, Matt Lucas and David Walliams' 'Ladies', and more recently, Mrs Brown, do not challenge the right for men to wear skirts and dresses. The humour in these portrayals is the same as the travesti – we are all in on the joke.

Chapter 13

Exposed to Ridicule and Insult

Throughout history, like many parts of their lives, women were restricted in the sports and leisure activities they could engage in. Running and jumping were seen as unfeminine and there was the concern that women could develop an unattractive 'masculine' physique:

> as regards the woman of today she has been of late much blamed for cultivating mannish habits. Cycling, lawn tennis, golf, and other forms of physical recreation have done wonders in cultivating the female physique … To say that of necessity a woman who cycles or golfs or fences is becoming unwomanly is a libel on the sex, which should be repudiated sternly and effectively.[1]

Most women who took part in sports and leisure activities did so in female attire and events were usually non-competitive. It was not until the mid-nineteenth century that organised competitive women's sports began, coinciding with the rise in the wearing of male attire and women's fight for freedom.

For those women who cross-dressed for leisure activities, only a few playing organised sports have been uncovered in this research. Tennis, as we understand the sport today, had developed from the early nineteenth century, although 'real tennis' had been played from the sixteenth. In 1760, Mademoiselle Bunel played regularly but would never wear male attire, preferring a short skirt and jacket.[2] No examples of women playing tennis in male clothing were discovered in this research; similarly, there are none playing golf or rugby. One woman, Caroline Winslow Hall of Boston, used sport as an excuse for cross-dressing. She was a watercolour painter of note in Milan but when dying of tuberculosis, she returned to New York. Accompanying her on the voyage home was Guisseppina Boriani, who was known on board as the wife. Guisseppina said they had been together for ten years and only three years earlier, Caroline had converted to male attire in order to enter rifle shooting contests.[3]

For centuries, the horse was the main means of transport and although women rode for both necessity and leisure, they did so mainly in female clothing – being astride a horse was seen as extremely unfeminine. There are Ancient Greek images of women riding astride, particularly Amazons, and Catherine the Great (1729–1796) had a portrait painted of herself riding astride in army uniform. However, it was not until the development of the side-saddle that riding became a common leisure activity for women. The saddle, which put both legs of the woman on one side of the horse, was considered a more modest means of riding and by some, as a misguided medical necessity to protect the hymen.

Early versions of the side-saddle were purportedly designed by women. Anne of Bohemia (1366–1394), wife of King Richard II, developed one which was not that practical as it gave no control of the horse, meaning it had to be led by someone else, usually a man. Catherine de' Medici (1519–1589) supposedly added a second pommel that allowed women to face forward and control their own horses; and a third pommel was added by a Frenchman in the 1830s that provided greater security – allowing the woman control, speed and even the ability to jump.

By the late nineteenth century, there was a growing concern that riding side-saddle was causing deformities in women's bodies, and more women were braving condemnation by riding astride. In 1897, Anna Held, a Polish actor and singer, was interviewed by a female reporter for the *Morning Leader* about her riding astride in man's attire. The reporter, who was very nervous about broaching the subject, asked if the rumours were true. Anna agreed they were, adding:

> Shocking – you think – shocking? Worse than the bicycle you think? But why? I say to my doctor, I sit on the saddle not straight, my body is twisted, and when I have a fall my boot is caught, with the elastics, you know, in my Amazon – my habit – and I cannot get free, but hurt myself. My doctor says, 'Sit like a man.' I did. I was astonished, it was so easy my body is no more twisted, and I am much more mistress of my horse.

When asked if she was going to ride in Rotten Row, Anna replied no because 'in England… I find you do not like it … for people to talk – for notoriety', but added that she rode astride in France and America because it was 'not good to ride twisted'.[4]

As more women took to riding and hunting, new clothing was required and the riding 'habit' was developed in the mid-seventeenth century. It consisted of breeches covered by an apron or half-skirt draped over the legs and attached to the foot to hold it in place. Once dismounted, the apron was joined together at the back and held in place on a button to look like a full skirt. For practical purposes, it became extremely popular among women, even when not riding and the famous image of the Ladies of Llangollen shows them wearing black riding habits. However, the attire was considered by some to be too masculine and a Birmingham paper in 1890 asked whether it could even be regarded as male attire, adding, 'if the police authorities regard this as a distinctly manly garb it will be awkward for the wearers.'[5]

The question of whether the riding habit could be regarded as 'male' had been asked since its invention. An 1862 Canadian writer was very specific about which was which: he had been seeking information about a 'mysterious female who delights to exhibit her fair proportions in male attire and rejoices in her ability to ride in public astraddle of a horse.' With her, was another 'mysterious female … feminine, who seemed to possess a little more modesty – not to mention decency – than her companion, and sported a lady's black riding habit.'[6]

Writing in 1666, diarist Samuel Pepys complained that such clothing was too like his own and that nobody could take them for women. A sight that did not please him, but then he was an infamous lecher.

Other men were, however, lecherous for women wearing male attire and it became a common feature in commentaries on women in sports and leisure. At a meeting in 1890, the increase in attendance was attributed to 'the report that several female leaders of fashion intended to appear at the meet mounted *en cavalier*.' However, 'people were disappointed, for no fair ladies donned male attire.'[7]

In countries with laws prohibiting women from wearing male attire, it could be confusing. In France, it was banned, unless the woman had a police permit; rules were relaxed in the late nineteenth century to allow for horse-riding or cycling but women could still be arrested for other activities. This law was not rescinded until 2003; it was last invoked in the 1930s when the French Women's Sports Federation banned Violette Morris, a gay (and possibly transmasculine) athlete, from entering the Olympic Games, because of her 'lifestyle' and insistence on wearing trousers.

Women's involvement in horse racing has always been challenging, and continues so today. An attempt was made to allow female jockeys in 1864 in Ireland but 'the Cork people are strongly opposed to the intention of permitting ladies to ride a public race, on account of the masculine and unwomanly nature of such a course.'[8] An unnamed woman in Melbourne, who 'looked like a man, being dressed in a suit of men's grey tweed', had been earning a living training and racing horses and was known as 'Jockey Jack.' When questioned as to why she adopted the male attire, she replied that she was fond of horses and was 'as good as any man'.[9]

As much as people were scandalised by women riding astride, the sports that horrified the public most were those that risked physical harm to 'delicate ladies'. Although women did take up many contact sports, most did so in female clothing. A rare example is the mother of the young Emperor of China who 'long ago' was dressed:

> in a sort of bloomer costume, she takes daily lessons in boxing from an old eunuch. Her appearance at the age of fifty in short skirts, hitting out her venerable preceptor, and occasionally receiving punishment herself, must be comical to the last degree, and the Hong Kong Times says the subject creates a most disrespectful merriment.[10]

Bullfighting occasionally featured women in male attire. In 1842, the *Morning Post* featured an article about six women 'unsexing themselves ... exposed to all kinds of danger, insult and ridicule' and that 'recklessness, coarse humour, and fierce passions are the principal characteristics of these Amazons: gentle and feminine feelings are stranger to their degenerate hearts.'

As with many writers, the *Morning Post* journalist discussed their appearance, being 'agreeably surprised to see two good-looking female countenances' but adding, 'I have always deemed it a melancholy thing to see a woman in breeches and gaiters, for it is a shame enough to shame her, were she not shameless.' Reluctantly, he added, 'to do these females justice, they managed and bestrode their horses well ... and a young woman, yes, *handsome* and young; good God! it was a terrible sight to see her, with her sword in her right hand and red flag in the other, approach the raging brute.'[11]

Forty-two years later, a bullfight of a 'novel kind' took place at Tarragona, with women clothed in the male 'torera' suit. Three took part but lasted only a short time and so disenchanted was the audience that the stewards had to promise to return the entrance fee; when this didn't happen, a riot broke out.[12]

Marie-Rose Astié de Valsayre was dedicated to overturning the ban on women wearing trousers in France. She continually and defiantly dressed in male attire, and had a love for duelling. In 1886, she caused a media sensation when she challenged an American woman to a duel over whether American or French female doctors were superior. Marie-Rose won easily and until her death in 1939, she continued to fight duels and for women's rights, including equal pay.

Other women also duelled or enjoyed fencing but few did so in male attire, although novelist Madam de Villecheu mentions a sword-fight in *The Memoires of the Life, and Rare Adventures of Henrietta Silvia Moliere*. The protagonist, Henrietta (apparently based on actress Armande Béjart), duels with another woman, both of them in male attire.

Of all the sports and leisure activities undertaken by women, there are three that dominate when it comes to the wearing of male attire: cricket, football and cycling.

The first recorded women's cricket match was held in 1745 at Hambledon and the 1884 publication of *The English Game of Cricket* by Charles Box included women's matches in a chapter entitled 'Curiosities of cricket'. It mentions a match in 1797 between eleven married women of Bury. An early match detailing male attire was held in 1823 in Norfolk when eleven married and eleven single women played for eleven pairs of gloves, which the married women won. 'It is remarkable,' wrote the *Flintshire Observer*, 'for the fact that on this occasion the players wore jackets and trousers.'[13]

In 1874, a match took place in Australia at the Sandhurst Easter Fete which, the *Mount Alexander Mail* pointed out

> certainly required a very considerable amount of courage on the part of the ladies to undertake to play a cricket match in public. The thing was unprecedented as far as Australia was concerned. They had originally intended to play in 'bloomer costume', as being less likely to interfere with the freedom of movement than any other; but the innovation was considered too startling for a British community, and the idea was given up in favour of an attire of the ordinary shaped dress.[14]

With so many women wearing bloomers and rational dress, by the late nineteenth century, sports commentaries became less concerned with appearance and would only mention in passing what women were wearing, as at a Lewes cricket match in 1884 when 'most of the fair players' were wearing bloomer costumes.[15]

The history of kicking a ball for sport is a long and varied one. Different types of play, rules, and teams have existed from the earliest of times, but the game which today is recognised as football (or soccer) had its roots in 1863 when the Football Association was formed. The first official recognition of a women's game was in 1881 in Scotland and the first team of note was formed in London in 1895. However, the desire to play competitively was considered an unwelcome reversal of gender roles. Writers, mainly men, believed their masculinity would be eroded and women players were labelled as masculine and ugly in an attempt to belittle them. Accounts of the games were obsessed with what women players wore – something that is still conspicuous in the coverage of women's sports today – yet few of the articles questioned why male identity was so fragile.

Early reports, such as the first commentary of a woman's football match in a Welsh paper, had a mocking tone, laced with lasciviousness:

> I was pleased to notice that nearly all my male fellow-passengers were going "merely out of curiosity, you know," and that they, without a dissentient voice, strongly deprecated such an exhibition. Still they were going, sir. Much profitable and ingenious speculation was indulged in as to what sort of apparel the ladies would wear.[16]

The first public match by the British Ladies' Football Club took place on Saturday, 23 March 1895 at Crouch End, London and was covered by most of the press. The controversial game attracted nearly 10,000 spectators and almost all the coverage debated the costume of 'knickerbockers, after the style of the divided skirt.'[17] This was a type of dress heavily promoted by the founder of the British Ladies' Football Club, Nettie Honeyball, and its patron, Lady Florence Dixie. Most reviews of the match were scathing and similar to this report in the *Western Mail*:

> No one upholds athletics for girls more than we do. Did we not wage a battle of words with that terrible Mrs Longshore Potts when she came here preaching the twaddle that our bonnie English (and Welsh) girls were not to ride or jump, or skip or skate, or play tennis (and cricket at home in strict privacy)? But the line must be drawn somewhere, and, thank goodness, we were not asked or required to go and see our fellow-women making fools of themselves – slipping, sloshing, and sprawling about in a muddy field. A woman can hunt or fish or shoot, and even

cycle in decent and feminine clothes. How she can hope to play football in any clothes approaching the decency of her sex demand we cannot imagine. Anyhow, it is with delight we have read all the various society papers' comments on the game, and a ludicrous fiasco it appears to have been.[18]

Of all the sport and leisure activities, perhaps cycling was the most contentious when it came to wearing male attire. Tied up as it was in wider issues of women's freedoms, one journalist asked: 'the question is beginning to be discussed whether anything so revolutionary in effect upon the human race has been introduced since the steam-engine.'[19]

This new-found freedom, however, was dogged by controversy over what the women were wearing when they rode their bicycles. While it was generally accepted that riding in a skirt could be troublesome, the onus was on the woman to ride in a sedate and ladylike fashion to avoid any problems. However, a skirt could be blown up in a wind so some advocated a narrower design – but this was itself opposed by those who felt it would bring too much attention to the female form.

When they did brave the outside world, women were often followed by jeering crowds. In 1893, 'quite a sensation' was created on the streets of New Jersey when two young women in male attire rode through the streets. Retha M'Gill, a 'gay and shapely young widow' and her 'bosom friend', Mrs Annie Pancoast, were chased by a crowd of urchins, hooting and jeering until they were forced to seek refuge.[20] However, there could be advantages in wearing male attire. A year later, Nellie Bacon was on a cycling tour around the UK when, in North Wales, she was taken for a young man and she was treated better than a couple who had been riding a tricycle a few days previously. They had met with 'the rudest behaviour' and had been followed by fascinated crowds, despite the fact that the woman was wearing a skirt, which led Nellie to believe that there could be greater safety in wearing trousers. Nellie went on to say that she had visited cathedrals in her knickerbockers without attracting attention or creating any remark.[21]

As the new century dawned, women were still not safe when cycling. In 1900 in Perth, Scotland, a woman was riding a man's bicycle in knickerbockers, followed by a swarm of youths hooting and jeering as the police gazed in 'lofty disdain.' Eventually, the young woman took refuge in a restaurant, the traffic was blocked, a large crowd gathered and many climbed on the shoulders of others to gaze in through the windows. The proprietor, 'not relishing this advertisement', smuggled the female knickerbocker cyclist out by a back entrance.[22]

As with other sports, the language used to describe female cyclists could be vitriolic – and not just from men. Some women writing to the *Daily Telegraph* described cyclists as 'a scandal to their sex' who had 'further unsexed themselves by doing so in men's attire.'[23] A woman 'riding furious in bloomers' in Bankyfelin, Wales, crashed into the back of a cow and the concerned herdsman asked, 'Ydych chwi wedi cael dolur, Sir?'(Are you sore, sir?). She was described in the piece as a 'hermaphrodite cyclist.'[24]

Lady Jenne wrote, 'the movement of the legs in bicycling is not graceful, and the figure should certainly be draped to render this movement as little apparent as possible. Women clothed like men, and "unashamed," with their figure well bent over their machines perspiring at every pore, their hair flowing in the breeze (for your new woman bicyclist does nothing by halves), present as ugly and as ridiculous a picture as one can imagine.'[25]

The social class of these women was also a matter of debate. 'The lower orders,' argued a writer in the *Sheffield Independent*, 'have not yet shown any emphatic desire to transform themselves by adopting men's attire.[26] However, another writer, in the *Nottinghamshire Guardian*, argued 'the majority of refined gentlewomen revolt against the idea of appearing in public in a travesty of man's attire.' In reality, all classes of women were taking to the bicycle in male clothing.

In some countries, moves were made to try and ban the offending dress. In 1893 in France, the police had written to certain lady cyclists cautioning them that they were infringing the law.[27] In Chicago in 1895, Alderman Coughlin proposed a law to prohibit the wearing of bloomers or knickerbockers by women cyclists. The terms set out were:

> Whereas, a great number of young girls and ladies in this city are appearing in the streets and public places dressed in male attire, which is disguised by the friends of this raging craze by the name of bloomers and knickerbockers, and whereas this craze has assumed such proportions that it menaces the public morals of this good city, and whereas it is unhealthy, un-American, and unladylike to appear in such costumes.

The penalty suggested was a fine of between $3 and $8 but Alderman Coughlin and his ordinance were laughed out of Court.[28] In Toronto, Trustee

Bell of the Public-School Board asked if members knew that female teachers were in the habit of riding bicycles in male attire. The question was received with loud laughter and board member Dr Stowe Gullen, a leading suffragist and the first woman to graduate from a Canadian medical school, demanded to know what business it was of any trustee what dress a teacher wore? However, Bell was not to be intimidated and moved that 'the inspectors be instructed to report at the next meeting of the Teachers' Sub-Committee the names of all female teachers who have been riding bicycles in male attire, commonly called bloomers.'[29] The same year, another educational facility petitioned the French government to prevent women appearing upon the streets in male attire. The bizarre reason given was that the female knickerbockers were so unattractive that young men are 'much more arduous in pursuit of their studies since the girls took to bikes and bifurcated garments.'[30]

There was also the question of whether knickerbockers were indeed 'male attire' at all. Men certainly did not wear them and when complaints were made in France against women frequenting the Luxembourg Garden, the police refused to arrest them, arguing, 'the cycling costume is not man's attire in the strict sense of the word.' For some, the first difficulty was that it was 'not always possible to distinguish a woman from a man in cycling costume.'[31]

When ten riders were arrested in New York for riding without lights, the court added a charge of masquerading in male attire. However, one woman argued that her 'rig was a lady's costume for a gentleman's wheel.' Unlike the 'safety bicycle' that had been developed in the 1880s and 1890s, which had a v-shaped bar that allowed a woman to wear a skirt, a 'gentleman's machine' had a horizontal bar that meant the skirt had to be lifted up so it was easier, and more decorous, to ride in trousers. The woman won her argument and the group was discharged.[32]

Even if women were not arrested for being in male attire, they could still be refused service. In 1894 on Derby Day at Epsom, two young ladies 'arrayed in tunics and knickerbockers' arrived at an inn and asked whether dinner was yet served. The landlady frostily replied that the meal was certainly served but that she could not permit the two women to enter her dining-room, as the costume they wore would 'scandalise the ladies and gentlemen assembled there.' Despite their appeals, the landlady 'inexorably refused to countenance their appearance.' She did offer to lend them two of her own skirts, 'beneath which they might conceal the offending bifurcated garments,' but they indignantly declined and left.[33]

One of the arguments against women wearing male attire when cycling was that it would set a precedent for other pastimes. In 1895, when a young lady in knickerbockers strolled down to a frozen lake and leisurely put on a pair of ice skates, an *Evening Express* journalist mused that the 'rational dress,' had become so familiar in the streets that even when she strolled down Fleet Street in the afternoon with a cigarette between her dainty lips, she hardly excited attention. Having donned her skates, the girl was cutting figures of eights and executing Dutch rolls, as the journalist watched on. She was, he said,

> young and distinctly good-looking: lithe, but not slender. Her costume was of check tweed. The blouse bodice was belted with the same material, the skirts reaching to the swell of the rather full – one might say baggy – inexpressibles. The right and left sections of this garment terminated just below the knees, and the draping folds were held up by elastic garters. Heavy knit stockings enclosed calves that must have been developed by many hours of pedalling over the roads of town and country. She wore a glistening pair of club skates.'

However, she soon became a target for roughs: 'a mob of them – half-grown men and boys – surrounded her, and followed her everywhere, howling and yelling' calling her 'Tommy,' 'Pants,' and other names:

> She put on speed to distance her tormentors, but the lake is not so very large, and she could not shake them off. Red spots showed in her cheeks, which were pale with anger, and her eyes glittered with a wicked light. A boy who darted up and laid an impudent hand upon the slack of one leg of her knickerbockers, received a ringing box over the ears that must have made his head sing for an hour. After braving the persecution for fifteen minutes she skated up to a policeman, and said, 'I would thank you if you would see me safely off the ice. This is outrageous. You should arrest every one of these brutes and young devils.' 'I'll lock the first one up that lays a finger on you,' said the man in blue gallantly, and then he walked over the ice with her to the shore, where she quickly took off her skates, and strode rapidly out of the park gate and trembling with anger and vexation of spirit.[34]

It was not just those taking part in sports who came in for criticism. In 1895, a journalist, noting the defeat of the champion rugby team in Australia, wrote it was 'made worse' by a number of 'creatures' in male attire in the stands.[35]

As the new century dawned and more women were advancing into new areas of sport and leisure, one male journalist lamented, 'between smoking, golfing, playing football and cricket, and other masculine games, wearing men's collars, shirts and ties, fencing, fighting, etc. there is nothing left to a "mere man" except his vote, and the poor, clinging dears are trying to grab that just now.'[36]

Women did get equality in the vote but equality in sport is still a long way off.

Chapter 14

A Skirt for Each Leg

Wearing trousers as fashion is not the same as cross-dressing or cross-living as it includes no attempt to pass as a man and individuals remain identifiably female. Prior to the 1950s, women who wore bifurcated garments did so to challenge society's values and to avail themselves of clothes which made it easier to play sports, ride bikes and horses, or to take a wider range of employment. In this respect, the fight to wear trousers began in earnest in the 1850s.

Objections to masculine dress as fashion had existed earlier, particularly in those countries where it was not against the law. In 1847, Louise Lehmann, widow of a captain of the Prussian Lancers, dressed in male attire and visited public places on horseback. After visiting a café at the university, one scandalized professor asked the proprietor not to admit Louise again. A letter was sent claiming she would 'frighten away these grave frequenters of his establishment.' An enraged Louise dressed as a man, entered the café and beat the proprietor with her whip. She was arrested, fined 800 thalers and sentenced to three months' imprisonment; she was also banned from ever appearing in the costume of a man. However, having checked the law, Louisa proved there were no legal restrictions against 'assuming the masculine habiliments' and on her release, continued to do so.[1]

In France, there were various challenges to the law against women wearing male clothing. In 1799, at the end of the Revolution, press restrictions began to be lifted in France. This led to an increase in newspapers and periodicals, but also groups like the Vésuviennes, who were among the most radical of the new feminist groups. They believed in military service for women; equality in household duties; equality in dress; and demonstrated openly on the streets in support of their beliefs. They wore culottes and were so often lampooned that woman wearing culottes became a typical image of a feminist.

In 1849, the *Water-Cure Journal*, a popular health periodical in America, began urging female readers to adopt a garment that allowed more freedom of movement amidst concerns that women's clothes were damaging to their health. Fashion (not everyday wear for working women) was dominated at that time by a strict format designed to promote a silhouette shape. The basic design was a long skirt with layers of stiff, unyielding petticoats and whalebone corsets so tight they could cause physical deformity. The sheer inconvenience of female attire was summed up by Madame Astié de Valsayre (she who fought the duel over American and French doctors) in a letter to the police notifying them of her intention to defy the law:

> during the time of the deep snow, having, thanks to my skirts which got wet up to my waist, returned with a cold, and considering that the female costume is only suitable for women who have nothing to do, I hereby give you notice that henceforth I shall wear men's clothes as often as my occupation necessitates my doing so.[2]

Various doctors began to advise looser clothing for women on health grounds and various forms were experimented with, often copying the loose pantaloon-type worn by Middle Eastern and Central Asian women.

In 1851, the first of the famous 'fashion' trousers emerged when Elizabeth Smith Miller designed a garment to allow her freedom of movement when walking in the country. Amelia Bloomer, an American activist for women's rights, started to wear them and her name became forever attached to it. The bloomer came in for extensive ridicule. There were even riots in London and Amelia wrote to a London paper asking:

> why the British public is so horrified at the idea of women dressed in trowsers [sic], seeing that they have for many years tolerated a number of men (from the north of the Tweed) in wearing petticoats – and shocking short petticoats too?[3]

She was referring to the kilt.

Not all could afford bloomers but others were confused about what they were, thinking them the same as breeches or trousers, so believed bloomer wearers were simply assuming men's clothing. In 1851, Sophia Edwards was arrested in Marylebone, London because by 'deliberate assumption of the male costume' she had collected 'such a crowd that all kind of business, as well as cabs and buses, were brought to a stand-still' and she could therefore be charged as 'a nuisance.' In court, Sophia demanded of the police officer, 'Who do you call a nuisance, you muffin-faced blue bottle?' She admitted she had heard so much about the new style of dress, she was determined to try it and taking her husband's clothes, she had walked for a considerable time in the road and never felt so comfortable in the whole of her life. 'Ah, gentlemen, gentlemen,' she said, looking around, 'how cosey you must feel in those dear delicious "tights"!' to roars of laughter from the court. The magistrate advised her to go home and wear her breeches there, to which a voice from the back shouted, 'She has done that since the first day of our marriage!' Having been dismissed, Sophia refused to get in a cab and said that for the short time she could wear the trousers, she would enjoy them. She took off running followed by 'some half-dozen constables and as many hundreds of civilians.'[4]

Many were confused over whether the fashionable dress could now be called male attire at all. Men certainly did not wear them and some women only wore upper garments such as vests, jackets and coats without trousers or bloomers, while others went for the whole suit. When Mary Ann Smith appeared in court, the magistrate exclaimed, 'Why, the charge is against a woman, but that's a man in the dock.' (Laughter).' Was she, he asked, a 'bloomer' or 'a nymph' (prostitute)? Mary explained that her young man had just returned from sea and insisted on rigging her out in his clothes 'as it was all the fashion in America.'[5]

Some activists for dress reform became well-known, including Caroline Dexter who announced at her London lecture on Bloomerism that she would appear in 'the modern female costume.' An immense crowd turned up, dominated by men, that rushed the hall – many not paying the admittance fee. Mrs Dexter wore a skirt down to the knees and very wide trousers below that tied at the ankle.[6]

One significant article that was widely reprinted was F. L. Townsend's 'Women in Male Attire', published in 1850. Townsend quotes a Miss M. Weber, from Belgium, who claimed that in the earlier ages, men and women dressed precisely or very nearly alike and that the new distinction in dress 'was arbitrarily drawn by the male sex, in the tyrannical exercise of power which they derived solely from their greater physical superiority.'

Townsend agreed with Weber adding, 'There are many women, however, who are not satisfied with the boundless variety of feminine garments in their wardrobes; they delight in setting the rules of society at defiance by going about in the garments of the other sex … our natural repugnance to such sights has gradually worn away.'

Townsend pointed out that the law prohibiting people from wearing the clothes of the other gender was designed to discriminate against women as 'man is a species of monster in petticoats; he knows it, and therefore does not covet them.' She further asked if it is 'morally right for men to wear pantaloons' and was it 'immodest for a lady to look at them.' She ended by noting that it would not be long before 'the sanction, of female pantaloonery' would be accepted.[7] In fact, it was to take almost a century.

It is difficult to imagine the excitement women would have felt in this revolutionary costume and some put themselves in danger in their determination to learn more. Mary Benson's 'peculiar appearance' in a London court excited curiosity and attention when she appeared in the full bloomer costume: 'Her masculine attire being only partially shrouded by a loose muslin robe, which enveloped the upper part of her person.' She had been arrested for loitering outside a venue, surrounded by a crowd of people, waiting for Caroline Dexter to deliver a lecture. Mary had travelled from Gloucester 'to tender her assistance to that lady in her praiseworthy efforts to revolutionize the inconvenient and unbecoming attire at present worn by the women of this country.' The police officer moved her on but, on his return, found her there again and the crowd had increased to several hundred people. She was

> declaiming, at the highest pitch of her voice, upon her favourite topic, and expatiating upon the picturesque beauty of the new costume, in illustration of which she occasionally raised the lower part of her mantle, and displayed to the admiring eyes of her auditors the graceful sweep of her nether integuments.

As the street was rendered completely impassable and Mary refused to move, she was taken into custody. In answer to the charge, she appeared greatly embarrassed at her position and assured the magistrate that she was painfully aware of her indiscretion and hoped he would be lenient. The magistrate expressed the hope that she had been duly warned and discharged her. 'The fair Bloomer, after carefully adjusting her robe over her masculine gear, made a silent and graceful obeisance to the magistrate, and hurried out of court.'[8]

Some women would not be moved. At Devonport market, a 'Cornish matron' in bloomers was surrounded by a crowd and a constable requested her to leave. The woman refused, claiming a right to wear what clothes she pleased, provided she did not outrage decency, and demanded the protection of the constable who then had to remain until she had sold all of her butter and eggs.[9]

Over the next decade, women persisted in the wearing of bloomers, one American stating 'God helping me, I shall persevere unto the end. I encounter much unpleasantness upon the street in the way of Young America. But I am bound to outlive the storm that greets me. I have unbounded confidence in the power of conscience, will, and character, in overcoming such difficulties. Our cause is founded in all-subduing right, and must succeed, sooner or later.'[10]

Some women took advantage of the craze to dress openly in male clothes. In a piece entitled 'A Female Gentleman', Sallie M. Monroe, of New York, a 'practising physician of the hydropathic school', had 'permanently adopted the masculine attire – not merely bloomer's, but the veritable dress of a gentleman, from hat to boots … she wears the masculine in preference to the feminine dress, because she conceives the former to be better adapted to the active duties of her profession.'[11]

Lectures and conventions on the bloomer, which was often connected to women's rights, and on general dress reform were held everywhere. Dr Major Mary Walker fought tirelessly to promote women's right to wear male trousers (she had refused to use the word 'obey' when she got married). She was an inspiration to other women, having been arrested thirteen times for wearing men's clothes. One fan, Ida Price, was arrested in New York and in her cell was 'howling at the despotism of man,' the journalist noting, 'we earnestly hope that the injured lady will continue to howl until man, unable to sleep, ceases to interfere with her desire to adopt the uncomfortable and ungraceful attire.'[12] Agnes Matthews in Ohio was also arrested for following Dr Walker but was released without charge. The journalist worried if men, when undressing at night, might 'ever see their unmentionables again.'[13]

By the 1870s, the bloomer was falling out of favour (but many 'trouser' types were referred to as bloomers for several more decades). However, the calls for dress reform continued. The first US national convention of the Dress Reform League was held at Painesville, Ohio in 1874. 'I tell you,' cried Mary E. Tillottson, 'this reform means trousers. They are freedom to us, and they will afford us protection. Trousers are coming.' One of the resolutions was that:

> to her unphysiological, unnatural, and suicidal modes of dress woman owes her physical inferiority to man, and that until she so clothes her body as to be able to compete with her brother in the world of work she can never arise to a full quality with the sterner sex.

Female attire was referred to as a 'licentious and murderous invention'[14] and a hint of hypocrisy crept in:

> an actress, let us say of unimpeachable fame, will play her part without flinching in male attire in burlesque or opera and exhibit her well-turned limbs in silk tights and hose *a la* Henry VIII, to the admiration and criticism of even the Whitechapel "gods" in the gallery, yet, if asked to join a supper party, non-professional, an hour later, wearing the same costume instead of her ordinary mufti, would feel herself grossly insulted.[15]

Many people, of both sexes, fought against the idea of dress reform: in 1876, an editorial in the *Western Mail* argued that 'this agitation is a direct invasion of the rights of man. Trousers have always been a man's prerogative and their usurpation by women is not to be endured.' The writer also hinted that those who wore them were not interested in men:

> how can a woman hope to subdue a male heart when she has no better figure to present to him than a huge misshapen mass of broadcloth or tweed? Perhaps, however, these reformers do not want the man, and eschew matrimony. We are led to this reflection by the statement that three of the ladies who have already appeared in public in male costume are spinsters of uncertain age.[16]

By the 1880s, a new development in dress reform was the divided skirt. Lady Harberton, president of the Rational Dress Society, was keen to stress that there were no similarities between the divided skirt and bloomers. A bloomer was a form of loose trousers with a skirt over them; 'ours,' she said,

> is a skirt with trimmings as usual, only we have a skirt for each leg, and over this some drapery coming to below the knees, and arranged according to individual taste. Many ladies having worn it now publicly for some months without exciting attention, will, I hope, further prove there is an error in asserting it to be a revival of the Bloomer "costume."[17]

For some this was not enough. 'Why this feeble compromise?' one writer complained, 'Let us have trousers, or else continue to worship the petticoat of our unemancipated days?'[18] Another wrote,

> the resisting weight of petticoats just doubles the exertion required for walking, and fully trebles it for running or tennis … the only alternative

is that women should take to "trousers," at all events for morning dress – but trousers … which in no respect resemble a man's attire; and being, therefore, a distinctly different dress, we are warranted in calling it by a different name.'[19]

Semantics were important, as Annie Jenness-Miller pointed out:

> it must be remembered that these hygienic substitutes for petticoats are not called trousers … when it comes to matters of dress there is ever so much in a name … The future will be able to demonstrate whether a woman is any more strong-minded for the knowledge that she wears things like trousers, though not called trousers.[20]

Whatever the garments were called, more and more women were taking to them and magistrates were dismissing arrests. In Kansas City, one judge ruled there was no law in the US to prevent women from dressing in male attire, adding, 'It is the latest fad for ladies to dress in the garments of the opposite sex, and women are rapidly coming to it. It is the correct thing, not only for health but for comfort. I will discharge every woman brought before me under such conditions as the defendant in this case.' Accordingly, he discharged a woman who had been brought before him saying, 'You can go, Mary. I think you look as neat as if you had on a dress.'[21]

France, meanwhile, remained relentless in its decision to deny women the right to wear trousers (in Paris, the law was not revoked until 2013). In an often-repeated article, it was stated that by 1890, only ten women in Paris and the provinces had been authorised to wear full masculine costume. Among them were: George Sand; Rosa Bonheur; Mme Dieulafoy, the archaeologist; Mme Fousault, the bearded woman; two feminine stone-cutters; Mme Fourreau; La Jeauuette;[22] a female house painter and decorator; and a mannish-looking directress of a printing office. 'Several others had obtained certificates to show that they ought to discard the attire of their own sex for that of the stronger and sterner one. On the other hand, a humble potato merchant in the suburbs has been allowed to wear female garments for reasoning which satisfied the Prefecture of Police.'[23] For the privilege of wearing trousers, the French government charged the women a tax of £2 to £2 10 shillings a year, the equivalent of about £260 in today's money.

A number of pen portraits of the 'masculine' woman that mocked both her and the clothes she wore appeared regularly, one stating:

all the time she is essentially a woman and spiders, cockroaches, mice, and earwigs could make her scream with terror if they came within hail. Her masculinity is just a bit of pretty pretence for the betted breaking of hearts ... and she remains the coquette throughout, as the doll, whether dressed as a sailor, a queen, a baby ... never anything but a doll.[24]

However, as Lady Florence Dixie pointed out, a lot of women were a lot more serious,

> It will surprise some people to know that there are not a few voters in the United Kingdom who are women in men's clothes, who have been forced to adopt that attire in order to attain work, and who, passing as men, exercise those rights which are denied them as woman. I myself know several of these people, and am willing to confess that I have advised them and helped them to play their role.

The *Newcastle Weekly Courant* journalist sniffed, 'there is no touch of repentance in that awful confession; for her ladyship avows her determination always to give similar counsel and aid! who can say how far this insidious invasion of man's domain may go.' 'Women, as women, can write and lecture,' continued Florence,

> but this will avail nothing unless they enter the haunts of men, partake of their chances, go into Parliament, and prove themselves capable of ruling ... Let them disguise themselves. At the near meeting of Parliament, members are likely to eye each other with suspicion, and it may go hard with beardless legislators. In society marriageable daughters will have to be careful in discriminating between false beards and real beards; and the year on which we are entering will be thick with doubt and uncertainty.[25]

Lady Harberton even suggested that suffragists should walk into the House of Commons in male attire and thus 'gain admittance by stratagem.'[26]

Some were going even further, defying social mores and getting married wearing breeches. A much-repeated article concerned Kate Walker, a member of the New Zealand Dress Reform Association, who in 1897 was wed in a garment 'divided into two parts ... the upper part of the dress consisting of the conventional bride's veil and the lower sinking into a modified pair of breeches ... a lovely veil was worn – not, however, over the face, but thrown back, and falling in long graceful folds over the shoulder.' The bridesmaid, Nellie Walker, and other female friends wore suits of the same design, 'neatly-fitting knickers, long coat, with revers, and a long vest, the coat being edged with cord to match the material. Most of the gentlemen were in knicker costume.'[27]

More than anything, however, it was the bicycle that led to the growth of such clothing (although not all women agreed and many refused to wear 'rationals'), but both were condemned.

The *Western Mail* ran an essay competition entitled 'Shall bloomers be worn or not' – their opening line being, 'the question of wearing "bloomers" is getting beyond a joke' and amid the well-worn arguments mainly around the un-feminine appearance, one man was in favour. He believed:

> we shall hear of less assaults on women, and our newspapers will not be filled with loathsome details as at present … Why? Because with "Bloomers" they would be decent. If the lady footballers had worn ordinary dress on the football field what an outcry would have been raised; while, by wearing rationals (as a spectator was heard to say while leaving the field) it was actually decent … Men have the right to this freedom, and why, should women, who is the weaker vessel, be trammelled, by society roles, with heavy, clinging garments, which must not be raised over a certain height, from the ground for decency's sake. Instead of lifting her voice against it "Mother Grundy" should hail with delight the advent of the rational or bloomer costume.[28]

Not all agreed, particularly when it came to business. In 1899, a case came to court to decide if venue owners had the right to turn away women because of their attire. Martha Sprague of the Hautboy Hotel, Ockham, was charged with refusing to supply lunch to Lady Harberton because she was wearing 'rationals'. When turned away, Lady Harberton insisted on her rights and so Martha showed her into a room at the back of the bar where several men were smoking and drinking – much to her horror – so she sued. The landlady's defence was that were she to admit women 'who go in for advanced notions in the matter of dress', her hotel would lose its good name and its respectable custom. The jury decided the room was fitting and dismissed the case.[29]

As the century turned, more women were wearing divided skirts but hostility was still rife. In Connecticut in 1900, Mrs Redman was horsewhipped in the open street by her husband because she disobeyed his orders by wearing the 'bloomer' costume in public. Anna Dickerson, also in 'bloomers', attempted to assist her and was severely lashed by the infuriated man. Mr Redman was fined but the judge overturned the punishment, saying that while legally guilty, Mr Redman deserved the thanks of society for his courage in resisting this immodest practice that was becoming all too common among women of the State. The judge went on to suggest that he would have been glad to fine Mrs Redman had she been brought before him charged with wearing man's attire.[30]

In 1910, Dr Mary Walker introduced a Bill into the Albany Legislature stating that women would not be deemed 'in disguise' because of their dress and that any 'policeman who arrested a woman not guilty of a crime, but because she was wearing a certain style of clothing, should be guilty of a misdemeanour.'[31] Meanwhile, the *Law Journal* was reminding the British that 'there is said to have existed at common law the offence of 'travesty' – the wearing by one sex of the garb of the other; but we can find no authority or statute that the wearing of the attire of the opposite sex can of itself now be treated as a criminal offence.'[32]

That same year saw a new development – the harem, or hobble, skirt – designed by Frenchman Paul Poiret; like previous designs, it was based on Oriental loose trousers. Like the bloomer, they were unmercifully ridiculed and many postcards lampooned suffragists wearing the garment with the inevitable addition of horrified onlookers. Harem skirt luncheons, dinners, and dances became popular but many women were still afraid to wear them in public as they were likely to be mobbed.[33]

The real change came during the Second World War when many women began wearing men's clothes, partly because of rationing. It was more convenient to wear the stuff left hanging in the wardrobe by men serving in the forces, than using up precious coupons on female work clothes. Also, women were undertaking more manual work, such as Dorothy Curtis from Cardiff who took employment in a munitions factory in Birmingham. She had a photograph of herself taken and sent home, signing herself 'trousers.'

Attitudes did not change quickly. In 1916, the *Herald of Wales* article 'The Unfrocked Girl' included the sentiment that 'Women war-workers … have fallen in love with their dungarees, and, in one place at least, have flatly refused to return to their conventional costume.' It seems that Margam farm workers had worn their dungarees out one evening when they travelled to Aberdare – and Aberdare was shocked. 'It held up its hands in pious horror,' wrote the *Herald:*

Women in trousers, indeed to goodness, tut-tut! Whateffer next? Especially staggered were the ladies of the County Women's Field Labour Committee. 'Go home!' they cried, 'go home, you shameless hussies!' or words to that effect.

The 'unfrocked girls' (we would call them women today) pointed out that they could do what they wanted in their spare time and would strike if not left alone. So, the Women's Committee appealed to the County Agricultural Committee to instruct them to wear dresses, particularly as this sort of behaviour seemed to be increasing. The Committee's reply was that the complaint was preposterous and inquiries showed that nobody had been aggrieved or shocked. The *Daily Mirror* picked up the story and asked of its readers, 'Should women wear trousers in war time?' Miss Farquharson, the organiser of the Women's Land Army told the *Mirror* that it struck her as:

> unreasonable when a woman works a ten-hour day and has only an hour or so of leisure, that more than half of it should be spent in changing her gown. 'Take for instance,' she said, 'our farms at Evesham where 300 girls work, or our camp of girls on Colonel Raike's estate in Warwick. Here they cook by camp fires, clear the woods, and generally do both men and women's work. It would be hard to make them waste their precious leisure time.'

The Women's Land Army uniform, the *Herald* told its readers, consisting of 'brown knickers, gaiters and smock to the knee denotes work for one's country. True, in peace time officers get into mufti; but then this isn't peace.' They reluctantly reminded their readers that times were changing, 'Our new bus conductors have long ago discarded petticoats in favour of the more masculine garments, partly draped by an abbreviated skirt.' But they also drew attention to certain hypocrisies, 'if the war girl may not go abroad in her tempestuous dungarees,' they wrote, 'why should her civilian sister be allowed to lounge on the sands and take afternoon tea in a deck chair, clad in a scanty bathing costume?'[34]

In the period after the Second World War, there was a vast rise in women wearing masculine or boyish clothes, smoking cigars and affecting accessories such as monocles. There are no singular reasons for this. Some women were deliberately flouting the rules of fashion or social etiquette; or were lesbians or transgender; some enjoyed the comfort; and still others were just copying the rest. In a 1927 *Punch* cartoon, an elderly aunt confronts her trousered, short-haired niece, 'Why, you would think you were a boy,' to which the niece replies, 'Oh, come, dear old thing, that's absurd. Who ever saw a boy wear earrings?'

Now boys wear earrings and girls wear trousers and some ask: if we all wear the same, what cultural codes can we rely on to identify each other? That's rather the point – we can't – and we never could.

Chapter 15

Loving Women

Historic stories of same-sex love between women have been published in many forms. Countless women we today recognise as lesbians, including the Ladies of Llangollen, Amy Dillwyn and Anne Lister, did wear 'mannish' clothes on the top half of the body, but not trousers. Others did cross-dress and cross-live and a number of these are well-known but as with other chapters in this book, the accounts here focus predominantly on those that have not been previously published.

For those who did cross-live for extended periods of time, it was necessary to use a number of devices to maintain the disguise. One was an association with other women in a 'romantic' manner. But the contemporary definition of romantic was something novel, or like a fiction rather than love – at least, that was how writers generally wished to portray same-sex relationships.

There are thousands of matchstick-type stories which flare up and are never heard of again, usually containing a reference to the individual 'gallanting a lass' or similar phrase. A London girl charged with masquerading in 1918 explained that she wore men's clothes because she could earn more and needed to keep her parents. 'She had been walking out with a young lady,' the journalist casually added.[1] These stories may raise questions but without further evidence, we cannot know if the association was a device or a relationship. We cannot assume homosexuality just because an individual cross-lived, nor can we assume a sexual orientation for those we may today regard as trans. However, with stories that involve multiple or extended relationships, engagements and marriages, there is an indication of something more than a simple device to maintain a disguise.

When discovered, the majority of women did not comment on their reasons for their relationships and for those that did, we have to consider that even though many excuses sound contrived, some may indeed be true. Therefore, deciding which stories concern love, and which do not, can be difficult.

One of the general difficulties with stories featuring relationships is that writers tended to be very subtle about it; after all, they did not want to encourage readers to 'try this at home'. Even at Oscar Wilde's trial, it was difficult to ascertain exactly what the charges were, leaving many readers unsure of what he had actually done. Many of the cases we would today refer to as lesbian were treated in a similar way, as the standards of decorum of the time left much to the reader's imagination. In 1843 a male servant in Ballaghaderreen was known as a 'great lady killer.' 'In fact,' reported the newspaper, 'this person could not stand at the house door but the girls would flock about him; and so jealous were they of each other, that one of them was fined by the magistrates of this district some time since for *scandal*, arising out of this strange partiality.' It turned out the servant had been born Catherine Reilly, who had been married for five years but left the husband due to domestic violence. Taking a job as a servant, a maid fell in love with the 'assumed man' and they were married four months before the discovery. 'We shall leave this part to the imagination of our readers,' wrote the reporter.[2]

Often, when covering these cases, the language used implied something not very serious and writers often described them as 'larks' or similar. In 1839, an unnamed Lincoln woman 'disguised' in male costume, 'pretended to be in love with a Miss B_y, whom she induced to accompany her in moonlight strolls.' It was said that this affair had carried on for months until Miss B_y was told by others of the hoax.[3] That the 'pretence' lasted months implies that there might have been more involved than simply keeping up the disguise.

In addition to 'the lark' was the satirical portrayal, such as in the case of two Leicestershire 'lasses' who were 'practical champions of women's rights,' who sallied into the streets of Castle Donnington in male attire in 1851 and 'gallantly called upon several young ladies'. But the 'roystering blades (or jades) were so rakish in their advances, that the girls took them for noblemen and refused to lend them their ears.'[4]

It was all considered such a laugh. Paul Downing, a rare example of a person of colour, was discharged from his job because he was continually seducing women. Following their discovery, the journalist noted, 'Flirting with the girls was her little joke!'[5]

When women lived with women, the language employed to describe them was intended to set them apart – words such as *strange* or *freak* – that left the reader in no doubt that this was not an ordinary friendship. However, the reader may not have fully understood the implications as rarely were the women presented as a threat or something which would destabilise society. The tone was usually amused, puzzled or neutral, such as the description of

Jack May and companion Miss Wittrick, who took a farm together. Some six years earlier, Jack had adopted male attire 'as a convenience in her duties of managing her large holdings' and could ride a horse and handle a plough like an expert. Jack had an excellent knowledge of livestock and had plenty of muscle, grit, and ambition. In what was presented as nothing more than a convenient arrangement, Miss Wittrick 'would do the housekeeping.'[6]

The nineteenth-century image of women was that they were essentially sexless and so the idea of females enjoying or wanting sex was inconceivable to many. This allowed women to maintain relationships with women as long as they did so quietly and out of the public eye. Few newspaper editors and journalists made an attempt to understand the relationships they described. Some did include other cross-living women to show the story was not in isolation, but mostly the articles were presented as a 'strange' case of humanity.

One of these 'strange' cases was that of Italian Giovanni Bordoni, born in 1719 as Catherine Vizzani. Giovanni lived almost a whole life as a man and was an infamous seducer of women. A post-mortem in 1743 was carried out to prove that the body must, in some way, be different from a 'normal' woman. It was not. In the late nineteenth century, there was scientific interest in women who enjoyed sex and they were often defined by having enlarged clitorises or genitals more akin to hermaphrodites. It is now accepted that woman have an enormous variety of genital shapes and features, and that there is no 'normal'.

It was not until the end of the nineteenth century and the beginning of the twentieth that interest in same-sex relationships and trans individuals increased, and stories abound from that period. Havelock Ellis' book, *Sexual Inversion* (1897), co-written with the writer and poet John Addington Symonds, was the first English language medical book on homosexuality. Both argued that male homosexuals should not be seen as effeminate, yet were willing to portray lesbians as mannish women.

Freud argued that everyone is born bisexual, but this theory had been around earlier: Otto Weininger in *Geschlect und Charakter* (Sex and Character) published in 1903 tried to explain the similarities between male and female. He stated that all organisms are born bisexual and in reality, there is no such thing as male and female because individuals contain elements of both and we oscillate between them, according to internal and external influences.

John Addington Symonds wrote about the development of the embryo, which he argued is unisex until further development and even then, does not always reach the heterosexual outcome because it leads to hermaphrodites, cross-dressers and those who desire their own sex.

As for the women themselves, they rarely discussed reasons for their relationships; if they did comment, the association was portrayed as sexually pure and an ideal 'companionship.' Numerous stories casually mention marriage, such as the female who had lived in men's apparel for six years, working as a labourer. When discovered in 1825, it was reported they had been married two years earlier 'to a female.'[7]

In 1871, Patrick M'Cormack died at the North Union workhouse having cross-lived for forty years. From childhood, Patrick had worn male dress and the journalist, tying himself in knots putting Patrick's name, or pronouns, in inverted commas finally gave up, stating 'we will speak of the deceased in the masculine gender'. Patrick worked as a gardener and 'had the reputation of being a capital workman' and 'extraordinary to relate, was actually married.' After seven years, Patrick and his wife separated and she survived him.[8]

As with other examples in this book, many women in relationships were found through their criminal records. Most were arrested for a specific crime and their situation came to light as a result.

Mary Field disappeared and was believed by her parents to be dead but in truth, she had become Henry Peck, a hop-picker, potboy and later a groom. While in the service of the vicar of Brenchley in Kent, Henry collected money for missionary societies but when a deficiency of 10 shillings became apparent, he was made to return it. To get the cash, Henry decided to burgle a grocer's shop but was soon tracked down by the police, who found a quantity of male attire; a rifleman's uniform and accoutrements; and a false beard and curls. The article also mentioned in passing that Henry had 'made love to a young lady in the neighbourhood.'[9]

Undoubtedly, many cross-living individuals were blackmailed but we will never know about most as to expose a blackmail meant exposing themselves. Occasionally, stories do appear such as that of a couple who lived together as man and wife for thirty-six years and kept a public house at Poplar. On her deathbed in 1776, the 'wife,' (the newspaper put the word in inverted commas for emphasis) told relatives that they had both been crossed in love when young and chose this method to 'avoid further importunities.' When a man discovered their secret, he tried to blackmail the 'husband' who took him to court for extortion. The blackmailer was sentenced to stand three times in the pillory and serve four years' imprisonment.[10]

The eighteenth century saw a number of stories about cross-dressing individuals who were regarded as con artists: marrying women to defraud them. In 1746, Lavinia Edwards (aka Mary, Charles or George Hamilton) was tried at the quarter sessions in Somersetshire for pretending to be a man and marrying fourteen wives. The last, Mary Price, stated in court that she was married to the prisoner and 'bedded, and lived as a man and wife a quarter of a year, during which time she thought the prisoner a man, owing to her vile and deceitful practices.' After a debate upon the nature of the crime and what to call it, the court agreed that Lavinia was a 'most infamous and notorious cheat' and sentenced her to be publicly whipped in Taunton, Glastonbury, Wells, and Shepton Mallet; imprisoned for six months; and to find security for her good behaviour for a period thought suitable by the Justices. Two men who attended the trial, one as a juryman, reported that the 'arts which the impostor practised were as curious as revolting, but of course are unfit for publication.' The purpose, apparently, was to obtain the women's property and once that was achieved, Charles, or George, moved on to another woman. At the trial, the thirteen wives gave evidence and all were convinced the prisoner was a male person. It was Mary who, after three months, discovered the truth and reported him to the police.[11]

Another case in 1777 that reappeared many times over the next century was of a cross-living individual who 'was constantly going about captivating her sisters, and marrying them!' Having finally been caught, the unnamed person was tried in London where it was proven they had married three women and 'defrauded them of their money and their clothes.' The magistrate decided that in order for women to become familiar with the 'face of the deceiver', they were to stand in the pillory at Cheapside after which they were imprisoned for six months.[12]

One case which does not appear to involve theft was treated just as harshly. In 1751, an unnamed individual at the Lancaster Assizes was 'prosecuted for the strange crime of marrying seven persons of her own sex in succession' and was duly transported. Apparently, the first six wives were virgins but the seventh, a widow, soon 'discovered her bedfellow.'[13]

As today, when a story was sufficiently sensational (particularly if it included a celebrity), it would run for days and was packed with as much salacious information as possible. In 1870, a story from Chicago that appeared widely concerned Lydia Thompson, a well-known actress and dancer who gained fame in 'leg shows', those burlesque or travesti shows where women's legs were covered in a thin hose-like material. At first, these were extremely popular until accusations of immodesty began, causing a backlash in a way that breeches roles never experienced. At least in the latter, legs were covered by trousers while 'leg shows' could seem as though the woman wore no covering at all.

Lydia had been arrested on the complaint of Ellen A. Griffin for assault and battery but in a surprise turn, she was released and Ellen was arrested. In court, Ellen sat gazing lovingly at Lydia, her features described as 'of imbecility or mental aberration' and 'coarse even for a man.' It turned out that Ellen sent a letter to Lydia who recognised the handwriting, declined to read it and had returned it with the information that Ellen would not be received. Infuriated, Ellen made her way to Lydia's hotel and attacked her.

The story had begun a year earlier when Lydia received a basket of flowers and a diamond ring, accompanied by a note signed by Ellen asking to meet her. Lydia agreed and during their conversation, Ellen told her she was in the habit of dressing herself in male attire and had become infatuated with Lydia's performances. When she said the ring was a family heirloom, an alarmed Lydia gave it back but later Ellen replaced it with another – which in reality was the same ring re-set. One night, as Lydia was on stage, a note was thrown down on which was written, 'If you don't return my dead sister's ring, I'll jump down and snatch it from your finger.' For a year, Ellen inundated Lydia with messages, sending her three or four hundred letters and the ring was sent back and forth. Even Ellen's mother wanted her committed for lunacy. An exasperated Lydia told the court, 'I go in bodily fear of this woman – in fear of my life,' so she had bought a pistol. The county physician brought in to examine Ellen said he thought that, although very intelligent, she possessed an uncontrollable obsession and was a monomaniac. Finally, she was released on her own recognisance if she paid $300 to keep the peace, provided she leave the city immediately. That seemed to put an end to Ellen's infatuation.[14] This is the only story found of what we would today regard as stalking.

One of the most familiar arguments put forward for women cohabiting was to avoid forced marriages. Arguably the story of the most famous couple in history today defined as lesbian – the Ladies of Llangollen – has been dogged by the erroneous idea that they ran away together to avoid marriages. From family records, it can be seen they ran away because they wanted to be together. Similarly, retiring after the loss of a man through death or abandonment crops up frequently. Mary East (the Woman-Man of Poplar) was 'landlord' of the White Horse public-house, a councillor and served as a juryman as James Howes. The explanation provided was that Mary's 'eccentricities' originated in 'an unfortunate love affair' when her sweetheart committed a highway robbery and was transported. Nearby lived another woman, who like Mary had been disappointed in love, and they decided to live together – but as man and wife. In 1750, a Mrs Bentley, who had known Mary from childhood, discovered their whereabouts and blackmailed them. James paid up but fifteen years later, Mrs Bentley returned wanting another pay-out, then continued to demand more. During this time, James's wife died. Mrs Bentley hired some thugs to accuse James of a robbery committed some forty years previously; again, James paid but the two men were arrested and sentenced to stand in the pillory and go to prison for four years. Due to the publicity, Mary 'resumed the habit of her sex' and lived the rest of her life as a woman.[15]

In 1878, Mary O'Keefe died of Bright's disease in a New York hospital. Known to the police and local residents as 'Sergeant Mary', they often regaled people with their story. It began with the familiar cliché: the end of a heterosexual love affair. In this case, a lover was arrested for highway robbery, found guilty and sentenced to twenty years in prison. This affected Mary so much that they resolved to remain single. Meeting a woman also blighted in love, they resolved to live together. Having drawn lots, Mary agreed to be the man. Some years later while walking down the street, they were recognised by a former friend who threatened to expose Mary, so the couple agreed to part. In the following years, Mary took to drinking; but having met a soldier got him drunk, stole his money and uniform, and enlisted. They had only been serving a few weeks before becoming drunk, was arrested and confessed their biological sex to the guard. Mary was dismissed but was thereafter known as 'Sergeant Mary.' They lived the rest of their life as a drunkard with periodic arrests until a menial position was acquired on Blackwell's Island, where they remained until death and burial in a pauper's grave.[16] If Mary was lesbian or trans, one has to wonder if it was mental health issues that drove her to drink.

Harry Norman had lived in Buffalo for ten years and been married for six, although the couple had recently parted. In 1902, an accident saw Harry in hospital in New York with them imploring the surgeon not to reveal their biological sex, and threatening, if exposed, to commit suicide.[17]

As has been seen in previous stories, the avoidance of shame has often played a prominent role. This was the case in the story of John Smith, an

Being drunk, everyone went to sleep and did not realise until the afternoon that Jacky was dead.[24]

In Manchester, John Jones was prosecuted for creating a disturbance and threatening to beat his wife, Sarah. Prosecuted under the birth name of Ann M'Gaul, or Ann Hughes, they were accused of passing as a man for six years in order to earn 2s. 6d. a day as a banksman in a colliery, instead of 1s a day at 'women's work'. John was discharged on the condition he would not create any further disturbance, but had to be kept in the dock for a time because of the mob outside the court.[25]

Despite the extraordinary amount of news reports about women living and working as men, journalists, even at the end of the century, seemed amazed by the fact. One writer felt that:

> the novelist who would dare to introduce into one of his works a woman who, for close upon half a century, should live and work as a man, amongst men, in the hardest and most exhausting forms of manual toil, who, moreover, was twice married to persons of her own sex, and yet whose secret was only revealed by the hand of death, would be held up (says a writer in the *Westminster Gazette*) to universal ridicule by all the critics for the gross improbability of his story. Yet that such an exceedingly improbable thing did occur, in a mining district of the county of Durham, is a fact within the writer's personal knowledge, and attested by an entry in the parish registers of Etherley.

The story concerned Joseph Josiah Charles Stephenson who had died in the quiet colliery village of Etherley, Durham in 1869 and 'the motive which underlay her extraordinary imposture apparently as impenetrable as the identity of the Man with the Iron Mask.' A man, about 30, obtained work in one of the colliery pits and soon afterwards married Sally, who was employed as a domestic at the Black Bull Inn. After the custom of the colliery villages, when an outsider married a girl born in the village, he became known as 'Sally's Joe.' The birth of a son followed much earlier after the marriage than was regarded as fitting by the gossips, but did not appear to mar the harmony of Sally and Joe, who lived contentedly and happily together. Joe worked at the pits in winter, and in the harvest and other field work in summer, being renowned as the fastest shearer in the district and so in great demand at a time when all corn was reaped with a sickle. After thirty years of marriage, Sally died, and Joe buried her with 'much, and apparently sincere' mourning. However, the *Sheffield & Rotherham Independent* dismissed Josiah's grief, claiming he 'professed' to lament her loss. Joe, it was argued, had saved her from disgrace and in return, Sally had faithfully kept Joe's secret through all the intervening years. Whether 'advancing age had brought the reverse of wisdom' to Joe is uncertain, but he later married a widow. The union was not a happy one and the pair soon separated. Village tradition had two accounts of their quarrel. One was that the woman declared her second husband a woman, but that the story was doubted by those who had known Joe for many years as a ridiculous fabrication. The other version is that the pair parted friends and the second wife kept her husband's secret as faithfully as Sally had done. After that, Joe lived alone, at first in a little cottage attached to a turnpike gate, which led to him being called 'Joe Pike'. He ended his life in a miserable two-roomed cottage in a court-yard, where he fell ill in the latter part of 1869, steadfastly refusing to allow anyone to approach him and 'persisted in wearing trousers in bed.' It was only when some kindly neighbours went to perform the last offices for the body that Joe's well-kept secret was revealed and the twice-married pitman, who had gone in and out among the villagers for nearly fifty years, was discovered to be a woman. Joe always claimed to hail from Berwick-on-Tweed and spoke in a strong border dialect but enquiries by the then rector, Reverend W. B. Findlay, failed to throw any light on either Joe's history or motives.[26]

Of course, it is entirely feasible that there were platonic relationships where the woman kept the cross-living individual's secret in order for them to live as they chose, in return for saving them from shame by having a child out of wedlock.

As with all marriages, some of these arrangements ended in divorce. In 1869 in Santiago, police became suspicious of an egg-seller because he always wore a cloak. On investigation, they found the man was a biological woman so his wife sued for divorce. She was described as 'of a simplicity and innocence so great that for some time after the marriage she had no suspicion as to the nullity of her husband's pretentions.' The man had married her for her money and made purchases and contracts in his wife's name but in court, complications emerged on how to separate the property. The question was whether the wife should be responsible for the debts incurred by the husband and whether he could be prosecuted for falsely signing contracts and the marriage certificate. Unfortunately, the records go quiet so we do not know if the husband was prosecuted.[27]

In 1850, a case of bigamy came into the courts regarding John Curtis, a labourer of the village of Strensham, Worcester who had married Anna Maria Wilkins in 1835. They remained together until 1840 when Anna, who was of a 'masculine character', decided to adopt male attire, move to Staffordshire and work as a labourer. Sometime later, having taken up with a maid, they were admonished for their unseemly closeness, so they married. However, it did not work out and they separated, the 'wife' then marrying a man. In the meantime, John wanted to remarry but needed a death certificate to prove that Anna had died. Unable to acquire this proof, John went to another county and married there but Anna heard of this, reverted to female attire and accused him of bigamy. John was found guilty and sentenced to three months in prison.[28] Why Anna chose to prosecute him is unknown and it seems a little churlish given that she remarried – perhaps it was revenge for domestic violence but we can only speculate.

Even when separated by death, things could become more complicated for some individuals. When a man named Joseph Deitchen died in Indianapolis, a chest was found in his house containing £23,000 ($115,000 or about £3 million today) in gold and banknotes. Joseph's relations decided to contest the will, which left the wealth to his wife, on the grounds that he was a woman and never had the right to marry. They asserted that until fifteen years previously, 'she' wore dresses and was called Josephine but had decided to become a boy and change his attire.[29] Again, it is not known what happened and if the wife got to keep her money.

One fact not explored by writers was that there was rarely a traditional heterosexual outcome to the stories they reported on. In both fictional and real-life stories of cross-dressing and cross-living, a common outcome was that 'normality' was restored when individuals went back to heterosexual marriages, returned to families, or resumed their 'proper' dress. However, in accounts of real-life 'same-sex relationships' (they would have been defined as same-sex at the time), those concerned usually continued in their lives and lived with the women they loved.

Chapter 16

Questioning Gender

Individuals who have gender dysphoria – to put it succinctly – do not identify with their birth gender and many transition. However, transposing an understanding of gender dysphoria to individuals from the past presents problems as we cannot ascribe definitions of gender identity to individuals based on short articles. We can say that some people conform to what we know today of transmen but we cannot know if they had gender dysphoria; or if they were women who wanted to live free of the restrictions on their lives; or were lesbians (as we understand the term today). All these individuals can be described as gender-fluid because they were understood by society to be men, but there are a number of stories which allow us to consider gender dysphoria in more depth.

Where applicable, the pronouns used for these individuals, in keeping with current usage, is 'they' or 'their'.

One story that stands out is of an unnamed individual who arrived in New York in 1897. Discovered to be a biological woman, they begged the doctor not to expose them saying, 'I'll kill myself before I will wear women's clothes. It is my life's desire to be a man. That the Almighty made me a woman is no fault of mine.' They absolutely refused to dress in 'proper' clothing and instead asked for the family's lawyer who explained:

> When only six years old she began to manifest peculiar traits of character, all of a masculine nature, declaring that she was unhappy at being a girl, and she was always insisting on wearing boy's clothing. If dresses were put upon her, she would tear them into shreds. As her parents could not overcome her freakishness they allowed her to grow up as a boy. When fifteen years old she drifted away from them and came to this country. For two years she worked as a hostler in a stable in this city. Later she went south, where she took to farming. Then she went to the West Indies, where she also followed the vocation of farming, because she liked to be in a place where she could 'boss.' … All attempts of her mother and father to induce her to give up her inclination to dress as a man have proved futile.

The individual was allowed to leave on the promise of leaving the USA at once.[1] One feature of this story that conforms to the stories of many trans people of today is an awareness of their dysphoria from an early age. This is reflected in the opening lines of Jan Morris's autobiography, *Conundrum* (1974): 'I was three or perhaps four years old when I realized that I had been born into the wrong body, and should really be a girl. I remember the moment well, and it is the earliest memory of my life.'

One theme of gender diversity that has been studied extensively is the 'female husband' and certain individuals have become quite well-known.

The term first appeared in 1746 when Henry Fielding wrote a fictional account of Mary/Charles Hamilton (mentioned in the previous chapter) in *The Female Husband*. The term was often used in the eighteenth and nineteenth centuries until it died out in the late nineteenth century with just a few examples existing until the 1910s. By using the heading 'female husband' in press articles, it was accepted that the reading public would recognise the nature of the story. In fact, the phrase became a cliché and so-called 'true' stories were either invented or over-dramatised to emphasise the femininity of the 'husband' and so make the story more socially acceptable.

The term 'husband' carried associations of respect because this was the ideal society was aiming for: that men should be married, responsible, hard-working, decent and someone with authority. It was understood why women would want to aspire to such heights and as many female husbands were hard-working and respectable, they were often held up as shining examples of what a man should be. Consequently, the language used to describe female husbands was generally benign. However, coupling the word with 'female' did set up a conundrum – something against nature – and according to standards of decorum of the time, nothing was discussed as to sexual relations.

Most of the more famous female husbands are covered widely on the internet including Edward de Lacy Evans; Mary East of Poplar; Count Sándor Vay; Joseph Israel Lobdell; Nicholas de Raylan; Amy Bock; James Allen and others, however, this chapter will focus on individuals who are less well-known.

Often when stories appeared, they generated a spate of letter writers recalling people they knew personally or citing something they had read. In 1829 'an inhabitant' writing to the *Cheltenham Chronicle* had been inspired by a female husband story to quote from a work published in 1787 about a court case in Birmingham. A plaintiff wished to sue someone for debt but did not know whether the party was male or female, and was at a loss as to what name should be on the documents. The defendant had been known for many years in both:

> the dress and character of a woman, called Elizabeth, and had been many years known in the dress and character of a man, who answered to the name of John.

In the end, the plaintiff covered all his options and entered 'Elizabeth alias John Haywood' on the summons. The press report added:

> Whatever was the gender, the animal appeared before the Court in a female habit, was rather elegant, of a moderate size, tolerably handsome, about thirty-two, had a firm countenance and manly step, no beard, susceptible of love, a voice tending to the masculine, with engaging manners, and was rather sensible.

The trial continued for four days in an 'uncommonly crowded' courtroom, where the defendant was nicknamed *Betty John*. The writer noted, 'as it appeared in the Court in female dress, I shall take the liberty of treating it with a feminine epithet.'

From the evidence it appeared that:

> whilst she drest like a man, she was suspected to be a woman, but in both dresses was strongly suspected to be a man. The common opinion of the ignorant, who knew her, was, that she was an hermaphrodite, partaking of both sexes.

While dressed in male clothes, they spent the evening at the pub with male companions and:

> could, like them, swear with a tolerable grace, get drunk, smoke tobacco, make love to the girls, and now and then kick a bully. Though she pleaded being a wife, she had really been a husband; for she courted a young woman, married her, & they lived together in wedlock till the young woman died, which was some years after, she afterwards, like the people of higher rank, kept a mistress, and ran away with her.

In court, the mistress gave evidence that her partner was a man and that they lived together 'peaceably … without one complaint of a breach of the marriage covenant, evinced there was no defect. Neither would a girl sacrifice her reputation, by becoming a mistress to a woman in breeches.'

The magistrates asked if Elizabeth could prove the marriage, which they tried to do, even producing a certificate, but it was rejected and the magistrates concluded that Elizabeth was really John in disguise. John was ordered to make payment but having failed to do so, was sent to a male prison, where it was discovered they were a biological woman. After forty days in a female prison, they were released.[2]

A decade later in 1834, another story headed 'The late female husband at Kennington' described a recently deceased Captain Wright, who had a predilection for pretty girls who were courted by the dozens 'without exciting any jealousy in *her* wife!' On one occasion, the Captain was invited to a dance where, 'notwithstanding his enormous size … ogled each fair face with the devotion of an Adonis, scarcely knowing how to choose from so large and captivating a circle of the graces.' Having made a choice of 'graces' he:

> waddled, and sometimes strode, along the room. His partner's activity was, however, more than a match for his ardour, and after puffing and blowing till the perspiration literally poured from his forehead, he was constrained to give in, and hand his fair partner to a seat. … During the remainder of the evening he was observed to be whispering to his *inamorata*, in words of soft and tender import, as might be readily perceived from the blushing countenance of the lady. It was a subject of general surprise among the visitors, that his wife, who was present, scarcely noticed the apparent infidelity of her spouse; at all events, she was very far from being annoyed at it.

Rumour had it that the purpose of the disguise was to inherit a dead brother's property or that he was receiving considerable sums from someone to keep up an 'amusing charade'. Whatever the reason, the coffin was engraved with the words 'Eliza Wright.'[3]

The veracity of one female husband story which appeared in 1838 was much debated. It began when a wife visited an attorney in Manchester to ask for advice because, after running her husband's business for years, they had recently refused to give her the weekly house-keeping money and generally treated her unkindly, especially when intoxicated. She wanted to know how to proceed because her husband, to the astonishment of the attorney, was a biological woman. The lawyer reported them to the magistrates where the husband admitted the charge. The wife said she had accidentally made the discovery about two or three years earlier but had kept it a secret. The 'woman-man', as described in the papers, was around 25 years old and had assumed the garb and character of a boy at an early age. He was now a master bricklayer, having established a good business. While still an apprentice, he was 'rather handsome' and attracted the attention of many females, one of whom became his wife. They were married at the Old Parish Church of Sheffield in 1816 and during the following seventeen years of marriage, the business was extremely successful and the husband was a highly respected townsman, even becoming a special constable. However, as soon as the story became public, the couple separated. 'Altogether,' the story ran:

> this is by far the most singular case of the kind which has ever reached our knowledge. The celebrated Chevalier D'Eon was not married; and James Davis (so-called), the discovery of whose sex took place only after death, had not been married for so long a period as the woman whose case is now under notice. There, too, the discovery was made too late to obtain from the party herself any clue to the motives which led her to so unfeminine a course of deception; but here both parties to the supposed marriage are alive, and the one who assumed the male sex is still alive to give, if she chooses, the true history of her reasons or fancy for laying aside the garb and character of her own, and assuming the appearance, and undertaking the toil of the other sex, which would certainly be a very curious chapter of biography.[4]

The husband did not give an account and as soon as the story broke, it was claimed to be a hoax. The *Manchester Times* called it 'a silly report' adding 'as it was not impossible for such a circumstance to have occurred, although very improbable, we had curiosity enough to make inquiries on the subject, and found that the alleged "remarkable discovery" was a gross fabrication.' However, the *Morning Chronicle* did its own digging and claimed the story was true, adding that 'the husband, who, so far as we have heard, has not offered any reparation to the wife for the cruel and painful position in which she is now placed.' The husband lost their reputation and the business, while those who knew the couple chorused the usual refrain of 'we never knew'.

One of the most common words found in 'female husband' stories is 'extraordinary' and one story sums this up when it was described as an 'extraordinary application' and an 'extraordinary marriage'.

In 1852, a Mrs Roberts applied to the magistrates at Westminster for assistance and advice about her 17-year-old daughter who had gone through the ceremony of marriage 'without being blessed with a husband.' The couple had met several months earlier when Mrs Roberts had lodged a Mrs Panton who, on several occasions, had shared a bed with her daughter. However, 'after an intimacy of some months', Mrs Panton suddenly appeared in the 'costume of a gentleman' by the name of Albert Guelph. Albert explained that he was really a secret child of George IV and Queen Caroline who, for reasons not explained, could not keep him. Instead, he had been disguised as a woman and was required to meet 'a very benign old lady' regularly who kept him supplied with liberal amounts of cash. He now, he said, appeared to Mrs Roberts as his true self as he had fallen in love with her daughter. As he dressed very fashionably and always had plenty of money, Mrs Roberts accepted his story and gave her permission to marry her daughter. It was on the honeymoon that the new wife discovered her husband was a biological woman – and the mother of three children.[5]

In 1891, a writer called 'Kes' reproduced another extraordinary 'fact was stranger than fiction' story from 1781. His account concerned Jane West who was born in Wellington, Herefordshire in 1718 to farming parents. Jane's explanation for adopting male attire was the well-worn excuse of a 'lost love' when aged 17, her soldier sweetheart was killed in his first battle. 'Like many other young women similarly situated, Jane at once vowed to be "true to her first love," and to remain single all her life,' Kes wrote. The other cliché in the story is the coincidence of a schoolfellow who lost her lover to fever and she also made a vow to remain chaste – together. Having about £35 between them, they travelled to London, secured modest lodgings and Jane – the elder and more masculine-looking of the two – cut her hair and dressed in men's garments. She told the astonished landlady that she had only assumed female attire to avoid creditors. From then on, the two appeared as James and Mary Wood, 'Jane playing the role of the husband so well as to completely banish all suspicion as to her sex.' They decided to rent a small river-side tavern near Henley which they ran successfully for three years and amassed £300. This enabled them to take another tavern, the White Lion at Croydon, and once again, they were extremely successful and well-respected. James was often called onto juries and took a number of parochial offices. The only blot on their lives, as they frequently told friends, was not having any children so they adopted a 4-year-old orphaned girl. For twelve years, they lived pleasantly until a Wellington local entered the bar and at once recognised Mary. Calling James to one side, he casually asked if he knew what had happened to Jane West who had left with Mary. Noting James's discomfort, he asked for a loan of a couple of guineas, promising to pay the sum back when he passed that way again. James paid but this was just the beginning of the blackmail. A week later, the man returned claiming to have been robbed so he needed five guineas. A month later, he was back and even when James set the man up with a haberdashery shop nearby, it did not stop his blackmailing. Perhaps the worry undermined Mary's health because she became so unwell that her doctor told her she needed a change of air and was sent to Essex to stay with friends. Only a fortnight later came the news of her death. Relieved of marital responsibilities, James decided to confide in the local rector who immediately laid a trap for the blackmailer and they concealed a police constable behind the bar to overhear the demands. The following day, the blackmailer was in court on charges of extortion and despite outing James as a woman, which was dismissed as nonsense, he was sent to Bridewell where he caught gaol fever and died. For a further five years, James continued to run the White Lion until a 'buxom female of the village set her cap' at him but was rebuffed. Furious at the rejection, she brought a charge of seduction against James and the only defence open to him was to admit he was a biological woman. The woman was prosecuted for perjury but James's reputation had gone. Having sold the White Lion, he had a fortune of £5,000 (over £600,000 today), half of which he handed to relatives of Mary's. With the remainder, James retired to the village of Poplar where he lived alone until he died on 14 January 1781, aged 63. Kes assured readers that if anyone doubted the story, they could check the record of death in the Parish Church register.[6]

Aside from passing as men, the fluidity of gender can be considered in other areas, such as bearded women. The quantity and quality of hair on women's bodies varies enormously, particularly on the face – amounts can range from a fine fuzz on the upper lip to a full beard. One disorder where a great deal of hair grows naturally – hypertrichosis – can be caused by a variety of conditions. It can occur locally or all over the body and is caused by genetic mutations. Some of the very hairy people seen in what was referred to as 'Victorian freak shows' had this condition. Hirsutism is also another condition of excess hair, an imbalance of the endocrine system including an excess of androgen – the hormone that develops and maintains male characteristics. Approximately 40 per cent of women have some form of facial hair growth and an excess of 'male' hormones like androgen illustrates the porous line between the sexes.

However, women attempting to maintain a disguise who did not have excessive androgen could still encourage hair growth by shaving their faces, something they needed to imitate when trying to live in close proximity with men.

Many women who had moustaches or beards continued to present as women, despite discrimination – a situation that still exists today. Some women in the past took advantage of economic opportunities and joined shows such as those run by the American P. T. Barnum. Annie Jones, the bearded lady, was a popular attraction and the character Lettie Lutz in the film *The Greatest Showman* was based on her.

Hundreds of women with excess hair were written about, such as Barbara Van Beck, a German woman whose face was covered in hair. Their androgynous status was discussed at length but not all wore male attire or passed as men. Those who cross-dressed or cross-lived did so for a variety of reasons and sometimes it was the direct result of their greater hair growth that inspired them. In 1847 in Laon, France, an unnamed man with a long white beard was arrested for begging and sent to prison. For forty years, this man had been a butcher and would, in all probability, have 'gone on to the end of her career believed to be a man, had not her advanced age prevented her working'. It had been the growth of her beard that gave her the idea of passing as male[7] as, according to an eighteenth-century French law, any woman growing a beard had the right to dress like a man.[8]

Despite hundreds of articles about bearded women, most in relation to cross-dressing are from France. One unnamed Marseilles woman in 1887 who, blessed with a 'hirsute appendage' on her chin, was followed by a crowd of small boys whenever she appeared in public. She decided to 'discard the petticoat for ever' and 'don the trousers of the stronger sex.' She made an application to the police for a permit, which was granted at once.[9]

In 1845, a woman named Brouilard, who was about 40 years of age, with 'a pair of mustachios of which many a Parisian dandy would be proud' was arrested in Paris for 'wearing the habiliments of the male sex without having received the requisite permission from the authorities'. It appears that she had dressed as a man for several years working as a day labourer and had amassed a decent sum of money.[10]

Another aspect of gender-fluidity is the varying masculinity of women and a number found fame simply because of their extreme apparent masculinity.

There were those who dressed in female attire; those who dressed in male attire but continued to present as female; and those who passed as male.

Newspapers were fascinated by those who presented as women but dressed as male and would often delve into their backgrounds, allowing us better descriptions of those individuals. Women such as Molly Neville, 'who had led a very remarkable life' and who died aged about 70 in 1867. She was said to live by her gun, was an excellent fisher and would sell her produce every market day, but a short time before her death she had lost her right arm when her fowling gun exploded.

> In appearance she was masculine, and wore a peculiarly striking dress, having in general a man's hat and coat. Her comfortable little cabin was built by herself out of wrecked timber and seaweed, and the furniture it contained was also the works of her own hands. She principally favoured men with her society, and often competed in shooting contests, the accuracy of her aim being a matter of some surprise.

'Molly,' ended the piece, 'must have been a curiosity.'[11]

One writer in 1895 described ten women in France who were authorised to wear masculine clothes 'all the year around and not merely at Carnival time.' The list included 'a bearded woman, and some poor deformed creature who would be ridiculed if they were dressed according to their sex.'[12] Martha Ellis, alias John Sellis, of Lambeth was described as 'if dressed as a male, be more fitly attired than she or it then was.'[13]

A 'masculine woman' was arrested in Berlin because she looked mannish and had a growth of hair sprouting from the upper lip and cheeks. When she went about in female clothes, she was repeatedly arrested by the police for masquerading as a woman and each time she had to produce her birth certificate. She decided to live as a man and obtained a post in a large house, where her secret was known only to the proprietor. 'She is known to the entire staff as "Herr So-and- So," and they have not the least inkling of her sex.'[14]

Other writers described androgyny, such as this report by Joshua Vernal, in *A Jaunt to Wales*: 'we went a little further, and met a sort of hermaphrodite, a man's hat upon the head, a man's coat upon the back, and men's shoes upon the feet, but the petticoats were those of a woman. I suppose this is a woman though by her dress she seemeth not.'[15]

Perhaps the people who most clearly destabilise the notion of binary genders are those who were called hermaphrodites. These individuals were, putting it simplistically, born with both sets of genitals, however, the variations and confusion over definitions saw the term removed and replaced with the modern word, intersex.

There was a common view that hermaphrodites were 'deformed' women rather than men but in many cases, writers circumnavigated the issue by referring to the individual as 'it'. For most of history, hermaphrodites, and intersex people today, have been defined by their genitals rather than as people.

As with anything 'other', the media was fascinated by hermaphrodites and several became quite well-known, such as Marie Madeleine Lefort who was also bearded and had a licence to wear male attire. Many other examples exist but as they do not include cross-dressing, they are not included here.

In 1829 in the town of Dreux, France, a case 'excited much amusement as well as attention.' Rose Victoire Vivien had been registered as female at birth and was very feminine until the age of 26. When her uncle died and left her a small property, she tried to establish herself but no man would show any interest in her. Becoming despondent, she went to a doctor who, 'to her inexpressible surprise, assured her that, instead of being an old maid, she was neither more nor less than a young bachelor.' She therefore applied to have her birth certificate altered but before granting the application, the court had her examined by three doctors, who all confirmed she was 'to all intents and purposes a gentleman.' The judgement was given in her favour and '*Monsieur* Ross Victoire Vivien' now 'set off in search of a wife.'

A few years later in 1837, an article entitled 'More Funny Than Pleasant' concerned a woman baptized and educated as a girl. She demanded the right to marry a young woman, alleging that an error of sex had existed, and requiring to be publicly recognised as a man. 'The medical men, who have been consulted in this matter, have ascertained that the person in question is, in every sense of the word, androgynous.'[16]

According to the article, something similar happened in 1814 when Marie Marguerite Metey had applied to change her sex and was examined by the same doctors. Mr Metey became a 'thriving farmer in the Commune of Bu, with a very pretty wife, who is an excellent manager, and expects every day to present her husband with a fine little Master or Miss Metey.'[17] If this is a case of hermaphroditism, the wife would probably have waited in vain, as it is rare for hermaphrodites to retain the ability to have or father children.

One story entitled 'A Change of Sex' appeared in 1894 concerning Laure Bernard, a 24-year-old woman from Treschatel, France who was well-known as the founder and director of a school to treat stammering. She suddenly changed her sex and married one of her friends. It seems that at her birth, the question of sex was a difficult one to settle and 'the weaker sex was chosen.' As well as working at her school, she toured the country, teaching her methods with great success. She accumulated a small fortune and used this to study medicine, sometimes wearing male attire. 'Nothing,' wrote the journalists, 'in her outward appearance betrayed that she was of the masculine sex. The face had perhaps a certain hardness, and the voice was slightly manly in its tone, but on the whole, she wore her skirts "as to the manner born." Of beard or moustache there was not a trace.'[18]

Hundreds of similar stories exist which simply cannot fit in this book but all show that the dividing line between the sexes is gossamer-thin.

Conclusion

Today, there are women who never wear skirts or dresses because they have the freedom to choose. Sadly, a choice is not given to those men who wish to wear skirts and dresses – they are often seen as transvestites. Indeed, many women who only wear trousers state they would feel like a transvestite if they had to wear 'female' garments. So, questions inevitably arise as to what defines gender. The examples in this book indicate that it was clothing, rather than the body, that assigned gender in the eyes of the beholder – and distributed power accordingly.

However, the subject of gender boundaries was on the whole ignored when it came to the women's stories. Most of the newspaper articles were short, often buried in the page reserved for human interest stories; only rarely did they make the top of the page or the front cover.

What is missing from most of these accounts is the real sense of what these women felt and thought while passing as the other sex. Restrictions on women's roles as daughter, spinster, wife, mother or widow did not allow a public expression of what it meant to be different for society did not want other women to try this at home. So, for the most part we cannot know their real motivation, as we now might.

As has been seen, these restrictions could be broken with clothes and words: words that slip easily from one interpretation to another. Some Christian women today explain away Deuteronomy 22:5's edict about women not wearing men's clothes because they are 'women's trousers', the zips are on the other side and they are tailored differently. By simply refashioning and renaming a garment, rules can be broken. Other biblical passages are similarly open to interpretation. The Geneva Bible, the most important translation before the King James Version, was reproduced widely and in one 1579 version, Genesis 3:7 had Adam and Eve making 'breeches' to cover their nakedness:

> when the eyes of them both were opened, and they knew that they were naked, and they sewed figge tree leaves together and made themselves breeches.

This version was subsequently nicknamed the 'Breeches Bible'. When the King James Version was published in 1611, the word 'apron', which had appeared in Tyndale's first English translations of 1526, was restored. Since then, a whole range of translations have appeared including 'fig leaves', 'clothes', 'clothed themselves' or 'covered themselves.' Indeed, look up any biblical passage on the internet and a wide range of interpretations are offered.

As the twentieth century progressed, women began to break free of clothing restrictions. Trouser wearing became more prevalent during and after the First World War and arrests began to wane, although they didn't completely disappear. During the 1930s, celebrities such as Marlene Dietrich and Katherine Hepburn popularised trousers and by the Second World War, it was barely noticeable that women were wearing clothing more suitable for manual jobs. By the late twentieth century, women had the option to wear trousers in almost all situations. At least, this was true for Westerners – there are still rules or laws on religious and cultural traditions in other parts of the world that control what women wear. For example, in 2018, women in Sudan could still be fined and whipped for wearing trousers under Article 152 of the Sudanese Public Order Law which stipulates that woman cannot wear 'a revealing outfit' (but as with many restrictive laws, the word 'revealing' is not defined).[1]

As people became familiar with women in trousers, it ceased to be an entertainment. Male impersonators disappeared and were replaced by drag kings and drag queens, but their audience is mainly LGBT+. While cross-dressing has featured in film and TV, almost all portrayals are feminised and most have the character revert back to a female life. Various operas still include original cross-dressing roles, as do pantomimes and Shakespeare's plays but these excite little comment. Women in trousers are no longer considered to be 'cross-dressing'.

However, the stories in this book leave us pondering one point. The binary system failed – the gossamer nature of gender is torn. If one sex can so successfully reproduce the traits of the other, how stable are those boundaries separating the sexes? How secure are the powers and privileges of men when the justification for dominance fails?

I keep returning to the same point: the women featured in this book, for the most part, passed as men. They looked sufficiently like men to pass in public; they behaved like men and their behaviour was accepted by both men and women. Even those who had slight frames, a lack of an Adam's apple, a smooth chin, or a light-sounding voice were accepted and simply seen as a different form of a man. Where then does that leave us in defining a 'proper' man? And what value does the thin gender line have when it can be snapped so easily?

In the 1835 novel *Mademoiselle de Maupin* by Théophile Gautier about a cross-dressing woman, the heroine states, 'instead of a woman disguised as a man, I shall look like a man disguised as a woman. In truth neither sex is really mine ... I belong to a third sex, a sex apart, which has as yet no name.'

In reality, there is no third sex, nor first or second. There is only a fluidity of disguise. By conforming to society's demands that men and women adhere strictly to the dictates of dress and behaviour, many people deny those aspects of themselves which are masculine for a woman or feminine for a man. Most women get rid of any facial hair as it represents the masculine, while men with 'man boobs' cover them up.

Sadly, the notion of the 'proper' woman is still fought out on the pages of social media with many 'trolls' defining how women should look or behave. Dame Mary Beard, a classics professor at the University of Cambridge, was viciously 'trolled', particularly on her appearance as she does not wear make-up, dye her hair or wear what people consider 'fashionable attire'. Her response was a videoed lecture entitled *Oh Do Shut Up Dear!* (2014), which can be watched online, in which she explored the many ways that men have silenced women since the days of the ancients. 'It doesn't much matter what line of argument you take as a woman,' she says. 'If you venture into traditional male territory, the abuse comes anyway. It's not what you say that prompts it – it's the fact that you are saying it.'

Today, many women are still reluctant to enter the world of politics due to the vicious attacks of those who judge them on aspects of their personality and appearance – and not their politics. They are seen as failing to conform to the trolls' demands but if they were to conform, there would be others to argue against it. So where does that leave women? Perhaps nowhere.

In that respect, aren't we all still living in a masquerade?

Notes

Introduction
1. Shopland, Norena & Leeworthy, Daryl, *Queering Glamorgan: A Research Guide to Sources for the Study of LGBT History* (Glamorgan Archives, 2018)

Chapter 1
1. Barr, Pat, *A Curious Life for a Lady. The Story of Isabella Bird* (London: Faber & Faber Kindle edition, originally published 1970)
2. *Bury and Norwich Post*, 10 November 1802
3. *Aberdeen Weekly Journal*, 14 May 1890
4. *Belfast News-Letter*, 31 May 1887
5. *Morning Post*, 15 August 1834
6. *Pall Mall Gazette*, 11 November 1869
7. Burton, Lady Isabel & Wilkins, William Henry (ed.), *The Romance of Isabel Lady Burton* (New York: Dodd Meade & Company, 1897)
8. *Leeds Mercury*, 6 November 1880
9. *Birmingham Daily Post*, 9 September 1889
10. *Queenslander*, 30 October 1869
11. *Pall Mall Gazette*, 12 September 1888
12. Morris, Steven, 'Teenage boys wear skirts to school to protest against 'no shorts' policy' in *The Guardian* (22 June 2017)
13. 'South Wales Notes [by Cosmos]' in *South Wales Daily News* (2 June 1891)
14. *Chester Daily Times*, 3 August 1877
15. Wallach, Janet, *Desert Queen* (London: Hachette UK Kindle edition, 2015)
16. *Morning Post*, 24 March 1830
17. *Lancashire Gazette*, 24 December 1831
18. *Border Watch*, 8 July 1874
19. *Monmouthshire Merlin*, 16 November 1833
20. *Blackburn Standard*, 16 January 1839
21. *Northern Star*, 18 November 1847
22. *Daily News*, 12 March 1856
23. *Evening Express*, 22 August 1895
24. *Pall Mall Gazette*, 6 February 1889
25. *Abergavenny Chronicle*, 30 April 1915
26. *Sydney Mail*, 21 June 1890
27. *Yorkshire Herald*, 7 November 1896

28. *The Argus* (Melbourne), 14 March 1855
29. *Rockhampton Bulletin*, 5 November 1872
30. *Evening Journal*, 12 May 1873
31. *Welsh Gazette*, 11 December 1902
32. *Liverpool Mercury*, 2 March 1820
33. *Derby Mercury*, 15 April 1802
34. *Berrow's Worcester Journal*, 23 June 1836
35. *Hampshire Telegraph*, 4 December 1886
36. *Belfast News-Letter*, 4 May 1853
37. *Lloyd's Weekly Newspaper*, 28 November 1897
38. *Evening Express*, 7 November 1908

Chapter 2
1. *North Wales Chronicle*, 2 October 1858
2. *Daily Colonist*, 7 August 1909
3. Hugo, Victor, *The Man Who Laughs: L'Homme Qui Rit* (ebook: Floating Press, originally published 1869)
4. *Llangollen Advertiser*, 7 July 1876
5. *Cardiff Times*, 3 September 1904
6. *Evening Express*, 27 October 1904
7. *The Daily News*, 2 December 1896
8. *Daily Northern Argus*, 26 February 1892
9. *Evening Express*, 17 December 1906
10. *Bristol Mercury*, 27 October 1890
11. *South Wales Daily News*, 7 September 1900
12. *Evening Express*, 22 February 1910
13. *Evening Express*, 22 April 1904; *Weekly Mail*, 7 May 1904
14. *South Wales Echo*, 6 August 1889
15. *Evening Express*, 2 March 1907
16. *Illustrated Usk Observer*, 11 July 1863
17. *Newcastle Morning Herald*, 26 February 1879
18. *Ballarat Star*, 6 March 1879
19. *Bunyip*, 24 March 1876
20. *Aberdare Leader*, 26 September 1903
21. *Belfast News-Letter*, 1 May 1856
22. *Morning Chronicle*, 18 September 1828
23. *Cardiff Times*, 3 September 1904
24. *New York Journal*, 4 May 1897

Chapter 3
1. *Aberdare Times*, 20 December 1890
2. *Monmouthshire Merlin*, 22 August 1829; *Carmarthen Journal*, 21 August 1829

3. *The Era*, 13 March 1859
4. *The Standard*, 11 October 1871
5. *Illustrated Police News*, 2 August 1872
6. The Juvenile Protective Association of Chicago, *The Public Dance Halls of Chicago* (Chicago: The Juvenile Protective Association of Chicago, 1917)
7. Wilson, Harriette, *The Memoirs of Harriette Wilson: Written by Herself* (London: J. J. Stockdale, 1825)
8. *Morning Post*, 28 October 1854
9. *Morning Chronicle*, 17 September 1829
10. *Morning Chronicle*, 17 February 1834
11. *Glasgow Herald*, 31 March 1854
12. *Sydney Monitor*, 12 May 1837
13. *Evening Express*, 24 March 1899
14. Shopland, Norena, *Forbidden Lives: LGBT Stories from Wales* (Bridgend: Seren Books, 2018)
15. *Cardiff Times*, 8 May 1863
16. *Cardiff Times*, 23 July 1887
17. *Cardiff and Merthyr Guardian*, 9 February 1855
18. *Aberdeen Weekly Journal*, 3 July 1894
19. *South Wales Echo*, 13 March 1890
20. *South Wales Daily News*, 18 October 1900
21. *Weekly Mail*, 4 January 1890
22. *Pontypool Free Press*, 1 January 1892
23. *Morning Post*, 19 July 1843
24. *Morning Post*, 17 January 1844
25. *Western Star*, 3 January 1885
26. *Leicester Chronicle*, 12 March 1898
27. *South Wales Daily News*, 7 June 1895
28. *Northern Echo*, 7 August 1896
29. *Birmingham Daily Post*, 9 October 1877
30. *The Argus* (Melbourne), 24 March 1877
31. *Newcastle Courant*, 25 October 1850
32. *Hampshire Telegraph*, 8 March 1851
33. *Daily News*, 18 September 1860
34. *Cheshire Observer*, 19 August 1871
35. *North Eastern Daily Gazette*, 17 April 1889
36. *The Times*, 29 August 1872
37. *Pembrokeshire Herald*, 19 April 1872
38. *County Observer*, 24 February 1877
39. *The Era*, 20 August 1881
40. *Evening News* (Sydney), 4 February 1876

Chapter 4

1. Shopland, Norena, *Forbidden Lives: LGBT Stories from Wales* (Bridgend: Seren Books, 2017)
2. *Weekly Mail*, 24 December 1910
3. *Evening News* (Sydney), 15 March 1871
4. *Leicester Chronicle*, 24 August 1849
5. *North Wales Chronicle*, 6 December 1827
6. *Belfast News-Letter*, 5 January 1864
7. *Morning Post*, 7 August 1805
8. *Bristol Mercury*, 30 December 1837
9. *Hull Packet*, 26 February 1858
10. *Cardiff Times*, 26 August 1881
11. *Hampshire Advertiser*, 20 January 1900
12. *County Observer*, 18 February 1905
13. *Bury and Norwich Post*, 5 May 1841
14. *County Observer*, 21 May 1904
15. *Evening Express*, 12 December 1908
16. *Freeman's Journal*, 5 August 1882
17. *Flintshire Observer*, 23 March 1889
18. *Evening Express*, 27 February 1905
19. *South Australian Chronicle*, 13 March 1880
20. *Aberystwyth Observer*, 14 January 1865
21. *Morning Post*, 25 March 1822
22. Genlis, Countess de & Colburn, Henry, *Memoirs of the Countess de Genlis, illustrative of the history of the eighteenth and nineteenth centuries* (London: New Burlington, 1825)
23. *Illustrated Sydney News*, 10 June 1854
24. *The Cambrian*, 7 September 1883
25. *Pembrokeshire Herald*, 24 January 1862
26. *North Wales Chronicle*, 9 January 1844
27. *The Spectator*, 11 September 1830
28. *The Australian Star*, 22 January 1897
29. *Richmond Times*, 14 January 1902
30. *Hull Packet and Humber Mercury*, 13 January 1829
31. *Florence Times* (Alabama), 9 April 1892
32. *Pittsburgh Commercial Gazette*, 27 August 1884
33. *New York Tribune*, 10 July 1910
34. *Colac Herald*, 14 October 1887
35. *San Francisco Call*, 22 June 1904
36. *Cardiff Times*, 27 August 1880
37. *Monmouthshire Merlin*, 3 December 1880
38. *Evening Express*, 24 June 1910
39. *Bradford Observer*, 15 December 1859
40. *Evening Express*, 2 August 1906

Chapter 5
1. *Monmouthshire Merlin*, 22 June 1861
2. *Liverpool Mercury*, 30 September 1857
3. *South Wales Echo*, 13 August 1888
4. *Western Mail*, 23 January 1871
5. *Mount Alexander Mail*, 20 April 1882
6. *Sheffield and Rotherham Independent*, 22 January 1863
7. *Hull Packet*, 18 March 1864
8. *Aberdare Times*, 30 October 1886
9. *Dundee Courier*, 13 August 1880
10. *Cambrian News*, 1 October 1870
11. *South Wales Daily*, 24 July 1895
12. *Press* (Philadelphia), 7 May 1860
13. *Daily News*, 11 August 1849
14. *Liverpool Mercury*, 24 July 1858
15. *Sunbury American*, 17 July 1841
16. *Daily News*, 9 February 1852
17. *Evening Express*, 5 October 1910
18. *Sydney Mail*, 24 April 1893
19. *Troy Daily Times*, 13 July 1857
20. *Brisbane Courier*, 7 October 1865
21. *Illustrated Usk Observer*, 30 September 1865
22. *New York Journal*, 8 August 1897
23. *Reynolds Newspaper*, 22 March 1891
24. *Aberdare Times*, 25 January 1862

Chapter 6
1. *Morning Chronicle*, 27 June 1831
2. *Morning Chronicle*, 6 January 1830
3. *Monmouthshire Merlin*, 30 December 1848
4. *Cardiff and Merthyr Guardian*, 13 December 1856
5. *Western Mail*, 1 August 1874
6. Howard, Jean E., *The Stage and Social Struggle in Early Modern England* (London: Routledge, 1988)
7. *Morning Chronicle*, 20 October 1853
8. *Leicester Chronicle*, 17 April 1869
9. *Cardiff Times*, 29 January 1864
10. *Birmingham Daily Post*, 20 September 1886
11. *Daily News*, 17 October 1872
12. *Kyneton Observer*, 19 August 1880
13. *Cardiff Times*, 11 June 1870
14. *Essex Standard*, 12 July 1872
15. *Essex Standard*, 9 August 1872

16. *Essex Standard*, 10 September 1875
17. *Essex Standard*, 2 September 1870
18. *Essex Standard*, 15 May 1874
19. *Dundee Courier & Argus*, 9 September 1876
20. *York Herald*, 8 July 1871
21. *The Times*, 23 October 1854
22. *Newcastle Courant*, 20 February 1874
23. *Cardiff Times*, 6 December 1861
24. *Belfast News-Letter*, 6 August 1867
25. *Cardiff Times*, 14 May 1887
26. Ibid
27. *Hampshire Advertiser*, 8 May 1847
28. *Tasmania Colonist*, 29 December 1853
29. *Adelaide Observer*, 21 August 1885
30. Rhys, Anthony, 'Cross-dressing in Victorian Cardiff: Usurping the Male Prerogative' from *Upset Victorians* (2018). Accessed online.
31. *South Wales Daily News*, 2 January 1896
32. Trexler, Richard C., 'La prostitution florentine au XVe siècle: patronage et clientèles' in *Annales. Histoire, Sciences Sociales* (36e Année, No. 6 August – December 1981)
33. McGinn, Thomas A. J., *Prostitution, Sexuality, and the Law in Ancient Rome* (Oxford: Oxford University Press, 2013)
34. Bennett, Judith M & McSheffrey, Shannon, 'Early, Erotic and Alien: Women dressed as Men in Late Medieval London' in *History Workshop* (Vol. 77, Issue 1, Spring 2014)
35. Ibid
36. Toulalan, Sarah & Fisher, Kate (ed.), *The Routledge History of Sex and the Body: 1500 to the Present* (London: Routledge, 2016)
37. *Sydney Morning Herald*, 11 April 1882
38. *The Examiner*, 10 August 1833
39. *Hull Packet*, 2 March 1838
40. *Truth*, 11 January 1903
41. Bloch, Iwan, *The Sexual Life of our Time in its Relations to Modern Civilization* (London: Rebman, 1909)
42. *The Morning Post*, 17 March 1846
43. Cleland, John, *Memoirs of a Woman of Pleasure* (London, 1749)
44. *Illustrated Police News*, 5 August 1918

Chapter 7
1. *Richmond Enquirer*, 24 June 1853
2. *Flintshire Observer*, 11 September 1913
3. *San Francisco Call*, 5 October 1908
4. *Bay of Plenty Times*, 23 December 1914

5. *Belfast News-Letter*, 11 December 1883
6. Oram, Alison, *Her Husband was a Woman!* (London: Routledge, 2007)
7. *Monmouthshire Merlin*, 6 March 1869
8. *Preston Guardian*, 10 March 1860
9. *Morning Post*, 31 August 1836
10. *Weekly Mail*, 31 December 1910
11. *Lancaster Gazette*, 9 March 1805
12. *Welsh Gazette*, 8 August 1906
13. *Belfast News-Letter*, 6 February 1829
14. *Europische Mercurius*, Vol. 1, 1749
15. *Express and Telegraph*, 9 September 1911
16. *Sydney Mail*, 15 March 1890
17. *Eastern Daily Mail*, 30 October 1905
18. *Newcastle Weekly Courant*, 5 October 1888
19. *Pall Mall Gazette*, 28 March 1871
20. *Cardiff and Merthyr Guardian*, 1 April 1871
21. *Rhyl Record*, 9 March 1901
22. *Preston Guardian*, 15 January 1859
23. *Monmouthshire Merlin*, 14 October 1865
24. *Trewman's Exeter Flying Post*, 26 August 1858
25. *Pembrokeshire Herald*, 3 August 1855
26. *Royal Cornwall Gazette*, 27 August 1858
27. *Troy Daily Times*, 13 July 1857
28. *Preston Guardian*, 10 August 1878
29. *The Welshman*, 2 August 1861
30. *Cambrian News*, 1 September 1916
31. *McIvor Times and Rodney Advertiser*, 30 October 1873
32. *South Wales Echo*, 11 June 1898
33. *South Wales Daily News*, 24 January 1896
34. *Cambrian News*, 22 May 1903
35. *North Wales Express*, 22 September 1905
36. *Cambrian Daily Leader*, 13 August 1913
37. *Morning Call*, 4 September 1892

Chapter 8
1. *Pall Mall Gazette*, 27 June 1871
2. Roberts, Michael & Clarke, Simone (ed.), *Women and Gender in Early Modern Wales* (Cardiff: University of Wales Press, 2000)
3. *Cardiff Times*, 2 September 1893
4. *Bradford & Wakefield Observer*, 24 September 1846
5. *Hull Packet*, 1 May 1840
6. *South Wales Echo*, 8 April 1885
7. *Cambrian News*, 8 December 1871

8. *Aberystwyth Observer*, 16 June 1860
9. *The Welshman*, 11 August 1853
10. *Cardiff Times*, 2 September 1893
11. *Leicester Chronicle*, 16 May 1829
12. *Cambrian News*, 10 February 1888
13. *Evening Express*, 10 April 1899
14. *York Herald*, 14 May 1842
15. *Derby Mercury*, 9 December 1846
16. *Leicester Chronicle*, 18 May 1844
17. *Merthyr Telegraph*, 4 October 1856
18. *Carmarthen Weekly Reporter*, 23 October 1908
19. *Monmouthshire Merlin*, 13 October 1854
20. *Sydney Morning Herald*, 27 January 1864
21. *Aberystwyth Observer*, 3 September 1864
22. *Cardiff and Merthyr Guardian*, 10 May 1867
23. *Pall Mall Gazette*, 3 December 1885
24. *South Wales Echo*, 28 December 1895
25. *Australian Star*, 18 April 1896
26. *South Wales Echo*, 22 June 1897
27. *South Wales Daily News*, 17 March 1888
28. *Evening Express*, 22 December 1896
29. *The Australian Star*, 10 August 1895
30. *Essex Standard*, 20 January 1854
31. *Monmouthshire Merlin*, 10 February 1854
32. *Trewman's Exeter Flying Post*, 10 June 1863
33. *Ashburton Guardian*, 2 December 1912
34. *South Wales Daily News*, 13 August 1890

Chapter 9

1. *Weekly Mail*, 19 March 1904
2. Powell, Gary, *Convicted: Landmark Cases in British Criminal History* (Stroud: Amberley Publishing, 2018)
3. *Morning Post*, 26 December 1849
4. *The Cambrian*, 27 June 1829
5. *The Welshman*, 23 January 1835
6. *Cardiff Times*, 6 December 1884
7. *Evening Express*, 19 July 1910
8. *Glasgow Herald*, 19 February 1867
9. *Morning Post*, 8 January 1869
10. *Sheffield & Rotherham Independent*, 20 February 1875
11. *Sheffield & Rotherham Independent*, 23 October 1886
12. *South Wales Daily News*, 29 August 1896
13. *Evening Express*, 9 August 1910

14. *Monmouthshire Merlin*, 10 January 1871; *Morning Post*, 20 January 1871
15. *Caledonian Mercury*, 28 April 1806
16. *Monmouthshire Merlin*, 27 March 1830
17. *The Australian*, 15 June 1826; *Sydney Gazette*, 4 January 1828
18. *Monmouthshire Merlin*, 16 August 1861; *Lloyd's Weekly Newspaper*, 17 August 1861; *Morning Chronicle*, 18 December 1861
19. *Western Mail*, 18 October 1893
20. *Straits Times*, 11 June 1907
21. *Abergavenny Chronicle*, 17 April 1914
22. *Daily Evening Bulletin*, 27 October 1866
23. *Leicester Chronicle*, 11 February 1832
24. *Aberdare Times*, 31 October 1891; *Missoula Weekly Gazette*, 13 October 1891
25. *Derby Mercury*, 31 July 1895
26. *Illustrated Usk Observer*, 28 June 1862
27. *Queensland Times*, 9 July 1910
28. *Evening Express*, 1 October 1898
29. *North Wales Chronicle*, 22 August 1827
30. *Glasgow Herald*, 30 December 1844
31. *Sydney Morning Herald*, 16 March 1849
32. *Evening Express*, 4 June 1906
33. *The Hangman's Record*, '22 December 1690' (c1920s)
34. Glamorgan Archives, 'Fingerprint Registers' (DCONC 3/2/1-7)

Chapter 10
1. Sala, George Augustus, *The Strange Adventures of Captain Dangerous* (Boston, 1863)
2. R.M. Dekker and L.C. van de Pol, *The Tradition of Female Transvestism in Early Modern Europe* (Basingstoke: Macmillan Press, 1989) p. 73
3. *Illustrated Usk Observer*, 26 January 1861
4. *Carmarthen Journal*, 26 May 1810
5. *Liverpool Mercury*, 23 January 1813
6. *National Advocate*, 29 September 1894
7. *Caledonian Mercury*, 4 September 1813
8. *The Times*, 22 August 1808
9. *Aberdare Times*, 14 February 1863
10. *Llais Llafur*, 12 August 1916
11. *Pontypool Free Press*, 17 September 1864
12. *Aberdare Times*, 20 August 1880
13. *Western Mail*, 7 September 1893
14. *Cardiff Times*, 20 August 1863
15. *Newcastle Courant*, 6 June 1879
16. *Evening Express*, 22 May 1900
17. *Weekly Mail*, 22 August 1904

18. *Morning Post*, 1 October 1870
19. *North Wales Chronicle*, 3 June 1871
20. *Cornwall Royal Gazette*, 13 September 1839
21. *Monmouthshire Merlin*, 14 April 1854
22. *Aberdare Times*, 22 August 1863
23. *Evening Express*, 16 February 1910
24. *Cardigan Observer*, 16 March 1889
25. *Belfast News-Letter*, 13 February 1829
26. *Aberdare Times*, 3 August 1864
27. *Carmarthen Journal*, 29 June 1811
28. *Cardiff Times*, 16 December 1893
29. *Morning Post*, 24 July 1866
30. *Newcastle Courant*, 17 February 1882
31. *North Wales Gazette*, 22 December 1814
32. *Evening Express*, 29 August 1898
33. *Liverpool Mercury*, 14 February 1873
34. *The Examiner*, 1 June 1828
35. *Cornwall Royal Gazette*, 13 September 1839
36. *Evening Express*, 17 March 1904
37. *The Cambrian*, 5 December 1902
38. *Monmouthshire Merlin*, 20 August 1830
39. *Dundee Courier*, 21 January 1864
40. *The Graphic*, 29 April 1871
41. *Western Mail*, 28 March 1885
42. *Lloyd's Weekly*, 12 January 1899
43. *Aberystwyth Observer*, 27 October 1860
44. *Morning Post*, 26 January 1850
45. *Illustrated Usk Observer*, 17 January 1857
46. *Cardiff Times*, 5 February 1859
47. *Newcastle Courant*, 17 Feb 1882
48. *Freeman's Journal*, 27 January 1830
49. *Daily Evening Bulletin*, 14 September 1867
50. *The Welshman*, 17 December 1858
51. *Evening Express*, 21 August 1908
52. *Blackburn Standard*, 5 October 1853
53. *South Wales Weekly Post*, 12 June 1915
54. *Strathmore Standard*, 10 January 1917
55. *Redcliffe Review*, 30 August 1917

Chapter 11

1. Simpson, James Young, Sir, *The Siamese Twins, Chang and Eng* (London, 1869)
2. *The Cambrian*, 9 September 1815

3. *Leeds Mercury*, 5 April 1872
4. *Bristol Mercury*, 1 January 1836
5. *The Welshman*, 31 March 1843
6. *Belfast News-Letter*, 24 July 1846
7. *Newcastle Weekly Courant*, 21 March 1891
8. *South Wales Echo*, 1 August 1898
9. *Caledonian Mercury*, 6 December 1800
10. *North Wales Gazette*, 21 March 1811
11. *North Wales Chronicle*, 30 June 1846
12. *Belfast News-Letter*, 15 January 1876
13. *Jackson's Oxford Journal*, 18 September 1813
14. *Morning Chronicle*, 22 May 1813
15. *Morning Post*, 12 August 1807
16. *Belfast News-Letter*, 21 August 1832
17. *The Era*, 12 September 1841
18. *The Welshman*, 7 December 1860
19. *The Cambrian*, 29 August 1807
20. *North Wales Chronicle*, 9 August 1841
21. *South Wales Echo*, 12 June 1897
22. *The Times*, 9 March 1827
23. *North Wales Chronicle*, 17 February 1835
24. *Morning Post*, 15 August 1844
25. *Monmouthshire Merlin*, 6 October 1849
26. *Bradford Observer*, 16 September 1841
27. *The Welshman*, 29 April 1842
28. *Glamorgan, Monmouth and Brecon Gazette*, 30 January 1836
29. *Cornwall Royal Gazette*, 18 August 1846
30. *Evening Express*, 29 October 1898
31. *Cardiff Times*, 30 March 1907
32. *Morning Chronicle*, 3 January 1857
33. *Cardiff Times*, 13 August 1859
34. *Hampshire Advertiser*, 12 December 1857
35. *Aberdare Times*, 31 August 1861
36. *Leicester Chronicle*, 23 June 1838
37. *Wrexham and Denbighshire Advertiser*, 25 June 1864
38. *Derby Mercury*, 14 September 1887
39. *Barry Dock News*, 22 August 1902
40. *Cardiff Times*, 16 December 1893
41. *Morning Chronicle*, 10 February 1814
42. *Monmouthshire Merlin*, 29 June 1833
43. *South Wales Echo*, 13 June 1890
44. *Pembrokeshire Herald*, 2 May 1873
45. *Lancaster Gazette*, 17 October 1877

46. *Liverpool Mercury*, 24 September 1852
47. *Bradford Observer*, 19 August 1857
48. *The Cambrian*, 19 July 1823
49. *Muswellbrook Chronicle*, 8 October 1910
50. *The Cambrian*, 18 February 1843
51. *Pembrokeshire Herald*, 24 August 1855
52. *Morning Chronicle*, 21 May 1847
53. *York Herald*, 23 April 1874
54. *The Cambrian*, 26 August 1904
55. *Cambrian Daily Leader*, 12 August 1915

Chapter 12
1. Rainolds, John, Gager, William and Gentili, Alberico, *The Overthrow of Stage Plays* (New York: Johnson Reprint Corp., 1, originally published 1599)
2. *The Era*, 31 July 1859
3. Howe, Elizabeth, *The English Actress: Women and Drama 1660–1700* (Cambridge: Cambridge University Press, 1992)
4. *The Times*, 30 January 1787
5. *Morning Post*, 21 October 1815
6. *The Times*, 18 August 1819
7. *Bristol Mercury*, 10 February 1829
8. *Morning Chronicle*, 22 October 1804
9. *The Spectator*, 23 August 1828
10. *Morning Chronicle*, 14 July 1817
11. *The Examiner*, 5 June 1808
12. *The Examiner*, 6 August 1825
13. *Brecon Reporter*, 19 January 1867
14. *The Era*, 17 June 1899
15. Croall, Jonathan, *Performing Hamlet* (London: The Arden Shakespeare, 2018)
16. Clapp, Susannah, 'Hamlet Review – Maxine Peake is a delicately ferocious Prince of Denmark' in *The Guardian* (21 September 2014)
17. *Preston Guardian*, 4 May 1850
18. *The Examiner*, 19 October 1828
19. Berlanstein, Lenard R., 'Breeches and Breaches: Cross-Dress Theatre and the Culture of Gender Ambiguity in Modern France' in *Comparative Studies in Society and History* (Vol. 38, No. 2. April, 1996)
20. *Evening Express*, 26 March 1895
21. *The Examiner*, 30 July 1820
22. *The Examiner*, 24 April 1814
23. *Manchester Times*, 5 February 1859
24. *Morning Post*, 10 February 1835
25. *Bradford Observer*, 15 December 1864

26. *Daily News*, 2 October 1875
27. *Morning Chronicle*, 21 August 1826
28. *Scots Magazine*, April 1823, Vol. 91
29. *Morning Post*, 12 July 1802
30. *Hampshire Telegraph*, 12 September 1885
31. *The Times*, 3 July 1789
32. *Pall Mall Gazette*, 15 August 1890
33. *North Wales Gazette*, 18 April 1816
34. Berlanstein, Lenard R., 'Breeches and Breaches: Cross-Dress Theatre and the Culture of Gender Ambiguity in Modern France' in *Comparative Studies in Society and History* (Vol. 38, No. 2. April 1996)
35. *Hampshire Advertiser*, 11 September 1897
36. *Kapunda Herald*, 20 January 1885
37. *Pall Mall Gazette*, 14 January 1869
38. *The Welshman*, 21 May 1858
39. *Daily Mail*, 11 August 1903
40. *Daily Mail*, 19 December 1896

Chapter 13
1. *Cardiff Times*, 15 September 1900
2. Marshall, Julian, *The Annals of Tennis* (London, 1878)
3. *Evening Express*, 5 October 1901
4. *Evening Express*, 1 July 1897
5. *Birmingham Daily Post*, 28 April 1890
6. *Daily Colonist*, 25 April 1862
7. *Wrexham Advertiser*, 7 June 1890
8. *Illustrated Usk Observer*, 25 June 1864
9. *The Telegraph* (Brisbane), 3 January 1911
10. *Weekly Mail*, 20 August 1887
11. *Morning Post*, 17 September 1842
12. *Weekly Mail*, 25 October 1884
13. *Flintshire Observer*, 12 June 1884
14. *Mount Alexander Mail*, 9 April 1874
15. *Wrexham Advertiser*, 27 September 1884
16. *Cardiff Times*, 2 April 1887
17. *Evening Express*, 9 February 1895
18. *Western Mail*, 6 April 1895
19. *The Advertiser*, 21 August 1896
20. *Evening Express*, 23 October 1893
21. *Carnarvon and Denbigh Herald*, 28 September 1894
22. *Evening Express*, 11 August 1900
23. *Yorkshire Herald*, 16 August 1893
24. *Carmarthen Weekly Reporter*, 19 June 1896

25. *Birmingham Daily Post*, 3 October 1895
26. *Sheffield Independent*, 3 January 1895
27. *Daily News*, 18 December 1893
28. *Glasgow Herald*, 7 June 1895
29. *Sheffield Independent*, 26 July 1895
30. *Melbourne Punch*, 26 September 1895
31. *Cheshire Observer*, 14 September 1895
32. *The Australasian*, 11 May 1895
33. *Evening Express*, 18 September 1894
34. *Evening Express*, 19 February 1895
35. *The Bird O' Freedom*, 3 August 1895
36. *Carmarthen Journal*, 18 September 1908

Chapter 14
1. *The Welshman*, 28 May 1847
2. *Pall Mall Gazette*, 4 March 1889
3. *Pembroke Herald*, 24 October 1851
4. *The Standard*, 6 October 1851
5. *The Morning Post*, 29 September 1851
6. *Monmouthshire Merlin*, 19 September 1851
7. *Holden's Dollar Magazine*, March 1850
8. *Lloyd's Weekly Newspaper*, 12 October 1851
9. *Pembrokeshire Herald*, 19 December 1851
10. *Aberystwyth Observer*, 9 June 1860
11. *Leeds Mercury*, 1 October 1864
12. *County Observer*, 23 January 1869
13. *Pall Mall Gazette*, 21 October 1869
14. *Monmouthshire Merlin*, 2 October 1874
15. *Dundee Courier*, 4 January 1877
16. *Western Mail*, 22 September 1876
17. *North Wales Express*, 14 April 1882
18. *The Graphic*, 26 May 1883
19. *The Standard*, 8 February 1887
20. *Aberdare Times*, 3 March 1888
21. *York Herald*, 12 October 1888
22. *Evening Express*, 24 February 1896
23. *Weekly Mail*, 15 August 1890
24. *Weekly Mail*, 28 February 1891
25. *Newcastle Weekly Courant*, 14 January 1893
26. *Pembroke County Guardian*, 5 April 1907
27. *Evening Express*, 5 September 1894
28. *Western Mail*, 16 August 1895
29. *Cheshire Observer*, 8 April 1899

30. *Evening Express*, 8 September 1900
31. *Evening Express*, 29 March 1910
32. *Weekly Mail*, 6 August 1910
33. *Penny Illustrated Paper*, 1 January 1911
34. *Herald of Wales*, 9 September 1916

Chapter 15
1. *Llangollen Advertiser*, 25 Jan 1918
2. *Morning Chronicle*, 1 June 1843
3. *Bradford Observer*, 21 February 1839
4. *Pembrokeshire Herald*, 30 May 1851
5. *Cardiff Times*, 16 September 1905
6. *Wetaskiwin Times*, 27 April 1911
7. *Derby Mercury*, 29 June 1825
8. *Ipswich Journal*, 6 May 1871
9. *Birmingham Daily Post*, 4 March 1869
10. Ibid
11. *Morning Chronicle*, 2 February 1833
12. *Caledonian Mercury*, 9 June 1862
13. *Lancaster Gazette*, 14 March 1877
14. *The Era*, 4 September 1870
15. *County Observer*, 24 April 1869
16. *New York Herald*, 13 January 1878
17. *Evening Express*, 17 December 1902
18. *Trewman's Exeter Flying Post*, 19 October 1848
19. *Cambrian Daily Leader*, 16 August 1916
20. *Brecon County Times*, 7 December 1867
21. *County Observer*, 13 January 1872
22. *Liverpool Mercury*, 11 June 1856
23. *Cambrian News*, 11 April 1902
24. *Glasgow Herald*, 23 April 1856
25. *Aberdare Times*, 5 April 1862
26. *Sheffield & Rotherham Independent*, 29 August 1869
27. *Sheffield & Rotherham Independent*, 22 October 1869
28. *Pembrokeshire Herald*, 5 April 1850
29. *The Telegraph* (Australia), 31 January 1894

Chapter 16
1. *Rhyl Record and Advertiser*, 7 August 1897
2. *Morning Chronicle*, 30 January 1829
3. *Bristol Mercury*, 27 December 1834
4. *Carnarvon and Denbigh Herald*, 21 April 1838

5. *Liverpool Mercury*, 14 October 1853; *Royal Cornwall Gazette*, 21 October 1853
6. *North Eastern Daily Gazette*, 2 July 1891
7. *The Examiner*, 27 March 1847
8. *Flintshire Observer*, 11 September 1913
9. *Queanbeyan Age*, 29 October 1887
10. *The Morning Post*, 12 December 1845
11. *Cardiff and Merthyr Guardian*, 25 October 1867
12. *North Eastern Daily*, 15 August 1895
13. *Morning Post*, 31 July 1848
14. *Evening Express*, 1 February, 1909
15. Vernal, Joshua, 'A Jaunt to Wales' in *Birmingham Daily Post* (27 September 1858)
16. *Morning Post*, 23 August 1837
17. *Morning Chronicle*, 6 June 1829
18. *South Wales Echo*, 20 August 1894

Conclusion
1. Hamdi, Yemina, 'Sudanese women can still be whipped for wearing pants' in *The Arab Weekly* (28 October 2018). Accessed online.

Bibliography

Bennett, Judith M. & McSheffrey, Shannon, 'Early, Erotic and Alien: Women dressed as Men in Late Medieval London' in *History Workshop* (Vol. 77, Issue 1, Spring 2014)

Berlanstein, Lenard R., 'Breeches and Breaches: Cross-Dress Theatre and the Culture of Gender Ambiguity in Modern France' in *Comparative Studies in Society and History* (Vol. 38, No. 2. April, 1996)

Bloch, Iwan, *The Sexual Life of our Time in its Relations to Modern Civilization* (London: Rebman, 1909)

Burton, Lady Isabel & Wilkins, William Henry (ed.), *The Romance of Isabel Lady Burton* (New York: Dodd Meade & Company, 1897)

Cardoza, Thomas, *Intrepid Women: Cantinieres and Vivandieres of the French Army* (Indiana: Indiana University Press, 2010)

Clayton, Ellen C. *Female Warriors: Memorials of Female Valour and Heroism from the Mythical Ages to the Present Era. In two Volumes* (London: Tinsley Brothers, 1879, public domain via Google Books)

Cleland, John, *Memoirs of a Woman of Pleasure* (London, 1749)

Creighton, Margaret S. & Norling, Lisa, *Iron Men, Wooden Women: Gender and Seafaring in the Atlantic World, 1700–1920* (Baltimore: The Johns Hopkins University Press, 1996)

Croall, Jonathan, *Performing Hamlet* (London: The Arden Shakespeare, 2018)

Dekker, R.M. and Pol, L.C. van de, *The Tradition of Female Transvestism in Early Modern Europe* (Basingstoke: Macmillan Press, 1989)

Genlis, Countess de & Colburn, Henry, *Memoirs of the Countess de Genlis, illustrative of the history of the eighteenth and nineteenth centuries* (London: New Burlington, 1825)

Hamdi, Yemina, 'Sudanese women can still be whipped for wearing pants' in *The Arab Weekly* (28 October 2018, accessed online)

Howard, Jean E., *The Stage and Social Struggle in Early Modern England* (London: Routledge, 1988)

Howe, Elizabeth, *The English Actress: Women and Drama 1660–1700* (Cambridge: Cambridge University Press, 1992)

McGinn, Thomas A. J., *Prostitution, Sexuality, and the Law in Ancient Rome* (Oxford: Oxford University Press, 2013)

Manion, Jen, *Female Husbands: A Trans History* (Cambridge: Cambridge University Press, 2020)

Merrill, Lisa, *When Romeo was a Woman: Charlette Cushman and Her Circle of Female Spectators* (Michigan: University of Michigan Press, 2000)
Oram, Alison, *Her Husband was a Woman!* (London: Routledge, 2007)
Powell, Gary, *Convicted: Landmark Cases in British Criminal History* (Stroud: Amberley Publishing, 2018)
Rainolds, John, Gager, William and Gentili, Alberico, *The Overthrow of Stage Playes* (New York: Johnson Reprint Corp., 1, originally published 1599)
Rhys, Anthony, 'Cross-dressing in Victorian Cardiff: Usurping the Male Prerogative' from *Upset Victorians* (2018, accessed online)
Roberts, Michael & Clarke, Simone (ed.), *Women and Gender in Early Modern Wales* (Cardiff: University of Wales Press, 2000)
Sala, George Augustus, *The Strange Adventures of Captain Dangerous* (Boston, 1863)
Shopland, Norena, *A Practical Guide to Searching LGBTQIA Historical Records* (London: Routledge Focus, 2020)
Shopland, Norena, *Forbidden Lives: LGBT Stories from Wales* (Bridgend: Seren Books, 2018)
Shopland, Norena & Leeworthy, Daryl, *Queering Glamorgan: A Research Guide to Sources for the Study of LGBT History* (Glamorgan Archives, 2018)
Stark, Suzanne J., *Female Tars: Women Aboard Ship in the Age of Sail* (Annapolis: Naval Institute Press, 1996)
Toulalan, Sarah & Fisher, Kate (ed.), *The Routledge History of Sex and the Body: 1500 to the Present* (London: Routledge, 2016)
Trexler, Richard C., 'La prostitution florentine au XVe siècle: patronage et clientèles' in *Annales. Histoire, Sciences Sociales* (36e Année, No. 6 August – December 1981)
Wallach, Janet, *Desert Queen* (London: Hachette UK Kindle edition, 2015)
Wilson, Harriette, *The Memoirs of Harriette Wilson: Written by Herself* (London: J. J. Stockdale, 1825)

Index

actresses, 32, 48, 54, 57, 94, 108, 122–132, 139, 151, 162
androgynous, 2, 9, 36, 67, 68, 70, 83, 103, 127, 133, 177, 179
asylum, sent to, 14, 15, 43, 44, 109, 127
Augspurg, Dr. Anita, 14

bal masqué, *see* masque balls
bandits, 95
Baret, Jeanne, 3
Beard, Dame Mary, 183
bearded women, 62, 69, 106, 152, 153, 161, 172, 176–179, 180
Bell, Gertrude, 1, 6
Bernhardt, Sarah, 125–126, 127, 131
Bialik, Mayim, 36
binding of the chest, 69
Bird, Isabella, 1
bisexuality, 87, 131, 160
blackmail, 89, 94, 161, 164, 176
bloomers, 30, 138, 139, 142, 143, 147, 148, 149, 150, 151, 154, 155
Breeches Bible, 182
breeches roles, 122, 125, 126, 128, 129, 131, 132, 134, 163
brick workers, 78, 79, 83, 86, 87, 174
bricklayers, 78, 174
builders, 72, 78
Burton, Isobel, 4

Calamity Jane, 100
cantinières, or vivandières, 102
carpenters, 78, 166
Charke, Charlotte, 65, 122, 126
Chevalier d'Éon, 24, 68, 174
chimney sweeps, 81
Choisy, Maryse, 7
Cleland, John, *Fanny Hill*, 65
colliers, 28, 34, 74, 84

con women, 98, 162, 168
Coombes, Catherine, 70, 72
cricket, playing, 139, 140, 145
Cushman, Charlotte, 127
cycling, 135, 137, 139, 141–144

Dahomey of Benin, 100
death, discovery through, 43, 72, 82, 85, 87, 101, 106, 107, 109, 118, 161, 165, 166, 167, 169, 174
destitution, 43, 86, 116
Deuteronomy 25, 121, 181
Dickens, Charles, *The Old Curiosity Shop*, 111
Dietrich, Marlene, 128, 182
Dieulafoy, Jane, 2, 152
dock workers, 73, 82, 87, 88
domestic violence, x, 159, 165, 166, 169
Dowie, Ménie Muriel, 5, 6
drivers, 5, 72, 85, 86, 91
Duchess of Gordon, 10
duels, fighting, 106, 139, 147

enlisting in the army or navy, 52, 102, 103, 105, 109, 112, 113, 115, 119, 120, 164

farm workers, 74, 85, 86, 155, 160, 170, 179
father's influence, 34, 38, 54, 81, 113
female husbands, 171–174
followed by crowds, 8, 25, 29, 30, 31, 32, 54, 59, 63, 90, 116, 118, 141, 144, 147, 148, 149, 167, 177
football, playing, 139, 140–141, 145, 154
freak, use of the word, 6, 15, 33, 46, 47, 75, 80, 92, 106, 159, 176
Freycinet, Rose de, 3

gardeners, 75–76, 161
Garnerin, Jeanne Geneviève, 1

Gautier, Théophile, *Mademoiselle de Maupin*, 131, 183
gender dysphoria, 170
gender pay gap, 67, 68, 72, 167
getting drunk, discovery through, 31, 32, 59, 60, 61, 71, 72, 87, 117, 119, 164
groom, working as, 161, 170

hair, 2, 13, 14, 17, 20–21, 31, 32, 37, 40, 47, 49, 57, 60, 63, 68, 72, 73, 90, 106, 107, 112, 127, 175, 176–177
Hamlet, women playing, 125–127
hangwomen, 71
harem skirt, 155
hermaphrodites, 142, 160–161, 172, 178–179
highwaywomen, 95–96, 129
hodwomen, 78, 83
homosexuality, viii, x, 16, 26, 42, 54, 63–66, 71, 121, 158, 160
horse riding, 42, 51, 82, 91, 97, 101, 129, 136–138, 160
Hugo, Victor, 12
husbands, 2, 3, 7, 10, 11, 29, 32, 39, 46, 47, 49, 50, 51, 52, 53, 62, 71, 72, 75, 86, 87, 89, 91, 93, 102, 117, 121, 130, 154, 159, 165

illness, discovery through, 24, 38, 43, 71, 106
injury, discovery through, 71, 87, 105, 113, 131

Jack the Ripper, 31
Joan of Arc, 100, 108

killed in battle, 100, 104, 106, 107, 109
knickerbockers, 140–144

labourers, working as, 65, 73, 74, 86, 87, 161, 166, 169, 177
Lawrence, Dorothy, 109
Légion d'honneur, 2, 101
lesbians, x, 43, 85, 127, 156, 158, 159, 160, 163, 164, 170
lodgings, 80, 87

male impersonators, 132–133, 182
masculinity, 9, 26, 38, 46, 51, 81–84, 87, 90, 92, 97, 103, 106, 116, 126, 127, 135, 140, 150, 152, 153, 169, 170, 177, 178, 180, 183
masons, 78
masque balls, 24–26, 57
mother's influence, 17, 34, 38, 70, 113
Mount Athos, Greece, 7–8
moustaches, 9, 13–14, 29, 32, 49, 62, 69, 123, 177
mummering, 23
murder, 31, 52, 75, 94

navvies, 78, 86

Order of the Iron Cross, 108

painters, house, 72, 78, 152
Peake, Maxine, playing *Hamlet*, 127
pensions, 107–108, 119
Pfeiffer, Ida Laura, 2
pit brow lasses and tip girls, 82, 83, 85
plasterers, 78
plumbers, 40, 78
Poimenidou, Maria, 7
police women, 76
post-traumatic stress disorder, 109
principal boy, in pantomime, 133
printing works, 75, 152, 165
prisons, in and escaping from, 37, 42, 43, 44, 49, 91, 96, 98, 99, 110, 111, 119, 166, 173, 177
pronouns, use of, vii, viii, 19, 37, 47, 49, 92, 161, 170
prostitutes, 24, 28, 31, 54–66, 121, 131, 148
punishment, discovery through, 106

railway workers, 39, 73, 78, 80, 86, 88
Rational Dress, ix, 21, 139, 144, 151, 154
reading novels, 12, 15, 37, 73, 94, 115
revenge, 51, 115, 166, 169
Romeo, played by women, 125–128
rugby, 135, 144

sailors, 3, 7, 34, 49, 52, 72, 74, 100, 103, 110–120, 129, 133
same-sex relationships, viii, 44, 51, 64, 112, 114, 119, 158–169
Sand, George, 152, 87

Sandes, Flora, 109
selective attention, 23
Shakespeare, William, 127
shaving, to create facial hair, 69, 86, 97, 177
Sheridan, Elizabeth Ann, 10
Siddons, Sarah, 122, 125, 126, 127
Snell, Hannah, 52, 100, 103, 106, 108, 110, 120
soldiers, 2, 75, 100–109, 110, 111, 119, 129, 133
soot, using as a moustache or beard, 14, 29, 62, 69
spies, 108
stalking, 163
Stanhope, Lady Hester, 4
steeplejacks, 71
suffragists, 143, 153, 143, 155
suicides, 27, 43, 44, 73, 109, 164

Talbot, Mary Anne, 100, 106, 108
tavern keepers, 175

Tinné, Alexandrine, 3–4
tramps, 16–17, 52
transported, 41, 90, 162, 166
travesti roles, 23, 122–125, 132, 133, 134, 162

Vauxhall Gardens, 24, 56
Vestris, Lucia Elizabeth, 20, 124, 128, 129
voice, betrayed by, 4, 13, 38, 57, 103

Walker, Dr. Major Mary, 100, 150, 155
Wallace, Lady, 10
Walpole, Horace, 24, 25
washing, discovery through, 87, 115
witches, 90
Wood, Mrs Henry, 7
Woolf, Virginia *Orlando*, ix
wounded in battle, discovery through, 102, 105–106

zouave trousers, 76